RICHARD "GOOSE" GOSSAGE

with Russ Pate

BALLANTINE BOOKS • NEW YORK

A Ballantine Book
Published by The Ballantine Publishing Group

Copyright © 2000 by Richard "Goose" Gossage

www.randomhouse.com/BB/

LIBRARY OF CONGRESS CATALOGING-IN PUBLICATION DATA
Gossage, Goose, 1951–
The Goose is loose : an autobiography / by Rich
"Goose" Gossage with Russ Pate. — 1st ed.
p.   cm.
ISBN 0-345-43068-9 (alk. paper)
1. Gossage, Goose, 1951–   2. Baseball players—
United States—Biography.   I. Pate, Russ.   II. Title

GV865.G64 A3   2000
796.357'092—dc21
[B]   99-055977

Text design by Holly Johnson

Manufactured in the United States of America

First Edition: March 2000

10 9 8 7 6 5 4 3 2 1

For Jick, Sue, and Jack Gossage,
who got me started in baseball and fueled my dream;
For Betty Ranals,
who invited me to try out for my first youth league;
For Bill Kimball,
the Chicago scout who gave me a shot at pro ball;
And for Corna, Jeff, Keith, and Todd,
who've made it all worthwhile.

CONTENTS

INTRODUCTION

This story is the truth—or at least my version of it. My mother and father taught me to tell the truth no matter what, even when it hurts. I suppose I've told a few tales in my time, but for the most part I'm a straight-shooting, no BS, let-the-chips-fall-where-they-may kind of guy.

I pitched with the same sort of straightforwardness. "Here comes the heat, batter, catch up with it if you can." I considered pitching a kind of warfare; batters were the enemy, and my job was to blow them away. I took no prisoners.

My approach to throwing a baseball for a living went something like this:

You're walking down an alley or through a vacant lot when a mean ol' junkyard dog sets upon you. His eyes are crossed, his teeth are bared, and he's drooling from the corners of his mouth. He looks at you like you're a greasy pork chop.

Ever have that happen? Then you know it elevates your senses to a state of emergency. At which point you have two choices: either stand there and get chewed up or run like hell.

Running to survive, as well as feeling the adrenaline that comes from being in a precarious situation but managing to escape, propelled my career in baseball. I learned to conquer the anxiety every pitcher feels in the late innings, when the bases are loaded or the game is on the line. I also learned, through experience, to control the rush of adrenaline so that it worked for me, not against me.

My philosophy about outrunning that mean ol' junkyard dog helped sustain my career for twenty-two years and allowed me to appear in 1,002 games and register 115 wins and 310 saves.

I had another pet theory about pitching, one that I shared with my pal and fellow closer Dennis Eckersley: *Don't get gay.*

Eck and I didn't mean gay as in homosexual, but gay as in happy. No matter how well things are going, a pitcher—especially a closer, the guy who's on the mound at crunch time—can't afford to get gay. If he becomes too happy, he runs the risk of becoming self-satisfied.

I learned through the years that closers must stay on an even keel emotionally—getting neither too high after success nor too low after failure. It's also imperative that closers realize that, no matter how overpowering their stuff, they are always one pitch away from disaster. Being a closer on a baseball team is like working a high wire without a net. There's no margin for error.

If there was another key component to the mental makeup that helped me become two-time winner of Fireman of the Year, baseball's top award for relief pitchers, it was this: *I remembered to forget.* By that I mean I didn't dwell on things. I learned, over time, to leave everything behind at the ballpark.

The best time to think about what transpired during a game—mistakes you made, things you did well—is in the clubhouse immediately afterward. The action is fresh and vivid in your memory, and adrenaline is still pumping, which means your senses are acute.

The worst thing any player can do is take the game home and mentally replay it over and over. I fell into this trap at several junctures during my career, but, through experience, I finally learned to let things go.

The lyric from a song written by Kris Kristofferson and recorded by my pal Willie Nelson says it best: "Yesterday is dead and gone/And tomorrow's out of sight. . . ." As soon as a game ends, it's history. You can't go back and change the outcome, so what's the point of dwelling on what happened?

I met more than a few relief pitchers who kept looking back and became consumed by what-ifs. What if I'd thrown that pitch? What if I'd pitched around that hitter? Two or three months later they'd still be talking about pitches they threw to a batter. That sort of second-guessing eats up a career faster than battery acid.

People have been pestering me for years about writing a book, but I resisted. For one reason, I had no desire to undertake such a project while I was still active in the major leagues. It seemed silly to write a book about my life in baseball until the final chapter was complete. For another, I didn't wish to rush anything into print. I needed to sort out my thoughts and opinions. Now I've had time to do that.

One of the messages I hope to get across in this book is this: *Do what you do for love, not money, and do it with great passion.*

I was fortunate to find my gift—being able to throw a baseball—at a young age. I loved the physical act of winding up and throwing the ball as hard as I could to my brother, Jack. I loved talking about baseball with my parents, Jick and Sue. I loved playing pickup games with my cousin, Rod Francis, and neighborhood friends like Sam Guadagnoli, Larry Ranals, Galen Miller, Eddie Barns, and all the Welch and Green brothers.

I loved baseball, period.

From the time I was twelve years old, riding to games with my buddies in the back of "The Binder," my dad's old International Harvester pickup truck, right on through my glory days in New York and San Diego and all the way to the end of the road in Seattle in 1994, I played for the love of the game and because it was fun.

The joy I derived from baseball kept me in the major leagues for more than two decades. Joy and a live fastball, I should say. I sincerely hope some of that joy comes through in these pages.

—Rich "Goose" Gossage

CHAPTER 1

1972

WELCOME TO THE SHOW, ROOK

Opening day for the 1972 major league season was delayed two weeks by the first general strike in baseball history. It wouldn't be the last work disruption over the next quarter century. Seven more stoppages would ensue, including lengthy strikes in 1981 and 1994, tarnishing the image of America's greatest game.

Labor and management were at odds in 1972 over the players' pension fund. To no one's surprise, baseball players demanded an increase in benefits, and team owners steadfastly refused to cough it up. Marvin Miller, executive director of the Players Association, put his own spin on the escalating situation. "Money is not the issue," Miller insisted. "The real issue is the owners' attempt to punish the players for having the audacity not to settle and having the audacity not to crawl."

Crawl, walk, run, or make a mad dash around the bases, it didn't matter. No sooner were stadiums dark and joy missing in Mudville than major leaguers became restless to play ball. Especially one antsy American League rookie from Colorado who, at the tender age of twenty, was making his debut in the show.

Me.

Commissioner Bowie Kuhn finally negotiated a settlement between the two contentious sides that resulted in a $500,000 increase to the pension fund but left bitterness lingering in clubhouses and front offices all around baseball.

The strike forced the cancellation of 86 contests, shortened the 1972 schedule to 153 games from its normal 162, and pushed season openers back to mid-April.

On Saturday, April 14, the Chicago White Sox, who a fortnight earlier made me a surprise addition to their roster, opened on the road at Kansas City, losing 2-1 in 11 innings. I watched my first major league game from the visitors' bullpen at Municipal Stadium, soaking up the atmosphere and marveling at how Royals groundskeeper George Toma had the infield and outfield grass looking as flawless as the felt on a new billiards table.

The next day, Chicago starter Stan Bahnsen sailed through the first three innings against the Royals and even drove in a run to stake the White Sox to a 1-0 lead.

In the fourth inning, however, Bahnsen's control temporarily deserted him. The Royals put a couple runners on base, prompting Chicago manager Chuck Tanner to tell pitching coach Johnny Sain to get on the dugout telephone and call the bullpen. Sain, in turn, uttered these three fateful words:

"Get Gossage up."

Get Gossage up. I had dreamed about pitching in the big leagues since my childhood days in Colorado, where I grew up a hardscrabble kid from the poor side of town. But those dreams seemed fantastic—unlikely, implausible, and in no way based in reality. The major leagues seemed like an unobtainable goal until the day the Chicago White Sox offered me a professional contract. Before that, I never really believed my dreams could come true.

My family lived in Colorado Springs, a picturesque city on the front range of the Rocky Mountains that had undergone a boom ever since the Air Force Academy was established there in the 1950s.

If you stand in the heart of downtown Colorado Springs and look due west, you're staring straight at one of the most celebrated landmarks in the American West—Pikes Peak, elevation 14,110 feet.

At times, my making it to the big leagues had seemed like an uphill struggle. Based on the evaluation of one manager in the minor leagues, who recommended that I be released, the challenge I faced might have been more like climbing Mount Everest than Pikes Peak. Thank goodness he was wrong.

I came from a family of baseball fans. Passion for the great game boiled in our blood. My dad, who passed away during my junior year in high school, worshiped the New York Yankees. On Saturday afternoons in the late 1950s and early 1960s, every activity in our house came to a halt when Dizzy Dean and Pee Wee Reese started broadcasting the national game of the week, which, for ratings purposes, usually featured the Bronx Bombers.

Jack Gossage, whom everyone called "Jick," had failed to dig his fortune out of the Colorado gold mines, and in his later years became a landscaper and lawn care specialist. He held his beloved New York Yankees in awe. Those pinstriped figures appearing on our small TV screen—Mickey Mantle, Whitey Ford, Yogi Berra, Roger Maris, and the rest—seemed to my dad like latter-day Knights of the Round Table. New York Yankees were brave and heroic.

My mom, Sue, who helped supplement our meager family income by working as a waitress at Colorado Springs eateries like Ruth's Oven and The Village Inn, shared my dad's passion. In addition to keeping tabs on the Yankees, she followed the fortunes of our hometown Colorado Springs Sky Sox, Chicago's Class A affiliate.

Sky Sox players would roll out of bed about noon and stroll into mom's place of business to eat a late breakfast or just hang out. Being ballplayers, they had long hours to fill each day. She treated them like sons. On summer evenings, after work, Mom would attend Sky Sox games at Memorial Park. I'd tag along.

My brother Jack, who is nearly seventeen years my senior, had been an outstanding amateur player in the Colorado Springs area. It often puzzled me growing up why Jack didn't land a job as a catcher in the big leagues. He possessed immense strength, a barrel chest, and a terrific throwing arm.

Jack once had a tryout in Denver with the Yankees, who invited him back for a second look. For whatever reason, though, things never progressed any further. He settled down in Colorado Springs, which presented a perfect opportunity for me to develop my skills as a pitcher. From the time I was eight or nine, I started throwing to Jack every chance I could.

By then I had discovered I could throw harder and farther than other kids my age. That talent, trust me, came in pretty handy during neighborhood rock fights. By the time I joined an organized league and put on a uniform for the first time, I could bring it to home plate. Other boys my age were scared to step in against me.

Besides baseball, my principal athletic interest was basketball. I demonstrated at an early age a pretty decent talent for shooting hoops. And shooting at targets too: I could wield a rifle or pistol pretty handily.

I also spent hour upon hour hunting, fishing, hiking, and just prowling around the countryside. Colorado is an ideal environment for anyone drawn to nature and the great outdoors. But baseball, primarily because of my family's unwavering loyalty to the New York Yankees, remained my first love.

Get Gossage up.

No sooner had Johnny Sain's message been relayed than I sprang to my feet, grabbed my glove, dashed up the seven or eight bullpen steps, took the mound, toed the rubber, and began tossing pitches to the White Sox backup catcher, Chuck Brinkman.

My heart raced. My knees shook. My palms sweated so much I kept picking up the rosin bag to dry them off. So fearful was I of hyperventilating that I had to pause and take several deep breaths just to calm down.

There I stood, quivering, a six-foot-three, twenty-year-old rookie not yet two years removed from high school. I was naive, innocent, and as green as an unripe banana. Throughout spring training in Sarasota I'd become a nuisance to veterans on the White Sox, repeatedly asking them if I had a chance to make the big-league club. Like they gave a damn.

To my everlasting surprise, Chuck Tanner and Johnny Sain decided to take me north that year. Never mind that I showed up in Sarasota as a nonroster invitee, or that I was making the jump straight from Class A ball. It's one thing to be overpowering at Appleton, Wisconsin, pitching to players who shave maybe twice a week; it's something else to contend with the best hitters on the planet.

Perhaps it should be mentioned here that the visiting team's bullpen at Municipal Stadium, located down the right-field foul line, was submerged below the playing field. And that the first time Stan Bahnsen got in trouble that day, he snuffed out the rally, which meant I could go sit down.

Being so hyped-up about my first dry hump—a term relief pitchers use to describe warming up without getting called into the game—I didn't have my bearings when I attempted to reenter the bullpen. I managed to miss the first step, and the next thing I knew I tumbled, head over heels, down the steps.

I landed in a heap and kissed the floor, a putrid mix of spit, bubble gum, tobacco juice, and no telling what else. The odor made me momentarily feel nauseous. I began checking body parts to see if anything had been broken. Fortunately, the only injury of note was a bruised ego.

What did my new Chicago teammates do upon witnessing such a severe case of stage fright? Did anyone try to catch me as I stumbled? Did anyone try to break my fall? Did anyone rush to my side to see if I was all right?

No, they stayed right where they were and laughed their butts off. They hooted at me: "What's wrong with you, big boy? You scared?"

Welcome to the show, rook.

I entered the game in the fifth inning that afternoon, inheriting from Bahnsen two base runners, one of whom subsequently scored to tie the game. I pitched one complete inning, surrendering a walk but no hits. The White Sox ultimately lost their second straight game, despite an RBI double in the top of the ninth by Dick Allen, which took the game into extra innings.

I'm proud to say I safely negotiated my way from the bullpen to the pitcher's mound for my one inning of work. After retiring the side, I didn't trip going down the steps into a major league dugout for the first time.

Taking one header that day had been enough.

But I have no recall of the batters I faced or pitches I threw. I might have faced Kansas City regulars like Freddie Patek, Cookie Rojas, Amos Otis, or John Mayberry, the slugging first baseman who'd come over from the Houston Astros. Then again, maybe not.

I might have faced my future New York Yankee team-mate Lou Piniella, who, as fate would have it, would become my last manager in the big leagues, some twenty-two years later in Seattle. Who knows?

I'm not sure whether I threw to Ed Herrmann, the White Sox's regular catcher, or his backup, Tom Egan. All I know is that rawboned and rangy Rick Gossage scaled a personal mountain on April 15, 1972. On a chilly and overcast afternoon, with dampness in the air, I arrived at the summit of my own Mount Everest. I became a big-leaguer. The impossible dream became a reality.

My debut in the major leagues went unheralded back in Chicago. The big news in the city that weekend was a pow-wow between Jimmy Hoffa, Mayor Richard Daley, and a thousand union stewards at Teamster Local 710. The last time Hoffa had been in Chicago, he was led away by authorities to serve a five-year term in federal prison for mail fraud and jury tampering.

Coverage of the White Sox game in Kansas City got

buried inside the sports section the next day. All the Chicago papers played up Cubs pitcher Burt Hooton's no-hitter against Philadelphia in front of 9,583 shivering fans at Wrigley Field.

Hooton's performance so impressed Phil Wrigley that the Cubs owner awarded the knuckle-curveball specialist a $2,500 bonus on the spot. And Wrigley tossed another $500 to catcher Randy Hundley for calling such a masterful game. Who said team owners were such tight-fists, anyway?

The other big sports story that Sunday concerned the Chicago Black Hawks 3-2 loss in an NHL playoff game with the New York Rangers at Chicago Stadium. Can you imagine, here it was mid-April, and the Stanley Cup finals were in full swing? Today, the National Hockey League season extends well into June, as does the NBA season, and World Series games have been pushed back so far in October that there's often the threat of postponement because of freezing weather or snow. World Series games no longer are played during the afternoon—when little boys and girls with athletic dreams of their own can watch them live—because of TV ratings and the demands of advertisers. Times have changed, eh?

My major league debut at Municipal Stadium in Kansas City wasn't the first time I'd pitched in a big-league park. During the summer of 1971, in the middle of a dominating season at Appleton in the Class A league, the White Sox summoned me to pitch an exhibition game against the Cubs at Wrigley Field.

The two major league franchises in Chicago—the White Sox and Cubs—played an exhibition game for charity each summer. This being 1971, more than a quarter century before the advent of baseball's interleague play, Chicago fans were eager to watch American Leaguers like Bill Melton and Walt "No-Neck" Williams go at it against National Leaguers like Ron Santo and Billy Williams. Such matchups between leagues only happened in spring training—or the World Series.

The exhibition drew a full house, which included a large contingent of the city's dignitaries. I remember seeing hizzoner, Mayor Daley, in a box seat near the dugout. Around him were the chief of police and no telling how many aldermen and county commissioners. Before the game, Leo Durocher, the legendary Cubs manager, posed for pictures with assorted big shots. So did Ernie Banks, reaching the end of a glittering Hall of Fame career that produced 512 home runs and two MVP awards.

A funny thing happened that day. The equipment manager for the White Sox issued me a cap a couple sizes too big. When I went into my windup, the bill of the cap would slide down over my eyes. I resembled one of those knights in armor whose face is covered by a shield. Only I didn't have any slots to see through.

The next day the *Chicago Sun-Times* carried a picture of me delivering the ball with my face buried behind that darn cap. The photo caption read something like "Blinding Speed."

If you ever saw me pitch, you know I had the unusual habit of not looking where I threw. This particular facet of my delivery, along with heat in the high nineties, explains why hitters didn't like to dig in against me.

I developed my windup as a kid, pitching to Jack. He would tease me, shouting things like, "Is that as hard as you can throw?" and, "That pitch wouldn't break an egg."

"C'mon, Rick," he'd say, "you gotta cut loose."

The more my brother ragged me, the harder I tried to

throw. I learned to put my whole body—arms, legs, butt—into each pitch, just so I could burn Jack's hand and shut him up. In the process of contorting my body to load up for maximum velocity, I'd jerk my head back, taking my eyes off his mitt.

Funny thing, though, the ball would still go to the target. My delivery may have been unorthodox, but my control wasn't half bad. As the saying goes, I was just wild enough to unsettle hitters.

That day in Chicago, though, became more than a matter of not looking at my target. I flat couldn't see.

And as the bill of the cap bearing the White Sox insignia slid down my forehead one more time, I suddenly had one of the most chilling thoughts of my entire career in the major leagues:

I'm going to kill Mr. Cub.

For there in the batter's box stood Ernie Banks, Mr. Cub, the most popular athlete in the history of Chicago sports—at least until the arrival of Michael Jordan. Ernie "Let's Play Two" Banks, the guy with the sunniest disposition in baseball. A beloved individual, about whom no one ever said an unkind word. Now, just because my cap didn't fit, Ernie Banks was about to be toast.

The White Sox, by bringing me in to pitch that exhibition, were making an unmistakable statement about my future with the team. At the time, I was en route to posting an 18-2 record in Appleton and winning all kinds of postseason honors in Class A ball. The Chicago brass had apparently decided to use this dress rehearsal against the Cubs to see how

I would handle the pressure of pitching to major league hitters.

Earlier in 1971, at spring training in Sarasota, I'd made a big impression on my employers. As part of our daily routine, minor league pitchers like me were sent to Payne Park, the big-league diamond, to throw fifteen minutes of batting practice to the starters.

I went over to Payne Park one afternoon and began throwing BP, not paying any particular attention to what I was doing. Gradually, though, I began to notice that the hitters weren't making solid contact. They kept fouling balls into the batting cage or swinging through the pitches.

I recall that Bill Melton and Tom Egan were two of the White Sox having trouble catching up with my fastball that day. They being big-leaguers, and me being some no-name pissant from the minors, I could tell Melton and Egan weren't pleased at the turn of events. Especially since their boss, Chuck Tanner, stood behind the cage, taking everything in.

The next thing I knew, they began yelling at me. Precisely what they yelled isn't the sort of language people repeat in polite company. They kept using the word "mother," but being a good Catholic boy, I could tell they weren't talking about Mother Teresa or Mother Superior.

Thinking they might be saying things about *my* mother, I turned up the heat. I began throwing BBs, and the White Sox hitters couldn't handle them. I left the mound, not a minute too soon, to a shower of obscenities.

To be honest, I lacked the awareness, or presence of mind, to know that a batting practice pitcher is supposed to groove the ball over the middle of the plate at half the normal velocity. The exercise is, after all, called batting practice. I'd been throwing fastballs like it was the seventh game of a World Series.

Chuck Tanner came over from the cage and stopped me. "Don't listen to those jerks," he said. "You were doing exactly what you're supposed to do. You blew them away. Great job, kid."

A month or two into the 1971 season, when the White Sox had a day off, Tanner and Sain traveled over to the Quad Cities in Iowa, where Appleton was playing, and taught me the mechanics for throwing a change-up. Sain, immortalized in baseball lore by the 1948 refrain of Boston Braves fans— "Spahn and Sain/And pray for rain"—possessed some of the best off-speed pitches ever.

Sain showed me that the key to throwing a change-up is to maintain the same motion and arm speed as with a fastball but to put the brakes on at the release point. Batters get fooled because the mechanics look the same but the ball travels 10 to 15 mph slower. By the time they realize the deception, they are out in front of the pitch. I valued the opportunity to learn from a master like Sain.

Among the highlights during my audition at Wrigley Field in 1971, besides showcasing my stuff for Tanner and Sain, was having White Sox third baseman Bill Melton tell me, "Throw like you did in spring training, kid, and you'll do fine." His words gave me a shot of confidence.

But the main highlight that day came when I didn't kill Mr. Cub. I got Ernie Banks to pop up. He lifted a lazy little fly ball that nearly fell into Mayor Daley's lap.

I also have a vivid memory about experiencing, for the

first time, the sound of major league baseball. As I walked down the catwalk from the clubhouse to the field, I became aware of an unfamiliar noise. The closer I ventured to the field, the louder the noise grew.

First it was a rumble. Then it turned into a roar. I suddenly realized all the commotion came from the bleachers and grandstands. My ears rang from the boisterous sound of a sold-out stadium. Baseball fans cheering their heroes.

Keep in mind that until that day at Wrigley Field, the largest crowd I'd ever pitched in front of might have been a couple thousand at a spring training game in Florida. I recognized immediately this was the sweetest sound—plus the loudest and most overwhelming—I'd ever heard.

What a turn-on it is for ballplayers to experience that kind of energy and enthusiasm. That root-root-rooting for the home team. The sheer sound of a baseball game—clamor generated by a full house of fans—is enough to pump you full of adrenaline and elevate your performance. The roar of the crowd goosed me plenty.

Speaking of noise, the hum of my fastball earned me an introduction to Chicago's resident superstar, Dick Allen. It happened the day before the 1972 opener in Kansas City. I'd been airing out my fastball, and the sound of the ball popping into catcher Tom Egan's mitt carried around Municipal Stadium.

Presently, here came a curious Dick Allen, carrying his massive forty-one-ounce bat, which resembled a telephone pole. He assumed his batting stance and motioned for me to continue throwing.

I hadn't met Allen during spring training. I'm not even

sure if he bothered to show up in Sarasota before we broke camp. What was the point of his working out in March, anyway? Everybody knew that, come April, Dick would be ready to play.

As a rookie, dumb as a box of rocks, I still had enough smarts to know that whatever else happened in the next few minutes, I'd better not have a pitch get away and hit Dick Allen. Allen was the cornerstone of the White Sox franchise, Chicago's alpha and omega. If I lost control of one of my pitches and inflicted any harm, my career would be over before it had begun. They'd either give me my walking papers or bury me in the lowest minor league.

Allen stayed in his stance until I finished throwing. He watched the movement of my pitches, listened to them, and apparently liked what he saw and heard. He waved me over, introduced himself and gave me a great piece of advice. "You got a good arm, so protect it, okay?" he told me. "Keep it covered up and wear a long sleeve when you pitch, kid. An arm like that, you have to keep warm."

I felt like a field grade officer getting some tactical advice from the commanding general. "Yes, sir," I said to myself, and offered an imaginary salute. From that day on, for the next twenty-two years, I always wore a long-sleeve T-shirt under my uniform. No one ever saw me throw bare-armed again.

Royals owner Ewing Kauffman petitioned the American League to force the White Sox to forfeit that opening series in Kansas City. His informants had reported that as many as a dozen Chicago players had been working out, using team facilities, during the strike. Such practice sessions violated one of the provisions of the strike.

I don't know if my new teammates had been practicing, illegally or otherwise, but I definitely didn't participate. This little dogie had been separated from the herd.

The day we flew north from Florida, I took a quick swing by Comiskey Park to drop off some personal items, then grabbed a ride downtown with one of the equipment managers. I had forty-eight dollars in my pocket and no immediate plans.

Displaying a homing instinct that would characterize my next two decades in the majors, I headed straight to a bar. Not just any of the hundreds of bars in Chicago, a great drinking city, either: I went to Joe Pepitone's Thing.

The former New York Yankee by then played for the Chicago Cubs. Cashing in on his fame and flamboyance, Pepitone had opened a popular watering hole in the downtown area. Like the rest of his baseball brethren, Joe Pep was eager to begin the season. In the meantime, though, he had customers to entertain.

I went into his bar, and there he stood, holding court. I wormed my way into his group at the bar and introduced myself. I told Joe that he'd been a hero to me and my family—I'm sure he'd never heard *that* before—and how sad we'd all been when the Yankees traded him in 1969 to Houston (which subsequently shipped him to the Cubs).

Joe's a fun guy, never at a loss for words. We had a few drinks, and a few more, and whiled away the night. His bar closed at something like four A.M., but Pepitone invited me to stay after he shut down for the night; a small group hung around and welcomed the dawn.

At six A.M., I stepped outside into the brisk morning air. I remember standing at a corner on Rush Street, pondering my next move, when two men approached and made a proposition.

"You want to come home with us and have a party?" they asked, and I knew instantly what they had in mind. They wanted to turn a tight end into a wide receiver, if you get my drift. They were the kind of guys in whose presence you didn't want to drop your car keys or loose change. I guess they figured me for the Jon Voight character in *Midnight Cowboy*—a country rube footloose in the big city.

I brushed them off, trying to hide my nervousness. That chance encounter frightened me and left me feeling vulnerable. I sensed an urgent need to formulate some kind of plan. So I called one of my older sisters, Lavonne, who lived in the Chicago suburbs, and spent most of my remaining money on a cab ride to her home in Des Plaines.

When I got there, I crashed. At dinner that night we started talking about Colorado Springs. Lavonne hadn't been back to visit Mom for a while, and I decided that when a ballplayer goes out on strike, there's no place like home.

By the next day, we were flying low across the Great Plains toward the Rockies. While Lavonne watched for the highway patrol, I drove a steady 100 mph, pedal to the metal. At one point we hit a bump in the road and heard the license plate fly off. We didn't bother to retrieve it.

Shortly after we got to Colorado Springs, I received word from the White Sox front office that the strike had been settled and players needed to report to Kansas City for opening day. Lavonne and I got back on the road and we drove—slower this time—east. She dropped me off in Kansas City and my career had begun.

———

When the White Sox returned to Chicago after opening on the road, starting pitcher Tom Bradley invited me to share his two-bedroom apartment on the South Side. Bradley, a native of North Carolina, was one of those pitchers whose IQ exceeded the top-end speed of his fastball. That's not always the case.

Four years my senior, he had three seasons under his belt. He started showing me the ropes of being a major-leaguer. Soon after, Bradley, whose native intelligence shone through in his quick wit, began calling me "Goss."

Then Bradley decided to change my nickname to Goose. "When you're out on the mound, looking in to read the signs, you resemble a big ol' long-necked goose," he said.

I had no comeback for him, so Goose I became.

Goss, Goose, Gossage—a few players in baseball's long history have had similar names to mine. For example, Howie Goss was an outfielder with Pittsburgh and Houston in the early 1960s. Fans affectionately called him "Home Run Howie," but after he produced only eleven homers in two seasons in the bigs, Goss left the scene.

Jim Gosger was a journeyman outfielder who lasted ten seasons in the majors and played on five different teams, most notably the Red Sox and Expos. In his career year (1966), Gosger hit ten homers. Not to be overlooked is Greg Goossen, a catcher for the New York Mets who later was converted to a first baseman and outfielder. When Goossen reached the majors in 1965, Mets manager Casey Stengel, evaluating his team's collection of talent, made this memorable remark in reference to him: "I got this kid who's nineteen, and in ten years he has a chance to be twenty-nine."

Then there was Leon "Goose" Goslin, a star with the Washington Senators during the 1920s and the American League batting champion (.379) in 1928. Goose Goslin helped lead the Senators to A.L. pennants in 1924 and 1925 and hit over .300 in the World Series each year.

In the 1935 World Series, playing for Detroit, Goslin drove home Mickey Cochrane with two out in the ninth inning of game six against the Cubs, giving the Tigers their first world championship. Goose Goslin was elected to baseball's Hall of Fame in 1968. He died three years later.

As a rookie, I was forced to endure some of the usual hazing rituals associated with being the new kid on the block. I had to carry bags through airports for Tom Bradley and the other pitchers. I had to haul their equipment to and from the practice field. I was subjected to the usual assortment of standard baseball pranks, like hot foots (which, as the name implies, involves setting a teammate's shoes on fire).

My teammates hounded me unmercifully about my taste in attire, or lack thereof. Guys like Bill Melton, Stan Bahnsen, Tom Egan, and Wilbur Wood would ridicule my slacks, sport jackets, and ties. One day I walked into the clubhouse wearing a new pair of wing-tipped shoes, which had a tonguelike device that popped up and down where shoelaces normally are found.

My teammates immediately called the fashion police. They humiliated me so much that before the night was over those shoes were in the trash. I went home wearing my shower shoes.

Say whatever else you will about big-leaguers, there's a Peter Pan quality to our existence: We never grow up. We're like big little kids. The vast majority of ballplayers have advanced degrees in horseplay.

I also learned some valuable lessons as a rookie, one of which is: Never fall asleep on an airplane. If you do, you're liable to wake up with shaving cream on your face and bubblegum in your hair. (Years later I made a major blunder by falling asleep on a Yankees charter, and woke up to the smell of burning leather. Dick Tidrow had set my shoes on fire. Burned 'em crisp.)

Or never fall asleep, period. We were on a road trip my rookie year, and at the hotel one evening, roaming the floors looking for mischief, we noticed a room door open and a teammate of ours lying naked across his bed. Upon further investigation, we discovered he had been seriously overserved that night. He was out cold.

Surveying the room, we saw that hotel management had been kind enough to provide our friend with a complimentary basket of fruit. Not wishing to see such a splendid gift go to waste, we used the fruit to administer a full body massage. We rubbed peaches on his legs, mangoes on his ankles, strawberries across his chest. We poured juices from all the various fruit into his hair. I'm surprised the odor didn't wake him up.

To top off our work, we took a banana and placed it in an oft-used orifice. I would have liked to seen his expression when he awoke during the night, or the next morning, and realized he was tutti-frutti.

One of the highlights of the 1972 season was making my first trip to Yankee Stadium, the House that Ruth Built. I jumped off the bus when we arrived at the stadium, and while my teammates went to the clubhouse to dress for the game, I dashed up to a security guard and asked for directions to the field.

Then I raced down a corridor, careened around a corner, and dashed toward light at the end of a tunnel. I emerged in the Yankees dugout, which is several feet below the field and not as spacious as you might think. In fact, I had to bend over to keep from hitting my head on the top.

But what a sight to behold! Yankee Stadium, the greatest citadel in sports. The place where Ruth and Gehrig stood. Where DiMaggio and Mantle roamed. The place where Roger Maris hit his record 61st homer and Don Larsen pitched his perfect game. My eyes bugged out like Will Clark's.

That night, when Chuck Tanner called me in for relief duty, I didn't stride to the mound at my normally rapid clip. I actually dallied. For once I felt in no hurry to rare back and fire. I was too busy taking in the sights of Yankee Stadium, every bit as beautiful to me as a Rocky Mountain sunset.

When I got the ball from Ed Herrmann, I stepped off the mound and rubbed it up and suddenly realized my knees were shaking. The feeling of actually playing in Yankee Stadium was awesome. I also thought about my dad and how proud of me he would have been at that moment.

From the time I was twelve years old, leading the Padgett Realty Angels to the championship of Colorado Springs youth ball, my dad told townspeople that one day I'd pitch in the big leagues. He didn't make that statement arrogantly, just in his usual low-key, subtle fashion. Jick made it sound more matter-of-fact than boastful, like the major leagues were my destiny. And now here I was, about to toe the rubber at Yankee Stadium.

I like to tell people that my dad had been born about a hundred years too late. He belonged up in the mountains, hunting and fishing, not in the city. He had more of an affinity for woods and nature than for concrete and glass.

My dad never was a much of a breadwinner. He never put any real effort into making money. When I was a youngster, our family had suffered the humiliation of having to downsize involuntarily. We moved from a two-story house with three bedrooms next door to a tiny one-story house with one bedroom. It was just a little box, with no paint on the exterior and no grass in the front yard. Rather ironic for a man who paid the bills by handling landscape projects, wouldn't you say?

When I reached high school and my pals who had their own cars picked me up or dropped me off, I felt too embarrassed about our humble home to invite them in. I wanted to protect the secret of how few material possessions we had. Some secret, all right: One look at the outside of the Gossage house said it all.

When the cupboard got bare, Dad and I would get out our rifles and go hunting—a polite way of saying that we poached. We would bring back a deer, skin and section it, and our family would eat venison for three meals a day until it ran out.

Or Dad and I would go out and shoot rabbits; my mother made a great rabbit stew.

By the time I arrived at Yankee Stadium, I still hadn't come totally to terms with my dad's death four years earlier. I still had feelings of guilt about the times when, as a selfish teenager, I would hassle him when he asked me to help him with his work.

By then his lungs had been ravaged. Too much time in the mines during his youth, too many cigarettes in adulthood. The emphysema that would kill him had already begun to sap his strength. As he grew weaker he needed my help on bigger jobs—like the grounds he maintained for a large insurance company—and rather than volunteering to go, I'd bitch about wanting to play ball instead.

I didn't visit my dad in the hospital during the last few weeks of his life. I lacked the maturity to deal with the looming death that filled his room. The last time I went to see him, I couldn't handle watching him breathe out of a respirator, hooked up with so many tubes.

I never told my dad good-bye. Mom came home from the hospital one afternoon and said simply, "Dad's gone." But standing on the mound at Yankee Stadium that evening, I had a peaceful feeling that my dad knew his dream for his youngest son had come true.

"Dad," I said, my eyes scanning the heavens, "this one's for you."

The most unforgettable aspect of my first season in the majors had to be the brilliant performance by Dick Allen. At the risk of using the most overused and devalued word in the lexicon of sports—what the hell, I'll go ahead—he was awesome. Capital A.

Allen carried us to a record of 87-67 in 1972, five and a half games behind the A.L. West champion Oakland A's. Oakland, beginning its three-year run of world championships under manager Dick Williams, had a star-studded lineup featuring Reggie Jackson, Joe Rudi, Sal Bando, and Bert Campaneris, as well as great pitchers like Catfish Hunter, Ken Holtzman, and Blue Moon Odom.

We had Dick.

Granted, having Dick was infinitely better than not having dick, er, Dick. But other than a few solid bats like Melton and Carlos May, we didn't have much punch in our attack.

Allen's selection as the American League's Most Valuable Player in 1972 amounted to a no-brainer. He had 37 homers, 113 RBIs, and led the universe in critical hits. He was our one-man wrecking crew.

Allen that year joined a small group of players in baseball history who won an MVP award after being named Rookie of the Year. He had won the latter award in 1964, when he played third base for the Phillies. Of historical note, Allen hit the first homer in the Astrodome on April 12, 1965, shortly after making the comment he didn't care for indoor baseball and artificial turf. "If a horse won't eat it, I don't want to play on it," he said.

It's a shame, but today's players have no idea about Dick Allen's ability. That's because he didn't suck up to the press like a lot of major-leaguers do. He wasn't a quote machine. He didn't play the publicity game at all. His reticence pissed off many members of the press, so they made him out to be a bad guy. For the record, he wasn't.

It's just that Dick didn't suck up to anyone, period. He didn't possess an ounce of BS in his makeup. Dick shot straight and played hardball.

He also studied the game intently. I can remember being in the dugout at times when some of the White Sox players would be horsing around, playing grab-ass and goofing around. Dick would suddenly pipe up with, "Cut the crap and get your heads in the game. Watch the pitcher. Learn something." The dugout would get as quiet as a funeral parlor, and those goofballs would start acting like pallbearers.

Allen played to win. The only stats that mattered to him were W's and L's—wins and losses. Many was the time he'd set up a pitcher by looking foolish on purpose. Early in a game, with the bases empty, Dick might let a pitcher make him look bad on a slider. Late in the game, with runners on base and the game hanging in the balance, Dick would come up again and the pitcher would say to himself, "Hey, this guy can't touch my slider."

So here would come a slider, and there a slider would go—either smashed off the outfield wall or into the cheap seats. Gone. White Sox win.

Other times, Dick would put us ahead early and then say, "I got you the lead, fellows. Now hold it." With that, he'd take himself out of the lineup in the sixth or seventh inning and retire to the clubhouse. He never stayed around to pad his stats in runaway victories. Dick interpreted his role as producing wins, not numbers.

That season, Allen hit some of the most wicked shots I ever saw. Against Detroit he hit a ball off the upper facade in center field in Tiger Stadium, and I promise you pieces of wood and paint chips fluttered down for the next five minutes. It was like the stadium was coming apart, piece by piece.

In another game against Detroit, Allen hit a rocket back through the box that nearly took off Mickey Lolich's head. Lolich hit the dirt and lay on the mound like Jell-O, quivering, while the ball kept rising and went over the Tiger center fielder's head. Lolich must have lain there for five minutes. When someone asked him after the game why he stayed down for so long, he replied, "Because I thought the ball was going to ricochet off the wall and kill me." It had been hit that hard.

In a road game against Minnesota, he hit not one but *two* wicked liners that knuckled on their way out to center field. The shots ate up Bobby Darwin. Darwin went to catch the ball over here, and—unbelievably—it landed over there. Dick trotted around the bases for two inside-the-park homers on the same day, only the second time that had occurred in the major leagues. It seemed like we were watching an instant replay.

Dick also hit a home run at Comiskey Park that defied every law of physics, including Newton's. It was a line drive to left field that went through some arches in a recessed area just below the upper deck. The ball wound up in a kids' park beyond the bleachers. For a baseball to stay that low and yet travel that far seems impossible. Yet we saw it happen.

I've wondered through the years whether I gush about Dick Allen in 1972 because I was a rookie and, at that point, had no basis for comparison. But I'm convinced his season really was as good as I thought.

I played in the major leagues through the season-ending strike in 1994. I've had teammates like Dave Parker in Pittsburgh, Reggie Jackson in New York, Mark McGwire and Jose Canseco in Oakland, Ken Griffey Jr. in Seattle. Some serious, serious power hitters. Yet in the time we were together, none of them had a year comparable to Dick Allen's in 1972.

Everything he hit was damage. In baseball jargon, *damage* refers to base hits that win a game or bring a team back from a deficit and give it a chance to win. Damage is like a coup de grâce. A finisher. Every time the 1972 White Sox needed a big hit late, we got damage from Dick.

One time he did some damage after having a mental lapse. We were playing at Cleveland, and when an Indian grounded out for what Dick thought was the final out, he flipped the ball to the first base umpire. Only the umpire jumped out of the way of the toss because, in fact, there were only two outs. What's worse, Cleveland had two runners on base and they both scored.

Dick came into the dugout and apologized for his mistake. "Guys, I'll get those runs back," he vowed. Then he made good on his promise, hitting a three-run homer that won the game.

I'll let my tribute go at this: If I were to pick an "All-Teammate Team" from my career, I'd put Dick Allen at first base. And bat him in the lineup wherever he damn well pleased.

Besides that little misstep in the visitor's bullpen on April 15, 1972, there were several other occasions when I fell flat on my face in baseball. Figuratively, if not literally.

I did a nosedive during an important showcase game during my senior year in high school. A dozen or so scouts had come to see me pitch, but they only got a cursory look at my stuff because I was rocked like a martyr. By the second or third inning, I was gone. So were the scouts.

During my banner season at Appleton in 1971, I got lit up like a firecracker during one start. The harder I threw the ball, the faster it came flying back over my head. Guys hit such wicked shots that I thought my catcher would come out and announce, "Get the married guys off the infield."

As it happened, that particular outing came on a Sunday afternoon. Coincidentally, I'd been out on the town partying with my teammates the night before. If my calculations are correct, for the twenty-four hours preceding game time the ratio of hours slept to beers consumed was 1:9 (two hours of sleep to three six-packs).

I didn't get out of the first inning that day. After Appleton manager Joe Sparks gave me the hook, he jumped in my face in the dugout. "I hope you learned your fucking lesson," Sparks snapped. He was so livid, that's all he could say.

Thereafter, I always made sure team parties and other extracurricular activities never interfered with my performance on the mound. Well, almost.

There *was* the occasion of the final day of the 1972 season. We were to play a meaningless game on the road in Minnesota. By then we had wrapped up second place in the A.L. West behind Oakland, the team en route to a World Series rendezvous with Cincinnati.

On Tuesday, October 3, on the eve of the final game of the year, White Sox players gathered for a farewell party in a suite at the Lemington Hotel. Spirits were high and joviality ruled the night. We deserved to blow off some steam; we'd had a great year. Or perhaps I should say that Dick Allen, and perhaps a handful of others, had great years.

Near sunrise, however, I came to the sobering realization that I was scheduled to be Chicago's starting pitcher that morning. The game had a ten A.M. starting time. Bummer. Sure enough, my spotless 7-0 record—which Tanner helped carefully cultivate all season, picking spots that never put me in jeopardy—got downed as quickly as cold beer in a chugalug contest.

My pitching line that day in Minnesota read:

	IP	H	R	ER	BB	SO
GOSSAGE (7-1)	3	13	9	9	3	3

Ouch. That constituted a different kind of damage. My respectable 3.49 ERA for the season shot up nearly a full point, to a less impressive 4.28. Cesar Tovar rattled the fences. So did Bobby Darwin. Even Twins pitcher Bert Blyleven got a hit. About the only thing I did right that day was hold future Hall of Famer Harmon Killebrew hitless. Everyone else in the Twins lineup lit me up. I felt like the Ned Beatty character in *Deliverance*. They made me squeal like a pig.

When I fell on my face in high school, in front of so many major league scouts, I figured I had blown any chance to be selected in baseball's 1970 amateur draft. So I started making plans to play college baseball and see what would develop down the road.

I'd received feelers from several schools in Colorado, plus national powerhouses like Arizona and Arizona State. But with shaky grades, junior college looked to be the only option. I had an eye on Mesa College, a good baseball school in Grand Junction, Colorado, and Southern Colorado State College in Pueblo.

While weighing scholarship offers for the fall, my most immediate concern in June 1970 was finding a job for the summer. I met with some people in the Parks and Recreation Department in Colorado Springs and they hired me to coach Little League baseball. The job only paid minimum wage, but in our house every extra dollar was precious.

I raced home to tell my mother. "Hey, Mom," I shouted, bolting through the front door. "Guess what? I got a job!"

She motioned at a stranger sitting in our living room and said, "Well, Rick, this man has a job for you too."

The man turned out to be Bill Kimball, from North Platte, Nebraska, an area scout for the White Sox. Based on his recommendation, Chicago had selected me in the ninth round of the 1970 draft. The news bowled me over like a collision at home plate. I flopped down on the sofa and tried to let things sink in.

Later that day we drove over to Bob's Cafe, where Kimball offered me $5,000 to sign. Instinctively, I knew what to do: Ask for more. I wasn't a math whiz, but I figured scholarships to play college baseball were worth at least $10,000.

After a little give-and-take we finally agreed to an $8,000 contract, with incentives that could potentially lift the deal to about $14,000. I immediately felt as rich as Rockefeller. I went out and bought a '57 Chevy and gave the rest of the money to Mom for bills and accumulated debts.

Speaking of rich, Kimball told me that day that I'd have to change my name from Rick to Rich (my full name is Richard Michael Gossage). I don't remember his rationale, but it had something to do with pronunciation. Kimball said "Rich" Gossage sounded easier on the ear than "Rick" Gossage.

So Rich Gossage I became. I made it to Chicago in 1972, met Tom Bradley, and became Goose. By that point I didn't care whether people with the White Sox called me Rick, Rich, or Goose, as long as they spelled my name right on the paycheck.

That first season in the majors produced one memorable encounter with Willie Horton that illustrates how I approached pitching throughout my career.

Granted, I didn't develop into a intimidator overnight. I didn't truly dominate until Pittsburgh in 1977, and afterward with the New York Yankees and San Diego Padres, when I grew my Fu Manchu moustache and went off the charts in intensity. But from the beginning in Chicago, I wanted hitters to have no doubts about who was boss. I did my best to exude confidence on the mound and never, ever backed down from a challenge.

Which is what Willie Horton, one of Detroit's best hitters, represented. The first time I faced Horton, he hunched forward in the batter's box and I knew that to beat him—to keep him from extending his huge arms and driving my pitches—I would have to throw inside.

I tried to come inside on the first pitch but my fastball accidentally got away. It tailed in too sharply and whizzed right under his chin.

As the saying goes, I undressed him. Horton's bat went in one direction, his batting helmet in another, and he spun around so fast he practically corkscrewed himself into the ground.

If you don't recall Willie Horton, he was the Mike Tyson of baseball. The baddest dude of his era. Horton had a build like a brick firehouse and guns (biceps) like anvils. Without question, Horton was the last guy in the majors anyone would want to tangle with.

As he began dusting himself off, I took the return peg from Ed Herrmann. I stood behind the mound, facing center field, when it suddenly dawned on me that for self-preservation I'd better make sure Horton hadn't headed out to pay me a visit.

I turned to face him and wished I hadn't. Horton's eyes bulged in their sockets. If looks could kill, his said it was time to dial 911.

But I realized I couldn't allow myself to be intimidated. I had to face down my fear, badass Willie Horton or not. On the next pitch I came inside again. It was no accident.

I spun Horton around like a carousel. He did another 360-degree dive, his bat and helmet flying all over the place. Once again he slowly picked himself up and dusted off his uniform.

This time, though, Horton didn't bother trying to stare me down. I had earned his respect. He'd tried to intimidate me and failed, so now we could get on with the at bat.

Baseball has changed dramatically in the past twenty-five years. Back then, pitchers would throw inside and batters respected their right to do so. That's how we played the game. Nowadays, Horton would probably come out to the mound and pinch my head off. Today's players will come out at the slightest provocation. It's ridiculous.

Today's hitters intimidate pitchers. As a member of the pitching fraternity, I believe there's something wrong with that. The guy holding the ball, not the one holding the bat, should be doing the intimidating.

Batters today want to be so comfortable at the plate that it's like they're hitting out of a rocking chair. I see batters taking all kinds of liberties, diving out over the plate and daring pitchers to throw inside. Believe me, that would never have happened when I broke into the big leagues.

As I used to tell anyone who asked, I would have drilled my own mother.

CHAPTER 2

1973–75

RIDE MY SEESAW

Were it not for that butt-kicking administered by the Minnesota Twins in the final game of 1972, I would have finished my rookie season undefeated. Coming off such a positive and productive year, my prospects rose like a blue-chip stock in a bull market.

One of the White Sox beat writers in Chicago, projecting the existing talent pool ahead to the 1973 season, wrote: "It's no stretch of the imagination to see Rich Gossage bursting into a starting role." That fit my plans exactly. I fully expected to join Wilbur Wood, Jim Kaat, and Stan Bahnsen in the rotation.

As things turned out, I got burned during 1973. I suffered a meltdown, a total eclipse. You've heard of baseball players going through bad stretches or slumps? My slump in 1973 lasted all season. I gave new meaning to the term sophomore jinx after compiling a glittering record of 0-4. That's right, I had zero wins. I registered the dreaded oh-fer. *Oh*-fer 1973.

My pitches were hit early and often. I suffered the indignity of being sent down—not once, but twice—to Chicago's Class AAA affiliate in Des Moines. To my credit, though, I achieved a level of consistency: I got hammered both as a starter and reliever.

How had I managed to go from prospect to suspect? I showed up for my second season in 1973 distracted, over-weight, and lacking control with the breaking stuff.

What's more, for the first time in my life my fastball went AWOL. I worked so hard trying to develop a slider and change-up that I neglected my best pitch. I took the fastball for granted and then discovered, much to my chagrin, that it had gone south.

That made me a pitcher with no pitches, which is the equivalent of being a one-armed paperhanger or a one-legged man in an ass-kicking contest.

But let's back up a bit.

On October 28, 1972, roughly three weeks after my rookie season with Chicago ended, I married Cornelia (Corna) Lukaszewicz in a wedding mass at Corpus Christi Catholic Church in Colorado Springs. My brother Jack served as best man. Corna's sister Michelle attended her.

Our wedding had its share of memorable moments. My six-year-old nephew Chris, Jack's son, served as ringbearer but was overcome by the occasion and also a bit confused. "I don't want to marry Corna," he blurted out, holding his ground at the back of the chapel and refusing to budge. The poor kid thought he was getting married. My sister-in-law Wanda finally got Chris headed down the aisle after bribing him with the promise of ice cream.

We exchanged vows without a hitch, although Corna immediately realized that all the flowers at the altar had been left over from a previous wedding. Our flowers had been delivered to the church, but remained in the foyer. Later, the cocktail napkins failed to make it to our reception. Visitors to our home during the first few years of our marriage were served drinks on napkins inscribed with wedding bells and "Corna and Rick."

After the wedding we stayed at my in-laws' house in Colorado Springs for a few days before leaving for Puerto Rico and winter ball. One of Corna's brothers-in-law, Al, joked that it was just like a Polish bride to spend her honeymoon with her parents.

What did we care? We were young and in love.

Corna was born in 1951 (the same year as I) in Lubsko, Poland, near the East German border. Her parents, Gerard and Herta Lukaszewicz, were both doctors engaged in private practice. They had seven children, of which Corna is the second youngest. (I'm the second youngest of six Gossage kids.)

In the late 1950s their peaceful world was shattered by communism. One day Corna's family was living life on the sunny side of the street; the next it was fleeing the country under the cover of night. The Lukaszewiczs had to abandon their home and all their possessions—not to mention friends and relatives—or risk being rounded up by communist oppressors. Their house later became the communist headquarters in the area.

Corna's family took temporary refuge in Vienna, Austria, and then spent a year in Switzerland while her parents made plans to migrate to the United States. The Lukaszewiczs came to America and lived for a year in Athens, Georgia, before finally settling down in Colorado Springs. Her dad, a geography buff, determined that the Rockies were the most beautiful mountains in the country.

Corna and I knew each other casually in high school; she was better acquainted with my younger sister, Paula. Although we were both members of the Wasson High School class of 1970, our schedules never overlapped. She took a precollege curriculum, while I slogged away at vocational studies like wood shop.

Academics never ranked high on my list of priorities. Perhaps I might have made better grades had I bothered to hit the books, but the point is moot. I went to high school solely to play sports. I majored in jock.

I would have played football in high school—and with my strong throwing arm, might have made a pretty decent passer—but the season overlaps with hunting. My football career ended in the ninth grade, when I informed our coach, Mike Larson, that I would have to miss an upcoming C squad game because of a conflict.

"Son, you'd better have a good excuse," he told me.

I did. I had to go hunting with my dad.

"Hunting!" Coach Larson spewed, airing me out like a mattress. "If you don't show up, I'll expect to see all your stuff on my desk Monday morning." He did.

During winter, I played basketball. As a senior, I averaged 18 points a game (with a high of 36 against Pueblo South) and 9 rebounds, displaying the same intensity on the hardwood that surfaced when I pitched. The coach took advantage of my strong arm to design special fast-break plays. The guards would take off down the court after the opponents scored, and I'd wheel the ball out of bounds and heave it the length of the court. My buddy Leroy Gortariz, who played one of the guard positions when he wasn't riding the pine, likes to tease about the time I took the ball out of bounds and threw it halfway up the bleachers beyond the other basket. C'mon, it slipped.

That same strong arm nearly fried my bacon during my senior year. As part of the Halloween celebration that fall, Wasson High teachers wore costumes. One of the assistant football coaches, Fred Lusted, came dressed as Broadway Joe Namath, the star quarterback of the New York Jets. He had on a full uniform, with pads.

Coach Lusted was strutting around in the cafeteria, showing off for the girls, when one of my buddies said, "Hey, Rick, see if you can hit him." I picked up a giant seedless purple grape off my plate and—as unlikely as it sounds—pegged it across the cafeteria and right through the ear hole in his helmet. The grape exploded at impact and left a large purple splotch on the side of Coach Lusted's head.

"Okay, who did it?" he demanded.

I owned up. "I did, Coach."

He went nuts. He grabbed me by my shirt, marched me out of the cafeteria and down to his office, bouncing me off lockers as we went down the hall. I'd just picked up a chair to defend myself when a couple of other football coaches burst in and managed to calm him down. For a minute I thought we were headed to fist city. That could have been ruinous.

—

With spring came baseball season, and I felt totally in my element. I made all-area both as a junior and senior, even though my record as a senior was only 6-5. People who saw me pitch, with a three-quarter motion and my fierce demeanor, said I had a chance to play professionally. Of course, city parks around the country are full of high school hotshots who never make the grade as a pro. Time would tell.

When I came home from rookie ball in the fall of 1970, I started hanging around with Corna and one of her good friends, Kathy Brotherton. One weekend the three of us drove up to Boulder to visit Leroy, who had enrolled for his freshman year at the University of Colorado. Corna and Kathy came roaring up in a '63 Ford Galaxy and honked the horn. I ran out, hopped in the back seat, and off we went on our big trip to Boulder.

My mom wondered who had hustled me off on a Friday afternoon and deposited me back on her doorstep Sunday night. Corna, Kathy, and I were just three post-high-school kids trying to find their way in the world and—to quote from Steppenwolf—"looking for adventure and whatever [came] our way."

It was all platonic. Good clean fun. We were simply friends.

After I left for spring training in 1971, I didn't see Corna again for six months. I didn't think of her the whole time I was gone. Nor, for that matter, did she ever think of me. But the following fall, when I got home after my big year at Appleton, we ran into each other at Giuseppe's East, one of the most popular hangouts in town.

Corna, a five-foot-six blonde, had always been cute. Yet

one look at her told me either she'd become a whole lot prettier or my vision had greatly improved after a summer in Wisconsin, eating cheese and drinking beer. She stopped me like a balk.

When I learned that a bunch of kids at Guiseppe's, including Corna, were going to a woodsie that night, I tagged along. I wanted to check her out. Woodsies, for purposes of clarity, were parties in the woods. Kids would build a campfire and hang out. I'm sure kids in other parts of the country have riversies or lakesies or swampsies or beachsies; in Colorado we had woodsies.

I drove Corna home at sunrise. We pulled into the driveway just as her mother was leaving for work. She gave us a stare.

The next day—after paying my sister Paula two dollars to clean my car—I called Corna and asked her out. When Corna told her parents she had a date with me, her mother said disapprovingly: "Is he the boy who brought you home at six-thirty?"

Let the record show that on our first date Corna and I went to dinner at Cork and Cleaver, a red meat emporium, and after gorging ourselves we caught the late showing of a Clint Eastwood flick, *Play Misty for Me.*

That movie sent out some serious vibrations. You had Eastwood and Donna Mills strolling hand in hand as surf pounded away on the Big Sur shoreline. You had Roberta Flack singing the romantic ballad "The First Time (Ever I Saw Your Face)." The movie also had enough action—an obsessed, whacked-out Jessica Walter carving up whomever stood between her and Clint—to keep male viewers from nodding off.

Corna and I shared a powerful aura that night. Something was in the air besides the smell of popcorn. I don't remember exactly what time we got home—but it was late and our hair was mussed.

For the rest of the winter we were inseparable and fell madly in love. We were stone-cold crazy about each other. No sooner had I left for spring training in Sarasota in February than we realized our lives weren't the same without the other one around.

Nor, as Corna discovered after putting the pencil to the telephone bills we were running up, could we afford to be apart. In March she flew down to Florida, and we started making plans to get married after the season.

Upon graduation from Wasson High, Corna had landed a civil service job. She worked as a steno/typist for the Defense Communications Agency (DCA), an affiliate of the U.S. Defense Department (NORAD) in Colorado Springs.

She had a good job making good money and showed no reluctance to travel. During the 1972 season Corna made several trips to join me, either in Chicago or on a road trip. She met and became friends with a number of the White Sox players and their wives. Being a liberated guy, I let Corna pay for all her airline tickets.

I turned twenty-one that July, but Corna, who's three months younger, was still twenty when we tried to enter a popular club in Chicago one night. I kept telling the doorman that Corna was of age but she'd left her driver's license at home. I could vouch for her.

He finally turned to Corna and asked her age. "Twenty," she said unwittingly. Which goes to show that you can take the girl out of Poland, but you can't take . . .

———

A few weeks after our wedding, Corna and I left for winter ball in Puerto Rico. The three months (November-January) we spent in the Caribbean served as an extended honeymoon.

We had a ball. We adopted the lifestyle of baseball couples by becoming night owls. We saw as much of dawn as Tony Orlando.

I pitched for Ponce, one of the largest cities on the island. We had a pretty decent club, featuring three Cruz brothers—José, Hector, and Cirilo. About the only problem with the situation was that the manager, Frank Verdi, thought I had my engine on cruise control. Verdi and I had several disagreements about my work ethic.

Although I pitched well in Ponce, Verdi might have had a point. Corna and I were heavily into our honeymoon mode. We spent most of our time eating, drinking, or in bed.

We developed a taste for the way Puerto Rican chefs produced spicy dishes of *pestado* (fish), *pollo* (chicken), and *carne* (beef). We developed a weakness for *langosta* (lobster). We wolfed down platters of *patatas* (potatoes) and *frijoles* (beans). We ate like dining was an Olympic sport and we were in medal contention.

Corna and I were in San Juan to celebrate the arrival of 1973 when reports surfaced on New Year's Eve that Roberto Clemente had been killed. Clemente had chartered a DC-7 to rush disaster relief and first-aid supplies to earthquake victims in Nicaragua.

He was on a mission of mercy. His plane was seriously

overloaded, however, and shortly after takeoff from San Juan the overtaxed engine conked out and the aircraft plummeted out of the sky.

Roberto Clemente was the patron saint of Puerto Rican baseball, his homeland's Babe Ruth. When news spread that the great outfielder had perished, his countrymen and countrywomen flocked to the coastline to look for signs of the wreckage. Rescue workers launched a flotilla of ships to seek any trace of survivors.

Plans for Puerto Ricans to celebrate a *prospero año* came to an immediate halt. Champagne corks went unpopped, fireworks unlit. Clemente's tragic death sucked the New Year's joy out of an entire island.

Corna and I recall staying at the same hotel in San Juan with Pittsburgh players and Pirate executives who came in for the funeral. Their faces were drawn, their lips pursed tight. They, and everyone else on the island, were still in shock.

Clemente was buried with the kind of ceremony reserved for a chief of state. The island mourned deeply for months afterward. It was such a sad, sad affair.

I'll never forget the look on my mother's face when Corna and I got back to Colorado Springs after three months of winter ball. The skinny son she'd seen off to Puerto Rico now resembled the Pillsbury Dough Boy. A running joke in the family had been about the time a local sportswriter, covering a Wasson High game, referred to me as a "stocky" righthander.

At the time, I was as stocky as Olive Oyl.

After three months in Puerto Rico, though, the word stocky would no longer suffice. I wasn't stocky—I was fat.

When I arrived in Sarasota for spring training in 1973, my teammates took one look at my girth and put the nickname Goose in storage. They called me "Pieface" instead. Granted, I resembled the second coming of Mickey Lolich. But after a few weeks in the Florida humidity—and a few thousand sit-ups and sprints—my gut began to recede. After that feeding frenzy in Puerto Rico, though, I never again weighed less than 200 pounds. Still don't.

My performance that spring was putrid. Simply awful. Not only did I fail to impress Tanner and Sain with my off-speed stuff, I also managed to misplace my fastball. My pitches were rocked like a hurricane. Fortunately, my last few outings were decent enough that Tanner took me north with the big-league team.

My first three appearances in April 1973—all against the Kansas City Royals, incidentally—caused everyone to shudder. I just couldn't get anyone out. When my ERA soared to double digits, Tanner and Sain had no choice but to bury me in the bullpen.

I didn't pitch again for nearly three weeks. In mid-May, Tanner gave me a start, and though saddled with a loss, I registered a complete game. Chuck liked what he'd seen. "If he pitches like that all year, gives up [only] three runs, he's going to win a lot of games for us," he said.

That one good start, though, proved to be a fluke, an illusion. The reality was I had regressed as a pitcher, and my confidence, consequently, had been snuffed like a candle.

After giving up a grand-slam homer to Joe Lahoud of Milwaukee in mid-June, I received the message every ballplayer dreads:

The boss wants to see you.

I knew Tanner didn't want to see me to discuss how the stock market was doing or the long-term weather forecast for Chicagoland. I might have been dumb, but I wasn't stupid.

Chuck came right to the point. "Kid, you're outta here. We're sending you down to Iowa [Class AAA]," he said. "Get your stuff together and get over to Des Moines. You're gone."

Okay, Tanner may have been a bit more diplomatic and encouraging than that. He probably tried to sell me on the idea that a change of scenery might do me some good.

Still, the demotion overwhelmed me. I had to borrow sunglasses from Terry Forster so that my other teammates, and fans hanging around Comiskey Park to get autographs, wouldn't see the tears in my eyes.

Corna and I packed up our things and skulked away to the American Association. We bawled like babies on the way to Des Moines. We thought our world had come to an end. Funny thing, though: When we got to Iowa, we discovered that we liked Des Moines. It's a great city with a lot of friendly people. The Iowa manager, Joe Sparks, had been my skipper in Appleton, so I immediately felt at ease.

It didn't take me long to have a misadventure, however. Iowa was scheduled to play a night game in Omaha, and rather than take a team bus, players often drove their own cars the 150 or so miles.

I suggested Corna drive ahead to Omaha. We could rendezvous that evening at a motel near the ballpark. Former Detroit star Denny McLain—the last 30-game winner in the majors (1968), who by then was toiling in the minor leagues trying to recapture his magic—had heard about a good golf course somewhere near Council Bluffs, Iowa. McLain wanted fellow pitchers Joe Keough and me to help him check it out.

Which we did. We left Des Moines early that morning, played golf in the afternoon, and then drove on toward Omaha. We were somewhere near the Nebraska line, far off the main highway, when we heard a tire blow. Denny pulled off to the side of the road, and we got out to inspect the damage. Sure enough, the tire was as flat as a two-by-four. McLain popped open the trunk and we discovered, much to our chagrin, that he had no spare.

Being the youngest and least tenured, I was deputized to go for help. I began walking down a dusty back road, cornfields in all directions, as far as the eye could see. The sun slowly began sinking. So did my spirits.

Meanwhile, over in Omaha, Joe Sparks began to panic. An hour before game time he called the motel where most of the players were staying and reached Corna.

"Where the hell is Rich?" he asked.

"Isn't he with you?" she replied.

Not exactly.

I must have walked six or seven miles before finally coming to a farmhouse. The farmer listened to my story and, thank goodness, showed some sympathy.

He drove me back to McLain's car—where we removed the flat tire—and then took me to a gas station in a nearby town. When we finally got a new tire on the McLain's car, we thanked the farmer repeatedly and then headed off to Omaha lickety-split, arriving in the middle of the game.

Sparks blew his top.

When we got back to Des Moines, Sparks evidently called back to Chicago and reported that the Gossage kid had fallen in with bad company. I guess people were worried that Denny McLain and others might have a negative influence on me, because within ten days I got recalled to the big leagues.

My performance during the remainder of 1973 showed little improvement. General Manager Roland Hemond and Chuck Tanner decided to ship me back down to Iowa again in August, before recalling me for good when team rosters expanded in September.

Corna, who had set up a household during our first stint in Des Moines, didn't even bother to unpack the second time around. If we needed a change of clothes, we had to fish them out of the car trunk.

About the only success I had during the second half of the 1973 season was lowering my ERA under double digits. Still, I finished the year with an ugly 7.43—not the kind of number associated with a pitcher with a future. Unless that future is in used-car sales.

The White Sox season had few peaks. The highlight reel for 1973 had the running time of a short subject. We won 77 games, ten fewer than the previous year. The few bright spots included Wilbur Wood, who won 24 games (with 20 losses), Stan Bahnsen, who won 18 (21 losses), and Terry Forster, who posted a team high 16 saves.

For all practical purposes, the White Sox were goners the

moment Dick Allen broke his ankle early in the year. The injury limited the 1972 MVP to 72 games and 250 at bats in 1973; when the one indispensable player in our lineup went to the sidelines, we dispensed with the season.

My season washed out totally. The only thing I won in 1973 was a bet. The pitchers were doing our pregame running one evening when we noticed a sparrow foraging around on the warning track in center field. Somebody piped up and said, "Hey, Goose, bet you can't hit that bird."

We were gathered along the left-field foul line, out near the fence. The sparrow hopped around innocently some 150 feet away. Never being the kind to shy away from a challenge, a dare, or a bet—in this case, ten bucks—I picked up a baseball, rared back and cut loose.

When the ball left my hand it flew as straight as William Tell's arrow. The sparrow, rest in peace, never knew what hit it.

Everyone was stunned. No one could believe I'd actually hit the unsuspecting sparrow. It truly was a long shot. We jogged over to where the bird had fallen, and I cradled its broken body in my cap. I felt terrible.

At least the little bird deserved a decent burial. I began walking to the bullpen, which would be its final resting place. Some fans who had arrived early and witnessed the fatal peg began booing as I passed by. "Sparrow killer," someone shouted. Others took up the cry. *Sparrow killer. Sparrow killer.*

For a couple days my teammates called me Sparrow Killer. Then, being ballplayers, with the attention span of tsetse flies, they started ragging on somebody else.

I could have thrown a hundred baseballs and not hit that bird. It was a total fluke. But then so was the time I heaved a baseball through my Aunt Pauline's kitchen window. Here's what happened.

My buddies and I frequently played pickup games in a vacant lot not far from her house. I was thirteen, fourteen tops. Playing shortstop one afternoon I had to go deep into the hole to stop a one-hopper. I caught the ball, planted for the long throw, then launched a missile that kept rising as it sailed over the first baseman.

When the ball went crashing through Aunt Pauline's window, we bolted like wild mustangs. I didn't learn for several hours that my uncle, Johnny Francis, her husband, had been standing in the kitchen, fixing a glass of iced tea, when my errant throw burst through the window and whacked him upside the head.

When Johnny finally regained his senses all he could say was, "One minute I looked out there and saw a diamond full of kids playing ball. The next minute I looked out and there was nothing but an empty lot."

When spring training rolled around in 1974, I felt ready to make up for the previous season. I wanted to prove to critics and doubters that 1973 had been an aberration.

Early at camp in Sarasota, I showed Tanner and Sain the right stuff. Or so I thought. They had a completely different take on what they were watching. Tanner called me into his office after one workout and waved a piece of paper in my face.

"See this list?" he said. "These are the guys who are going north with the team. And guess what, son? You're not on it."

Tanner's message—and his manner in delivering it—set me off. "What the hell are you talking about?" I screamed. "I'm the best damn pitcher on this staff."

"Like hell you are," scoffed Tanner. "You haven't improved one damn bit. You've been pitching like horseshit."

"I got the best arm in this fucking camp," I spewed, spit flying out of the corners of my mouth. "Just give me the ball and let me prove it."

Tanner and I were nose-to-nose and jaw-to-jaw. Which wasn't a picnic, because Tanner liked cheap cigars.

(Arguing with Chuck, who played outfield on those great Milwaukee Braves teams of the 1950s, amounted to risky business. He was tough as nails. I vividly recall the time White Sox catcher Tom Egan, who was pissed about striking out to end a game, stormed into the clubhouse and starting banging his shin guards.

Tanner hung Egan on the wall like he was a diploma. Egan was no small fry—about six-foot-four and 220 pounds—but Chuck grabbed him by the throat, lifted him up and pinned him against the wall. "Your shin guards had nothing to do with you playing like horseshit," Tanner roared. "Take a good look. It's your own fucking fault you screwed up. Now quit acting like a kid. Be a man.")

There I stood, toe-to-toe with Tanner, watching the veins in his neck begin to bulge. Whenever Chuck got mad, those veins started popping out like tulips in May.

Johnny Sain managed to play peacemaker, but not before our screams permeated the paper-thin walls. My teammates must have thought the Goose had hollered his way into a one-way trip back to Des Moines.

Not so. Tanner gave me the ball during the rest of

spring training. I didn't get things turned around all at once, but with steady work, I made progress. I didn't embarrass myself.

Standing up to Tanner that day convinced Chuck that I had the competitive fire he wanted to see in all his pitchers. My mechanics hadn't quite come together, but my attitude and desire were on target. When the White Sox went north in 1974, my name was on that precious piece of paper.

My comeback was under way.

The 1974 team played .500 ball, splitting 160 games. Jim Kaat won 21 games; Wilbur Wood won 20. Bart Johnson went 10-4. Dick Allen was healthy again and hit 32 home runs with 88 RBIs before packing it in with a couple weeks left.

My numbers weren't spectacular. Four wins, six losses, an ERA of 4.15. In the middle of the season I spent three weeks in Appleton on a medical rehab. I'd injured my ribs.

I continued to make mistakes that could be chalked up to immaturity. Like the afternoon in Texas when I went with Stan Bahnsen to visit one of his pals in Dallas. We got into a rousing game of water volleyball at Stan's friend's apartment complex and the broiling sun smoked me like sausage.

By the time I arrived at Arlington Stadium that night, my back, neck, and shoulders had turned fire-engine red. I've eaten lobsters that weren't as well cooked. I tried to sneak into my uniform without being caught, but Chuck Tanner somehow knew about my predicament. You couldn't sneak anything by him.

Tanner greeted me jovially as he strolled through the

clubhouse. "Goose," he said, slapping me on the back. "How are you doing? Ready to go tonight?"

As he moseyed on off, I nearly passed out in pain.

Tanner demonstrated his faith in my continued development by handing me the ball thirty-nine times in 1974. Toward the end of the year I got into a good rhythm and achieved some respectable results.

Terry Forster and I started getting noticed around American League dugouts. Harmon Killebrew, the veteran Minnesota Twins slugger, some years later told Tanner, "We knew that if we weren't ahead of you guys by the seventh inning, we might as well put the bats in the bags. Because you were going to bring in Forster or Gossage."

While I continued to take some lumps in 1974, Forster had another outstanding season. He saved 24 games, which won him the A.L.'s Fireman of the Year award. The left-handed part of Tanner's lefty-righty combination, at least, came through in a big way.

Terry and I first met in Appleton in 1970. We hit it off right away, probably because in addition to being members of the pitching fraternity, we were two strapping, fun-loving teenagers, as playful as bear cubs.

Terry had a heart as big as California, his home state. He'd give you the shirt off his back—even if it might be frayed at the cuff or have stains under the pits. If you needed it, he'd give you his last dollar.

A better, more loyal friend I've never had.

Shortstop Bucky Dent and I shared Forster's apartment in Appleton. The motif was a cross between Neanderthal and penal colony. It was cavelike and sparse. We had all the essentials of bachelorhood—a bed, TV, and refrigerator. That was it.

The apartment had one bedroom and one bed. We weren't the three bears, so bunking together was out of the question. One of us slept on the box springs, one got the mattress, and one, usually Bucky, got the couch in the den.

The apartment had a window air-conditioning unit in the bedroom which blew with such an Arctic vengeance that you knew for sure you'd wake up with a stiff neck. A cold was even money.

Once, on a road trip in 1970, Forster and I inadvertently trashed our motel room. We were sitting around, doing nothing in particular, when we found ourselves having a disagreement about what to watch on TV. Being the intellectuals we were, one of us probably wanted to catch something on PBS.

We started wrestling and Terry accidentally punched me in the face. That called for retribution, of course, so I popped him one back. Suddenly we were wrapped up in a bear hug and bouncing off the walls of the tiny room. We knocked over both nightstands and lamps, as well as the table on which the TV was placed. We broke a chair.

The melee ended when my ankle rolled over. For a moment I thought it might be broken. The dispute, though, was no big deal to Terry or me. We were buds again by bedtime.

———

Terry Forster possessed some of the best stuff I ever saw in the major leagues. He had the whole package, which explains why Tanner called him up to Chicago in 1971, when Terry was only nineteen. And also why Forster, the next year, broke Hoyt Wilhelm's White Sox record for saves in a season. Terry posted 29 saves in 1972, second in the American League behind Sparky Lyle (35) of New York.

Forster's fastball consistently clocked in the mid-nineties and was a "heavy" ball to hit. Guys might occasionally make solid contact, but even when they did, the ball didn't travel anywhere. I used to say that hitting Forster's fastball was like hitting a shot put or a bowling ball.

Terry had the best curveball this side of Sandy Koufax. Batters could see it coming and hear it coming, but they still couldn't hit it. Forster managed to get such wicked spin on his breaking ball that it sounded like a boiling kettle letting off steam.

Sssssss—here it came. *Sssssss*—there it went. The bottom would drop out of Forster's curveball like a trapdoor in a magic show.

Terry's stuff was so exceptional that he pitched in the major leagues for sixteen seasons. Had Forster not had to deal with a series of injuries to his arm and back, he could have pitched even longer. He was that good.

The one mistake Terry made in the 1974 season, in my opinion, was not giving his arm enough time to recover between outings. I can recall several occasions when we'd be sitting in the clubhouse and Terry would confide to me how much his arm ached.

Tanner or Sain would materialize out of nowhere and ask Forster if he was ready to go that night. Absolutely, Terry would lie through clenched teeth. You betcha, skip. Just give me the ball.

Forster's refusal to fess up about the pain in his ailing left wing probably compounded his problems. Then again, macho guys hate to admit they might be mortal. And Terry, need I say it, was as macho as guys come.

I have Terry Forster to thank for helping me get the uniform number—54—that I wore throughout my career. He set a precedent when he made the White Sox squad in 1971.

Terry went to camp as a nonroster invitee, or as they're commonly known, a turd. He was assigned number 51, a pretty good indicator that he was considered training camp fodder. Real players didn't wear numbers as high as 50 back then.

As soon as Tanner got a look at Forster's fastball and heard his curveball, Terry had a one-way ticket to the show. With his new status as the White Sox relief sensation, Forster could command whatever uniform number he wanted. And Terry wanted the same number he'd worn in Sarasota.

The next spring, I went through the same experience. I showed up in Sarasota as a nonroster invitee, a turd. And, like Forster, I impressed Tanner and Sain enough to make the unlikely jump from Class A ball to the major leagues.

When it became clear I would make the big club, Larry Licklider, the White Sox equipment manager, asked me what permanent number I wanted.

"Fifty-four," I replied. "It's been my lucky number."

"No, we're not giving out any more big numbers," Licklider countered. "Choose something smaller."

"Well, you let Forster wear number fifty-one, didn't you?" I argued.

"That was last year," he said. "We ain't doing that again."

I demanded that Licklider take the matter up with White Sox GM Roland Hemond, which he reluctantly did. Hemond gave me the go-ahead. End of discussion.

On August 11, 1974, the White Sox played an exhibition game in Cooperstown, New York, on the day of the Hall of Fame ceremonies. Among the legends inducted that day were two of my New York Yankee heroes, Mickey Mantle and Whitey Ford.

The exhibition game gave fans who flocked to Cooperstown a chance to see some big-league action, interact with players, and collect autographs. It was a casual, fun affair.

The night before, our charter flight had landed in Utica, New York. We were on the bus, headed for a hotel, when veteran Ron Santo called an impromptu team meeting to inform everyone that Utica was a "connected" town and that we should be careful where we stuck our noses.

Santo had come to the White Sox from the Cubs the previous winter in a trade involving, among others, pitcher Steve Stone. The Cubs originally intended to ship Santo to California, but Ron had invoked the new 10-and-5 rule—which stipulated that a ten-year veteran with five consecutive years of service with the same team could have a say in his future employment—and vetoed the deal.

Santo had become an established star in Chicago, and, with a range of business interests locally, he wasn't about to bail out on the Windy City. It would have cost him a small fortune.

That night, after checking into our hotel room, Forster and I headed to the bar. So many of our teammates were there we could have taken the official team photograph.

As hours crept by, pitchers of cold beer disappeared. Forster, claiming he needed some rest, returned to our room, but I maintained a vigil near the beer taps.

Near midnight I wobbled up to the bar to buy yet another round. Waiting to be served, I noticed that I happened to be standing next to two well-coiffed guys in black sharkskin suits.

They were having a heated conversation, which I couldn't help but overhear. One guy, who sounded like he could be auditioning for *The Godfather*, said to his pal, "I don't care. We gotta kill the motherfucker."

Feeling no pain, I piped up, "Yeah, just kill the motherfucker. Ba-bing. Ba-bang. Ba-boom."

These guys turned around and stared at me with four eyes as cold as bullets. I could see myself being fitted for a size 12 cement shoe.

One guy moved around behind me, and suddenly they had me flanked on each side. Just then the bartender intervened. He gave the two *paisanos* a nod of the head, which signaled to them that I was harmless (albeit drunk and stupid).

The sharp-dressed men took their business elsewhere, and I left the bartender a big tip. Scared sober, I went straight to the room.

What I didn't count on, though, was Terry Forster leaving his suitcase out in the middle of the room. His big, metal suitcase. The one with sharp edges.

I took off my shoes and tiptoed in, my heart still racing from my meeting with the mob. Being a considerate person and fearful of waking Forster, I didn't turn on any lights.

Major mistake. Halfway to the bathroom I stepped on the edge of his suitcase. Pain immediately shot through my ankle and up my leg. I hopped one-legged to the bathroom and leaned against the sink while I inspected the damage.

What kind of sorry so-and-so would leave a suitcase out in the middle of the floor? I was so pissed off that as soon as my foot felt better, I picked up the suitcase and dropped all its contents on Forster.

Terry, bless his heart, didn't even wake up. The next morning, though, he did ask why I was limping so badly.

After two years of constant struggle and self-doubt, I finally became grounded as a major league pitcher in 1975. Several events helped turn things around.

First, Corna and I went back to Puerto Rico for winter ball at the end of 1974, where I was reunited with catcher Pat Corrales. That season, Corrales was Ponce's manager, as well as the starting catcher. After catching me for a few minutes, he asked me where I had hidden the hopping fastball I'd flashed two winters earlier.

When I told Pat my fastball had been taking a siesta, he said, in effect, let's wake it up. We did.

Corna and I had a ball during our second trip to Puerto Rico. On New Year's Eve 1974 several couples decided to fly to San Juan to celebrate. We took a puddle-jumper to the capital, flying through such turbulence that the little plane bounced around like a pinball. We still laugh at the memory of my teammate, Roy Howell, who announced during the middle of the flight, "I'm really going to be pissed if we die tonight."

Corna and I also get a good chuckle remembering the day a bunch of the Ponce players piled into our little Ford Maverick, which we had affectionately dubbed "Marty Maverick." Five people were riding in the front seat and maybe six or eight were piled in the back. When I made a sharp turn, Corna slid against me and I discovered that I couldn't turn the wheel back. We started going around in circles through a service station, trying desperately to avoid running into one of the pumps.

Corna started laughing so hard that she momentarily lost control of her bladder—much to the chagrin of pitcher Rusty Gerhardt, in whose lap she was sitting. When we got back to the apartment, Rusty asked her ruefully, "Why did you do that?"

Then at spring training in Sarasota, I received a critical tip from pitcher Roger Nelson, an eight-year veteran who was getting a look to try and make the team. Nelson suggested that I move from the left side of the rubber to the right. It didn't seem like much of an adjustment, but that one subtle change produced a dramatic difference. The outside half of the strike zone suddenly looked as wide and inviting as the Grand Canyon.

The patience Chuck Tanner had steadfastly shown with me began to pay off. Johnny Sain, who constantly preached that the day a pitcher stops learning his craft is the day he's on the way out, finally saw the lights come on in this pupil's head. I started dusting people in Sarasota and didn't stop.

When the 1975 season opened in April, I shot out of the gate. My ERA hovered under 2.00, and for the first time I averaged nearly a strikeout an inning, one of the hallmarks of a genuine power pitcher.

I vaporized batters throughout the early part of the season. My fastball had plenty of hop and, working from the right side of the rubber, I painted my slider on the outside as never before. In a stretch of 15 relief appearances, covering 38 innings, I allowed only 12 hits and one earned run. By midseason my stats were so overwhelming I was selected to the A.L. All-Star team for the first time.

I was so juiced for the game, which unfolded in Milwaukee on July 15, that the night before I could barely sleep. Corna and I drove up from Chicago and arrived at the stadium two hours ahead of schedule. I walked into the home team's clubhouse and immediately spied someone sitting on a chair in front of a row of lockers.

He was stripped to the waist, just lounging around in cutoff long underwear. I couldn't see his face, but I noticed the thick, broad shoulders and heavily muscled neck and thought, Boy, this guy's huge. He's built like a brick wall.

He'd heard the door open, and as I approached he turned his head to greet me. "Hey, how are you doing?" asked the honorary captain for the American League team, Mickey Mantle.

Mickey Mantle! I nearly died. Like hundreds of thousands of kids who grew up in the 1950s and 1960s, I idolized Mickey Mantle. Worshiped the ground he walked on. All of that stuff.

Mantle, along with his contemporary, Willie Mays, possessed the rare combination of immense power and breathtaking speed that made them impossible for fans to ignore. They drew the spotlight the way a patio light draws moths.

Hit, run, throw—Mantle and Mays could do everything there is to do on a baseball field. They could beat you seven ways from Sunday. Both belong on the short list of baseball's greatest players.

Being a diehard Yankee fan, I always preferred Mickey Mantle to Willie Mays. And here he was, in the flesh, saying hello.

The experience numbed me. I muttered to myself, "It's Mickey!" then spun around and walked away without saying a word. What do you say to a god, anyway? I dressed quickly and silently on the other side of the clubhouse, then went out on the field to watch the National Leaguers take batting practice.

Presently, I felt a tap on the shoulder. It was Mantle. "What's the matter, kid, can't you talk?" he asked, scowling.

I nearly soiled my uniform. I tried stammering out an explanation for why I'd blown him off a few minutes before. I got tongue-tied trying to tell Mickey what a hero he had been to me and my family, how we always watched his games and rooted for him.

I babbled on until Mantle began laughing at my awkwardness. "Nice to meet you," he said. "Good luck in the game."

I was so nervous that day in Milwaukee that if reporters had bothered to ask me my name, I'm not sure I could have answered. I can't adequately describe my feelings at being surrounded by such rare talent. I suppose I felt like a kid making his first visit to FAO Schwarz: overjoyed, overcome, overwhelmed.

I had a case of the overs.

President Gerald Ford worked his way through each dugout before the game, shaking hands and posing for pictures. Me—a kid so poor that he sometimes had to scour streets in Colorado Springs looking for empty bottles to redeem for dinner money, a kid so ashamed of his home that he refused to invite friends inside—shaking hands with the President of the United States?

Forget about it; that stuff only happens in movies or books.

Yet there I was, being treated like somebody special. Getting to meet the Mickey Mantles and Gerald Fords of the world. Getting to hang out with Rollie Fingers, Joe Rudi, Sal Bando—all those stars from the three-time world champion Oakland A's. It seemed unreal, like a dream.

That day in Milwaukee was the first in a series of misadventures I endured in All-Star Games. The National League jumped to an early 3-0 lead on home runs by Steve Garvey and Jimmy Wynn. The American League rallied in the sixth, when a three-run homer by Carl Yastrzemski tied the score.

The 3-3 tie lasted until the top of the ninth inning. After Reggie Smith singled off Catfish Hunter and Al Oliver followed with a double, I got the call from A.L. manager Alvin Dark to come in and put out the fire.

Some fireman I turned out to be. Everything collapsed around us. I walked Larry Bowa, loading the bases, then surrendered a two-run single to Bill Madlock that skimmed under Graig Nettles's glove at third. Pete Rose followed with a sacrifice fly to complete the scoring in a 6-3 N.L. win.

I had gotten ahead of Madlock 0-2 on fastballs and was about to throw him a third, but in the middle of my windup I decided to throw him a change-up instead. Bad idea.

Smith scored easily. There would have been a play at the plate on Oliver, but the throw from the outfield sailed all the way to the backstop. Backing up the play, I saw Bowa make a break toward third base. I grabbed the ball, wheeled and fired.

It was, alas, my wildest pitch of all. The ball didn't sniff third base. But it did make a beeline for N.L. third base coach Red Schoendienst. Seeing the ball coming, Red tried desperately to scramble out of the way, but the ball tailed into him. Literally.

My peg hit him smack dab in the butt. The ball dropped straight down, Bowa held at third, and at that point there was nothing for everybody on both teams to do but laugh their asses off. In fact, the whole stadium erupted.

Under other circumstances I would have laughed too. But not then, not in that particular situation. For me, that inning was as funny as a heart attack. Catfish Hunter may have taken the loss; I knew who deserved the goat's horns.

Some of the press covering the game later asked Alvin Dark why, in that situation, he had pulled a veteran All-Star like Catfish for a first-timer like me. "If I can't bring in Gossage in a spot like that, I shouldn't have brought him to the game," Dark said. "I wanted the kid to strike out a couple of guys."

The sting of defeat passed quickly. I had nothing but good feelings about my first All-Star experience.

"It's a great honor to be here. I was never so excited in my life," I said in the postgame interview. "I just feel super at being in a super game with all these super players." (Okay, so my vocabulary was a bit limited in those days.)

When reporters asked me about the pitch to Madlock, I didn't second-guess myself. "Shoot, you can't get those National League hitters out by throwing fastballs all night," I said. "Shoot, I don't take that pitch back. I wanted to throw a change-up to Bill Madlock and I did."

I learned an important lesson that night, however: A pitcher should never get beat on his second-best pitch. When the game's on the line, you have to go with your best pitch. Win or lose.

Despite my breakthrough season, the White Sox were on the road to nowhere in 1975. It became widely rumored that the team was up for sale. Scuttlebutt surfaced that the franchise might be moved to another city. Financial limitations imposed by a lackluster season and dwindling fan base—fans generally aren't keen on supporting a club that might be deserting them—kept GM Roland Hemond from being able to make any major deals.

Hemond lacked the financial resources to go after serious talent. We had a clubhouse full of average-to-good players, but we'd been without a superstar since Dick Allen left at the end of 1974. The primary starters in 1975—Jim Kaat, Wilbur Wood, Claude Osteen—were nearing the end of outstanding careers. Terry Forster suffered arm trouble during most of the '75 season and pitched only 37 innings in 17 games.

Adding to the negative vibes were the barbs and brickbats of broadcaster Harry Caray. Larger-than-life Harry— so popular in Chicago he probably could have been elected mayor, or governor of Illinois—had strong opinions about White Sox players and no reluctance to voice them.

Harry Caray could be charming and gregarious or downright mean-spirited. He practically ran Ken Henderson and Bill Melton, to name two, out of town. He put their careers in a shredder and hit the start button. Thank goodness Harry Caray decided not to turn my career into confetti. With his clout, he could have.

What made me such a different pitcher during 1975 and thereafter? Two interrelated variables: consistency and confidence.

I already had combativeness. I could be mean as hell. The way I looked at it, batters were trying to take food off my dinner table, and Corna and I had good appetites. I was prepared to do whatever I could, within the rules, to feed my family.

I already had an out-pitch. My fastball consistently registered in the mid-nineties. It was one of the handful of hardest in the game and it had plenty of movement. I threw a sinking fastball and a high one with hop. Either could blow batters away.

In 1975, I added a much-improved slider to the mix. All the hours Johnny Sain had spent working on my mechanics began to pay off. I started shutting down batters on a consistent basis. That consistency, in turn, instilled in me a growing confidence that I could do it again and again.

Confidence isn't sold over the counter. You can't get it out of a dispenser. Confidence can't be conjured up. The only way to develop confidence is to give yourself a reason to be confident. It's trial by fire.

I've seen some pitchers with great arms who never made

it. Kids with can't-miss talent managed to miss anyway. Confidence was the missing ingredient. Those pitchers were tentative. They couldn't cut loose. They were consumed by the fear of failure.

During 1975, after years of grooming by Chuck Tanner and Johnny Sain, and based on an emerging pattern of success, I finally became a confident pitcher. The missing piece to the jigsaw puzzle had been found. I felt ready to kick some serious ass.

Watch out, world—the Goose was loose.

CHAPTER 3

1976

SEND IN THE CLOWNS

I'd come of age as a major-league pitcher in 1975, ratcheting up my fastball a couple miles per hour and gaining greater command of my off-speed stuff. I'd been selected for my first All-Star team—never mind the debacle in Milwaukee—and at season's end, having registered a league-leading 26 saves and a 1.84 ERA, I was cited as the A.L. Fireman of the Year.

Not bad for a twenty-four-year-old who two years earlier had been oh-fer 1973.

So what did the Chicago White Sox do with their star reliever in 1976? They turned me into a starter, that's what. They saw a shortage of starting pitching on the roster and asked me to fill a spot in the rotation.

Eager to help the club in any way possible, I didn't squawk. I just wanted them to give me the ball. If the new White Sox braintrust that took over in 1976 felt that should be every fourth or fifth game, so be it. I could adapt.

Despite my growing reputation as a reliever, I took a fancy to the idea of being the ace of a pitching staff. The Man. A pitcher along the lines of a Tom Seaver, Steve Carlton, or Catfish Hunter—the Beeg Guy who was going to get the ball, no doubt, whenever a crucial game came up on the schedule or a championship was at stake.

The 1976 season proved to be as zany and madcap as any I spent in the majors. Unpredictability had been ushered in the previous December, when Chicago underwent a change in ownership that kept the franchise from being shuffled off to the West Coast.

American League executives had the White Sox halfway out of town, headed for the fertile fields of Seattle, when riding in wearing a white hat and white chaps came that old wrangler himself, Bill Veeck. *Veeck—as in wreck.*

The American League had a hidden agenda to pack the White Sox off to the Pacific Northwest, satisfying an obligation to Seattle created five years earlier, when the expansion Seattle Pilots, after only one season, found themselves transformed into the Milwaukee Brewers.

Exiling the White Sox would allow Oakland owner Charlie O. Finley to move to Chicago. The A's teams of the mid-1970s might have been a powerhouse on the field but they were duds at the box office. The hearts of Bay Area baseball fans belonged to the San Francisco Giants.

Veeck spoiled all the plans at the eleventh hour, however, by arranging enough financing to buy majority ownership from John Allyn and keep the White Sox in Chicago. Veeck's appearance on the scene electrified the city; fans remembered that the previous time he had bought the team—in 1959— the White Sox won their first American League pennant in forty years (since the infamous Black Sox scandal of 1919). Could Veeck make magic again?

Anyone who follows baseball more than casually has

probably heard of Bill Veeck, who was born in 1914 and died on the second day of 1986 after a singular career in the sport.

Veeck may be best remembered for putting a midget (Eddie Gaedel) in a St. Louis Browns uniform (number ⅛) and sending him to the plate on August 19, 1951. But he contributed much more than just being baseball's equivalent of P. T. Barnum. Veeck combined showmanship and flair with a knack for producing winning teams—the 1948 Cleveland Indians and the 1959 Chicago White Sox, for example.

With Chicago in the late 1950s Veeck introduced the radical concept of putting players' names across the back of their uniforms. He installed an exploding scoreboard in Comiskey Park that erupted whenever a White Sox player went deep. He opened a picnic area beyond the outfield fence, combining baseball and dining in a way that's since become a given. Mind you, all of this was forty years ago. Way ahead of its time.

Bill Veeck was as fan-friendly an owner as baseball has ever seen or is likely to see again. He made himself totally accessible to fans. Unlike the majority of owners then and now, he didn't hide behind lawyers, advisers, or official spokesmen.

Anyone who wanted to talk baseball with Bill could. His phone number was listed in the book. The door to his office stayed open. He liked to sit in the bleachers with fans and, over a brewski or two, talk ball. He had a pet theory that the level of baseball intelligence among fans was in inverse proportion to the price they had paid for their seats.

Time-management gurus of today would frown on his actions, but Veeck's most valued hours were spent talking with his customers. And Bill could talk the ears off corn. The conversations seldom ceased either, because Veeck happened to be one of baseball's great night owls. "I have always hated to go to bed," he once said, "for fear I might miss something."

Bill Veeck's flamboyance ran him afoul of the lords of baseball, who considered him too much the maverick and not enough the team player. He, in turn, characterized baseball owners as stodgy, shortsighted stuffed shirts utterly devoid of marketing savvy. That's what he said when he was feeling charitable and complimentary about his colleagues. Concerning his tempestuous relationship with fellow owners, Veeck noted in his biography that he was "feared, despised and loathed, which means I must have been doing something right."

In January 1976, a month after Veeck bought the White Sox for a second time, I was one of a handful of players who accompanied Bill on a goodwill tour to spur interest and ticket sales. Our caravan traveled to Illinois, Indiana, and Iowa, banging pots and drums for baseball in general and the Sox in particular.

Give Veeck a podium to lean on and a microphone to speak into and he was as happy as a gopher with a hole. I've seldom seen a public speaker connect with an audience like Veeck. He always oozed humor, wit, and charm, but with a stage and audience, he could take his performance to a higher level. He'd have audiences shrieking with laughter, their cheeks streaked with tears, as he told one story after another.

Bill had grown up in and around major league baseball. His father, William Veeck Sr., made the improbable career switch from sportswriter for the *Chicago American* to front office executive. A column Veeck Sr. wrote about the deficiencies of the Chicago Cubs prompted a summons from owner William Wrigley. After listening to the reporter tell him about his team, Wrigley decided to see if the ink-stained wretch's theories had any merit. He hired Veeck Sr. as the team's president, a twist of fate that gave Bill Jr. the opportunity to hang out around Cubs stars like Grover Cleveland Alexander, Rabbit Maranville, and Hack Wilson. Bill's roots in baseball ran so deep that, in the 1930s, he worked on the grounds crew that planted ivy on the outfield wall at Wrigley Field.

Neither a serious combat injury suffered in World War II, which ultimately cost him his right leg, nor recurring bouts with cancer could dampen Bill Veeck's enthusiasm and zest for life. He was the classic free spirit.

Some of Bill's best stories were those he told about himself. He recounted how, after he and Charlie Grimm had scraped to buy a bankrupt Class AAA Milwaukee team in 1941, they showed up in town with eleven dollars between them. They immediately retired to a bar to celebrate their good fortune and spent ten dollars on toasts. Veeck noted that while businesspeople typically frame the first dollar they make, he framed the last dollar he had before he began his career flat broke.

Veeck told about how, when he owned the St. Louis Browns, a marginal talent named Bobo Holloman wheedled and cajoled him and manager Marty Marion into giving him a start. Miraculously graced by the baseball gods, Bobo went out and pitched a no-hitter—the first in modern history to do so in his first start.

That improbable performance forced Veeck to keep Holloman, whom he was trying to unload, on the roster for two more months. "Bobo could outtalk me, outpester me, and outcon me," Veeck would say. "Unfortunately, he couldn't outpitch me."

Veeck also told about how he tried to spark interest in his moribund St. Louis team by hiring the greatest player in that city's rich baseball history, Rogers Hornsby, as the Browns manager for the 1952 season.

Whatever attributes Hornsby, a seven-time N.L. batting champion, possessed, diplomacy and tact were not among them. Hornsby could be brutally honest, even if that meant telling some of his players they were better suited to selling shoes than trying to hit major league pitching. Legend has it Hornsby so disdained most of his players that after games he liked to urinate on their legs in the shower.

Veeck joked that his mother knew he'd made a grievous error handing over the reins to the immortal Rajah. She wrote him a letter inquiring, "What makes you think you're smarter than your father was?"—a reference to reservations Bill Veeck Sr. had expressed about Hornsby's managerial talents two decades earlier. Hornsby had been hired (over the elder Veeck's objections) as field boss for the Cubs.

Early in the 1952 season Veeck realized he faced a player mutiny if he didn't dump Hornsby. Fifty-one games into the schedule Veeck pulled the plug on Rogers, and promptly received a terse telegram from his mother: "What did I tell you?"

At one of those whistle stops on the White Sox's 1976 goodwill tour, I saw Bill Veeck perform an amazing feat of agility and dexterity. I can't recall where we were, but, as was Veeck's wont, he headed to the nearest watering hole as soon as our dog-and-pony show ended. We were seated at a table underneath a large, expensive chandelier, which was filled with tapered lightbulbs. The bottom of the chandelier was bowl-shaped and made of copper.

I don't know if Bill had a bum bladder as well as a bum leg. But every fifteen minutes, like clockwork, he'd get up and head to the john. As he arose he would swing his peg leg upward and smash the copper base of the chandelier. BAM! Lightbulbs exploded, and the chandelier swayed from side to side, like it was going to topple.

By Bill's sixth or seventh trip to the head, everyone in the joint egged him on. Never one to disappoint a crowd, Bill would whirl his leg around over his head and—WHAM!—glass and debris came raining down. It was the damnedest show I'd ever seen for free.

When we'd arrived at the saloon, the chandelier had been a collector's item. By the time we left, it was so dented and dinged it wouldn't have fetched five dollars at a flea market. But Bill whipped out his money clip as we were leaving and asked the barkeep, "How much for the damage?" He tossed a wad of bills on the bar, and we were on our way.

One other night on that goodwill tour, we were stumbling in late from another nocturnal adventure when Bill's peg leg fell off. We were climbing out of the backseat of a taxicab and, just like that, Bill went down like he'd been shot.

I knelt down to see if he was all right, but Bill shooed me away.

"Damn thing's more trouble than it's worth," Veeck muttered, sitting up on the curb. He took a tool kit out of his coat pocket and started screwing in the nuts and bolts. A few minutes later he hopped to his feet. Inside the hotel we went.

———

One of Bill Veeck's first moves as the new owner of the White Sox was to hire Paul Richards as manager for the 1976 season. He offered Chuck Tanner his choice of jobs in the front office, or as the third-base coach, but told Tanner he wanted Richards on the bench for one season purely for purposes of nostalgia. Chuck could have his old job back in 1977.

In keeping with the theme, Veeck next announced that White Sox uniforms would have a retro look and include such breakthrough fashions as clamdiggers, knickers, and shorts. The players talked it over and decided Bill might as well have issued us Ronald McDonald costumes and fright wigs. If we were going to look like clowns, why not go all the way?

Paul Richards's last field job had been with the Baltimore Orioles in 1961, but in the interim he had served in several front office jobs, including general manager for the expansion Houston Colt 45s. Paul enjoyed a reputation as an outstanding baseball strategist, although somewhat cold and aloof in his approach.

What encouraged White Sox pitchers was the fact that Richards had developed the Orioles "Baby Bird" hurlers of the late 1950s and early 1960s—Milt Pappas, Chuck Estrada, Steve Barber, and the rest. Maybe he could do the same with our beleaguered staff.

As the 1976 opener approached, Richards expressed cautious optimism about our chances. "This team has good enthusiasm," he said. "If we have good execution and good health, we could fool some people."

Alas, the only person we fooled that year was Paul. We

couldn't fool the Comiskey Park fans, who stayed away in droves despite the nonstop promotions and giveaways Bill Veeck dreamed up. Veeck's brain, as usual, worked overtime. He had circus acts—elephants, clowns, wire-walkers, sword swallowers, dancing bears, and belly dancers—working the perimeter of the playing field before game time.

On at least two occasions I started a game cold—that is to say, not properly warmed up—because of all the tomfoolery Veeck had going on before the game.

The 1976 White Sox were, in a word, awful. We finished with a record of 64-97 (the fewest victories of any team in my career) and wound up a mere 25½ games behind A.L. West champion Kansas City.

How bad were we? Well, we couldn't hit for average. We lacked power. Our defense was brutal at best, comical at worst. Our pitching was patchwork. We had a manager who at times seemed out of touch with the game—more than once, coaches had to awaken Paul Richards from a siesta to flash signs—and an owner who was more interested in booking circus acts than stocking the roster with talent.

Other than that, the 1976 Chicago White Sox were bonafide contenders. A juggernaut waiting to jugger.

Although I had pitched only fourteen innings in Sarasota that spring—the owners delayed spring training again, until Commissioner Bowie Kuhn intervened—Richards tapped me to start the season opener in Minnesota. I responded to his vote of confidence by silencing the Twins on three singles and notching just the second complete game of my career.

Paul was effusive in praising my first outing: "Gossage is about as good a pitcher as there is in the league right now," he said. Then, taking a shot at the departed Chuck Tanner—who, rather than accept Veeck's offer to stay in Chicago, replaced Alvin Dark as manager in Oakland—Richards added, "I don't want to criticize anybody, but how can you have a kid who can throw like that and not start him? It will be very rare if I ever relieve with him."

Four days later I got the first inkling that Paul, at age sixty-six, might have been a couple cans short of a six-pack. On the road in Boston, who did he bring in to relieve Terry Forster in the fifth inning? Me! So much for making those rare relief appearances. I got batted around like a piñata and took the loss.

When we came back to Chicago for our home opener, Veeck, in the spirit of America's bicentennial celebration, dressed up in a Revolutionary War outfit. So did Paul Richards and business manager Rudie Schaffer. The trio came for pregame introductions looking like they had gotten lost on the way to Lord Cornwallis's surrender at Yorktown. They carried a fife and drum and waved a flag. Veeck received a resounding ovation as he hopped out to home plate.

Surprisingly, after a slow start in April the White Sox managed to play decent baseball in May and early June. We really did fool some people, albeit for only six weeks. I fooled enough batters to have the best stretch in my brief tenure as a starter.

On May 20, I limited Minnesota to two runs and got eight K's pitching a complete game. On May 25, I went the route again and held California to one run, fanning nine. On May 30, I won a third straight complete game against Cleveland. On June 5, I beat the Indians again, outdueling Dennis

Eckersley (who would, years later, also make a name for himself in the bullpen, and become my teammate and good friend).

Everything positive about our season came to a halt after June 10, however. We went on a nine-game losing streak and never recovered. I injured my right elbow pitching in the rain in Minnesota on June 24 and subsequently missed three starts. After the June 5 win against Eckersley, I didn't win another game until August 1. Seven long weeks.

By the second half of the season, losses started stacking up and outcomes became such a foregone conclusion that, in the immortal words of pitcher Ken Brett (who led the 1976 team with ten wins), "Concessionaires at Comiskey Park were selling hot dogs to go by the fifth inning."

At the core of the problem was our defense. More to the point, our lack of defense. Every ball hit to the outfield had the potential for disaster.

There was the time a tough out came to the plate, and Paul Richards went strolling to the mound to chat with Bart Johnson.

"Son, Ah believe you better pitch around this hit-ah," drawled Richards, a slow-talking Texan.

Johnson agreed with the soundness of the strategy. "Okay, skip, I'll pitch around this guy," said Bart, a good all-around athlete who had played basketball at BYU. Then suddenly Johnson wheeled around, pointed at our outfield and shouted, "But how in hell do you expect me to pitch around those assholes?"

Everybody in our dugout fell over laughing. We got on the phone and called down to the bullpen to let the rest of the guys know what Bart had said.

The assholes Johnson referred to consisted of Ralph Garr

in right field, Jorge Orta in left field, and Chet Lemon in center field. Garr had great speed but bad instincts. Orta was a natural infielder playing out of position. Chet Lemon, who would in time become one of the best defensive outfielders in the major leagues, was still new to his craft.

Lemon reminded me of a Labrador puppy, game and willing. He would try to chase down anything. Likely as not, however, Garr or Orta would hear Lemon bearing down on them and, at the last moment, shy away from making the catch.

Their Keystone Kops imitation would have been even funnier if we hadn't been losing all the time.

Perhaps the funniest moment of all the outfielders' misadventures came the night someone rifled a shot down the left-field line. Orta, a shy and soft-spoken Mexican with one of the sweetest strokes in the game, went scampering after the ball until a sudden gust of wind blew off his cap.

Instead of going after the ball, Orta opted to go after his headwear. He raced back and picked up his cap, got it adjusted and secure on his head, and then tracked down the ball in the corner.

The hitter steamed into third base with a triple. It was a good thing Jorge hadn't stopped to check the crease in the cap's bill or it would have been an inside-the-park home run.

I think it's safe to assume that the producers who dreamed up all those baseball-blooper TV shows that began airing in the 1980s had grown up in Chicago and watched the 1976 White Sox from the bleachers. We couldn't get through nine innings without botching a routine play or committing a memorable blunder.

The agony I experienced at having to play for a ragamuffin outfit that won only 64 games, wore short pants, and was the laughingstock of the American League was matched by some equally painful moments on the mound.

We were playing the Yankees one day, and Mickey Rivers led off an inning with a rocket that ricocheted off my right shin before I had time to blink. It was an absolute bullet, square on the bone. I went down like a sack of flour.

I began rolling around in front of the mound, writhing in pain. Here came Paul Richards ambling out from the dugout like he was on a Sunday stroll. He surveyed the damage and said, "You okay, son? That was a pretty good knock you took there."

The home plate umpire came out to see if I could continue. I asked for a couple minutes to try to walk off the pain. He consented.

I stayed in the game and got the first out of the inning. Then Oscar Gamble, the third hitter, came up and on the first pitch lined a Screaming Mimi off my left shinbone. It was a billion-to-one shot.

Down I went again. This time I was completely laid out, screaming "Oh my God, oh my God." I looked over in the Yankees dugout and all their players had put towels over their heads to keep me from seeing how hard they were laughing.

Everyone but Catfish Hunter, that is. Catfish roared in full view. He laughed so hard that he doubled over. If I could have found a ball, I would have drilled him, I swear.

Here came Paul Richards again. "Son," he drawled, "looks to me like we might ought to get you out of here." When he said that, Brian Downing, our catcher, put his mitt over his face. He too couldn't keep from cracking up.

When I awoke the next morning, I couldn't get out of bed. I took one step and fell back on the mattress. I couldn't walk. I looked down and saw these two huge knots on my shins. A tattoo artist couldn't have etched two big blotches on my legs more perfectly.

As much as those Rivers and Gamble rockets hurt, they weren't the scariest moments of the season. In a game against the Minnesota Twins, I threw Rod Carew a low fastball on the outside corner. Carew, whose bat control was amazing, dropped the head on the ball and hit a rising bullet right at my crotch.

Fortunately, I had on a metal cup that day. The ball knicked the heel of my glove just before it flushed me right in the family jewels. The air went out of me like a popped balloon.

As the ball fell straight down, I fell straight back. My head hit the rubber. I thought I was going to die. I couldn't catch my breath and pain shot all the way up through my head. My vision grew fuzzy.

No one even bothered to wait for Paul Richards to stroll out and assess the damage. They didn't have to. The trainers came running out and hauled me off. Stick a fork in me—I was done.

Later, when I perked up in the clubhouse, I pulled out the metal cup and examined it. It was dented. The only thing that saved me was that I'd pulled my legs together right before impact. Had my legs been spread when Carew's wicked shot made contact, it's doubtful I would have become the father of three boys.

When I came home that evening, Corna greeted me at the door. "Honey, how's your knee?" she asked. Chicago's crack radio crew, ever ready with euphemisms, had informed viewers I'd taken a hard shot off the kneecap.

"My knee?" I laughed. "It's not my knee. Carew got me a little higher up than that."

I didn't just take punishment in 1976. I dished some out. In another game against New York, I plunked Thurman Munson right on the point of the elbow. Smoked him as solidly as you can hit someone.

Munson, being a manly man, insisted on walking down to first base under his own power. But then the Yankees decided to take their All-Star catcher out of the game and send him to the hospital for X rays (which proved negative).

Before he left the park, though, Munson tore a tiny piece of paper off a tablet and wrote me a personal message.

I took your best fucking shot, you motherfucker, he scrawled. He signed the note "The White Gorrilla."

It being Thurman, he misspelled the word gorilla.

That was the first exchange we ever had. Later, when I joined the Yankees, Thurman Munson and I became close buds. We'd always laugh about the White Gorilla incident.

In general, though, laughs were hard to come by in 1976. Any athlete with any competitiveness hates to endure a season where you get spiked like a volleyball.

Not even the antics of Bill Veeck, who on September 12 activated fifty-three-year-old Orestes "Minnie" Minoso, just so the Chicago fan favorite could play in four different decades, masked the disaster we experienced between the white lines.

(Minnie, incidentally, singled off California Angel pitcher Sid Monge on September 13, becoming the oldest player in history to get a base hit.)

It was a long, long season. I finished with a 9-17 record and 3.94 ERA. Bart Johnson went 9-16. Terry Forster, with a clipped left wing, went 2-12.

The personal highlight during a season of lowlights was my surprising—to many—selection to the A.L. All-Star team by Boston manager Darrell Johnson. The A.L. pilot by virtue of the Red Sox's pennant in 1975, Johnson had the prerogative to fill the pitching roster as he saw fit.

Going against the protocol of awarding All-Star slots to starting pitchers, Johnson named four relief specialists— Sparky Lyle of the Yankees, Rollie Fingers of the A's, Dave LaRoche of the Indians, and me—to the squad. "Even though he's starting for Chicago, I still consider Gossage a reliever," said Johnson, attempting to explain—or justify— his decision.

Naturally, I felt thrilled to be named an A.L. All-Star for the second straight year. Several pitchers around the league, however, were less than amused by Johnson's choices. The most vocal critic of the departure from protocol was Jim Palmer, ace of the Baltimore Orioles. Palmer, who'd been bypassed, made several unflattering remarks about the selections. Palmer went so far as to call Johnson "an idiot."

The 1976 All-Star Game, played at Veterans Stadium in Philadelphia, became yet another in a series of romps for the senior circuit. The National League won 7-1. For whatever reason, in those days the American League couldn't match up.

The irony of the evening was that after taking all sorts of verbal abuse about the composition of his pitching staff, Johnson didn't use any of his deep corps of relievers. Not one. Every guy who threw for the American League that night—Mark Fidrych, Catfish Hunter, Luis Tiant, and Frank Tanana—was a starting pitcher. We relievers sat in the bullpen and twiddled our thumbs.

That made as much sense as anything else that happened in 1976, a wacky year all the way around.

CHAPTER 4

1977

THE OTHER SIDE OF THE MAJORS

In the early 1960s, Cincinnati Reds pitcher Jim Brosnan wrote an insightful book about a year in the major leagues and called his opus *The Long Season*. Brosnan's title took on special meaning for me after the 1976 fiasco with the White Sox.

Play for a team that wins 64 games (out of 161) in six months and you'll discover just how interminable a baseball season can be. Try keeping your composure, never mind a straight face, when you're forced to play in short pants. See what it's like when baseball becomes the third act in a three-ring circus. You'll learn the meaning of the term "theater of the absurd."

It was, for all of Bill Veeck's fun, games, and sideshows, a season from hell. A long season from hell.

I spent the first part of the off-season up in the mountains in Colorado, fishing and hunting elk. I needed to decompress from all the weirdness. When I got back in early November, I learned that my mentor Chuck Tanner had been traded by the A's to Pittsburgh, where he would replace veteran manager Danny Murtaugh, whose health was failing. (The popular Murtaugh would pass away on December 2, 1976.)

In exchange for Chuck's managerial services, Pittsburgh had worked out a deal with Oakland that sent the A's catcher Manny Sanguillen and $100,000. It was the first—and only—time in baseball history that a manager had been traded for a player and cash.

A month later, two weeks before Christmas, I found out I was going to be reunited with Chuck. It was the best Christmas present I could have received. Tanner had engineered a four-player deal that took Terry Forster and me to Pittsburgh in exchange for Richie Zisk and Silvio Martinez.

Tanner placed a premium on having a lefty-righty combination like Forster and me. He liked having the luxury late in a game of bringing in a power pitcher from either side. The trade kept the long-running Terry-and-the-Goose act alive and well, albeit at a new venue—Three Rivers Stadium.

On paper, the deal looked good for both clubs. Of course, trades always appear to be flashes of genius at the moment they occur. It usually takes weeks or months for a deal to go sour.

Martinez, from the Dominican Republic, was one of the Pirates top pitching prospects. And, lord knows, the White Sox needed help with their pitching. But the key acquisition for Chicago figured to be Richie Zisk, an outfielder with plenty of pop in his bat.

The 21 homers Zisk hit for Pittsburgh in 1976 represented the third most in major league history by a guy whose last name began with the letter Z. Only Gus Zernial and Norm Zauchin had gone deep more often in a single season.

In addition, Zisk, who was of Polish descent, could be counted on to become a fan favorite at Comiskey Park. The South Side of Chicago, from which the White Sox draw their primary fan base, has more Poles than a slalom run.

My trade to Pittsburgh proved to be a blessing. I needed out of the carnival atmosphere in Chicago. When Tanner called to inform me of it, the first words out of his mouth were: "Rich, guess where you're going?"

"Let me guess—back to the bullpen?"

"You got it," he said.

"That's great, Chuck," I rejoined. "That's just great."

When I came up with Chicago in 1972, bullpens had yet to evolve into their modern-day structure. Specialized roles like closer, setup man, or long reliever were not yet defined and delineated.

Basically, in those days the bullpen was the repository for broken-down starters or guys with injured arms. A few relief specialists had surfaced in the previous ten to fifteen years—guys like Elroy Face, Lindy McDaniel, Hoyt Wilhelm, Don McMahon, Rollie Fingers, and two of the Gossage family's beloved New York Yankees, Ryne Duren and Luis Arroyo.

Most teams, though, hadn't sorted out pitching roles beyond starter and nonstarter. You were either fish or fowl.

When I made Chicago's major league squad in 1972, I was so overjoyed to be in the big leagues I went to the bullpen without a whimper. I would have done anything to keep my job, except scrub the toilets and urinals. Come to think of it, I would have done those things too.

By the beginning of my second season in Chicago, I was bucking for a spot in Tanner's starting rotation. The trouble was, as you now know, I went overboard in trying to develop off-speed pitches and lost my good fastball. I wandered in the wilderness in 1973 and 1974, groping around for command of my pitches and in desparate need of confidence.

When I finally established myself as an All-Star in 1975, it was as a relief pitcher, a closer. That's how Tanner knew me best, and it was why, now that I was going to the Pirates, I once again was bullpen bound.

I had a great year with the Pirates—arguably the most dominant of my career. I possessed great command with the slider, which allowed me to work the outside part of the strike zone and nicely complemented the resurgent fastball.

My heat had started drawing comparisons to Nolan Ryan's. My mechanics were solid and I got into such a rhythm, a groove, that I began obliterating batters. For the first time, "Goose" cries began reverberating around stadiums when I came in.

Goosemania—or something similar—started during a series against the Los Angeles Dodgers in mid-May. I totally dominated.

In one game, I worked three perfect innings and got eight K's. In one of those innings, I threw nine pitches, all strikes. Pirates fans started going bonkers; the whole stadium rocked.

Afterward, Dodger manager Tommy Lasorda said, "That's the first time I've seen Gossage. I wouldn't know him if I bumped into him. But I know this, he can throw the ball. That was one of the best exhibitions I've seen."

In another game in the same series, after striking out several Dodgers with fastballs, I threw Steve Yeager a slider and he popped it up to the infield. Yeager ran back to the dugout and from the top step screamed at me, "Challenge somebody, you chickenshit."

At the instant Yeager hollered, the ballpark had a sudden moment of silence, so players on both teams and in both dugouts heard what he yelled. Everybody cracked up.

Challenge somebody? That's an old baseball term that means throw your best fastball to a hitter and see if he can handle it. I'd been vaporizing Dodger hitters all night with my heat, which made me wonder what game Yeager had been watching. Challenge somebody? Who did Yeager think he was kidding?

"Screw you," I yelled back at him. I'd done him a favor by throwing him a slider; at least he could get his bat on the ball.

After the Dodgers series, the Pirates p.a. system started blaring the sound of honking geese whenever I came into a game. And a week later, John Hallahan, the team's veteran equipment manager, showed up at the park with a real goose, which a local farm had donated to the Pirates as a mascot.

We called her Lucy Goose at first. Lucy was set up with her own cage in the Pirate bullpen and assigned a handler. Fans would pose for pictures with Lucy before games. Then a local radio station, WWSW, sponsored a "Name the Goose" contest. The winning entry, in tribute to the strikeouts I'd been posting, was Dr. K (the same name given years later to New York Mets phenom Dwight Gooden).

Terry Forster got into the spirit of the occasion. "Maybe if I start going good, they'll bring an elephant or hippo out to the bullpen for me," said Forster, who besides his pitches was known for his girth.

After a month or so, however, Dr. K (née Lucy) became old news. She required too much care and nurturing. Besides, have you ever had to hang around goose droppings for any length of time? They get pretty pungent.

Forster never really got things going that year, and Tanner's lefty-righty strategy went by the boards. My partner in relief crime became fellow right-hander Kent Tekulve.

Teke was perhaps the least-athletic-looking guy in the majors. With his aquiline face covered by thick, tinted glasses, and a slight frame with a sunken chest, he looked like an eighth grade science teacher or a male librarian. He could have been the model for the "Before" guy in one of those Charles Atlas magazine ads.

The guys gave Teke a lot of guff about his looks. The joke around the clubhouse was that Teke was so ugly, when he checked into a hotel room his pillow would take off running down the hall.

Appearances notwithstanding, Kent Tekulve was a tough and durable competitor. Plus he had a submarine delivery that batters had difficulty picking up. Teke became the principal setup guy and I became the closer. He fooled hitters with his motion, and I intimidated them with power.

We became quite a pair that year, each making 72 appearances, a Pittsburgh record. Teke, who finished the season with a 10-1 record and 7 saves, later had a great run as the primary Pirate closer.

Despite the reputation I had rapidly acquired around the National League, I wasn't selected for the All-Star Game.

Not at first, anyway. Tommy Lasorda chose two relievers for the N.L. team, Bruce Sutter of Chicago and Gary Lavelle of San Francisco. When Sutter came down with a bad back, though, Lasorda made me a last-minute replacement.

That same year, Billy Martin picked Frank Tanana from the California Angels for the A.L. team. When Frank hurt his arm the week before the game, Martin tried to fill his spot with Tanana's teammate, Nolan Ryan. Nolan pitched a fit because he hadn't been named to the team originally and refused Billy's offer. At which point Martin blew up and tried to get the American League office to suspend Ryan for insubordination, dereliction of duty, or some equally heinous act.

Nolan may have been too proud to schlep to the 1977 All-Star Game as a replacement, but I sure as hell wasn't. I was as pleased as a peacock to preen before a national audience. And for the first time, I played on a winning team. The National League dusted the American League once again, 7-5.

Sad to say, my string of lousy performances in the mid-season classic continued. Lasorda brought me into to mop up in the ninth inning, and Boston's George "Boomer" Scott jacked a fastball I left out over the plate into the center-field stands at Yankee Stadium.

The one major glitch in the 1977 season was that I was unable to reach contract terms with Pittsburgh. During spring training my agent, Jerry Kapstein—to whom several Oakland A's had introduced me at the 1975 All-Star Game—made what we felt was a fair and reasonable offer. But Pirate GM Pete Peterson, for whatever reason, wouldn't sign off.

Peterson could have sewn up my services for three years for just over $400,000. As I recall, Kapstein and I were asking for a pay scale of $125,000, $130,000, and $150,000. When negotiations reached an impasse early in the season, however, I decided to play out the season under my existing contract (which was $58,000). At the end of the year I would become a free agent eligible for the reentry draft; I'd take my chances on the open market.

That decision would ultimately provide Corna and me with a windfall.

I finished the year with an 11-9 record, 26 saves, and a career-low 1.62 ERA. I struck out 151 batters in 133 innings, approaching Dick Radatz's record of 181 in 1964 for the Boston Red Sox.

With the manner in which relief pitchers are being used today, it's possible that Radatz's record will endure. It's not uncommon now for a closer to wait until the ninth inning to make his appearance. Closers today might appear in 65 or 70 games and log only 70 or 75 innings.

Back in the mid-1970s closers came into the game as early as the seventh or eighth inning. Instead of being asked to get just three outs, we were counted on to get at least eight or nine. And seldom did we get to start an inning with a clean slate. Calls from the dugout typically didn't come until a teammate was already in a world of hurt.

That year with Pittsburgh, I finally came to terms with the fact that relief pitching represented my real calling in the game. Success and celebrity were part of the equation, true, but so was growing self-awareness. I finally realized I didn't have the temperament to be a starting pitcher. I hated sitting around four or five days between assignments.

I craved action. I wanted the ball.

When you're a closer, there's a natural high that comes with the territory. Your pulse quickens when the game's on the line, and you can actually feel your blood pumping. All the adrenaline racing through your body lifts you to a different realm.

In 1977, I became an adrenaline junkie. I got hooked on the high. When that occurred, I knew my starting days were history. And do you know what?

I wouldn't have had it any other way.

The Pittsburgh Pirates won 96 games in 1977 and were without question the best team I had played on. Sadly, the Philadelphia Phillies were even better. Propelled by the one-two punch of Mike Schmidt and Greg Luzinski and the pitching duo of Steve Carlton and Larry Christenson, the Phillies won 101 games. Which meant that, once again, I went hunting in Colorado earlier in the fall than I wanted. Postseason games continued to elude me.

The Pirates were on the verge of winning a championship (which would come at the 1979 World Series). People who knew baseball could see that Chuck Tanner had most of the ingredients for success already in place.

Pittsburgh had great hitters like Dave "the Cobra" Parker, who won the N.L. batting title in 1977 with a .338 average; Al "Scoop" Oliver, a consistent .300 hitter; and Rennie Stennett, who put together a terrific season before being seriously injured.

The 1977 Pirates also enjoyed career years from Bill Robinson, who hit 26 homers and drove in 104 runs, and John Candelaria, who, as ace of the staff, was 20-5.

The Pirates also had outstanding clubhouse leaders, guys like Parker, Phil Garner, and Willie "Pops" Stargell, who was injured for much of the season and played only 63 games. At thirty-seven, a holdover from the Roberto Clemente era, Stargell remained the club's bell cow.

Like all true leaders in team sports, Stargell did his leading by example. On rare occasions when something needed to be said to a teammate, Pops wouldn't hesitate to speak up. But talking in sports, especially pro sports, is vastly overrated: What really counts is performance.

Stargell, Parker, Garner, and the rest of the team's leaders let their actions on the field set the proper tone. The Pirates played the game with passion and enthusiasm. There wasn't a slacker in the group.

Dave Parker was one of the real characters on the Pirates.

Along with Dick Allen, he was also one of the most gifted athletes I've ever seen or been around. Parker had power, speed, and absolute confidence in his abilities. Like Allen, he was a pure physical specimen, chiseled like one of Michelangelo's statues.

And, like Allen, Dave Parker lived in his own universe. I was in the clubhouse one afternoon when he came walking in. "Here, boy," he called. "Come on, fella. Come on."

Parker took a few steps and looked back at the door. Then he took a few more steps. "Here boy," he called out again. "Here, boy!"

There was no dog in sight. By now we were all wondering what the hell was going on. Was Parker hallucinating? Did he actually expect a dog to scurry over to his side?

Just then Parker gave a tug to his trouser leg, and into the clubhouse rolled his bat.

His bat? We all laughed so hard we cried. Dave had wrapped a thin fishing line, which none of us could see, around the bat handle and tied the other end to his pants. Where did he get that idea? You never knew with Dave.

Parker always was a bit nutty about his lumber. He liked to go around hugging the bat, kissing it and petting it. You can get away with a lot of bizarre behavior when you hit .338 and lead the league, but I wouldn't recommend it for .250 hitters. They'd get hooted out of the clubhouse.

I was sitting next to Parker in the dugout when Rennie Stennett tore up his ankle that summer. Rennie was racing toward second base, stretching a single, and got caught in between. That is, he didn't know whether to slide or take the base standing up. When Rennie tried to split the difference with a semislide, his cleats caught on the bag and his ankle snapped in horrific fashion.

The injury was gruesome. Stennett's ankle got absolutely mangled. It twisted terribly out of shape. The anklebone protruded from the skin, and his foot rotated 180 degrees. It pointed back at his head.

Anyone who remembers an NFL game between New York and Washington several years later, where Lawrence Taylor's tackle broke Joe Theismann's leg, has an idea how serious—and sickening—Stennett's injury was.

When they carried Rennie through our dugout on a

stretcher, I turned green. Dave Parker turned white. It was difficult to look at Stennett's ankle and keep your last meal down.

I doubt if many fans recall just how good a hitter Rennie had become before that injury. His name is in the record books for getting seven hits in a nine-inning game (in 1975), which tied a major league record. In 1977, Stennett really blossomed, putting together a twenty-game hitting streak. At the time of his injury, he was batting .336 and contending for the batting title Parker ultimately won.

Sad to say, Stennett never again hit .300. He wasn't the same player after the injury, not by any stretch of the imagination. At least Rennie was still on the Pirates roster in 1979—though no longer the starter at second base—and shared in their world championship. But his injury was too severe to overcome.

Stennett's ankle injury was probably the second worst I ever saw in baseball. The dubious distinction for worst belonged to my former White Sox teammate Wilbur Wood.

It had happened the previous year. Because everything else in Chicago went wrong during the madcap 1976 season, losing a veteran ace like Wilbur early in the season hardly seemed out of the ordinary.

We were playing on the road at Tiger Stadium. Detroit's Ron LeFlore timed one of Wood's flutterballs perfectly and hit a smash that caught Wilbur squarely on the kneecap.

Wood went down like a gored hog. Everyone in the park cringed at the sight of him lying in a heap at the base of the mound and shuddered at his screams of agony.

Tests subsequently showed that LeFlore's wicked shot

had shattered Wilbur's kneecap in seven or eight places. Wood missed the rest of the 1976 season and, although he pitched a couple more seasons, never regained his winning form. LeFlore's blast effectively ended his career.

I witnessed another serious baseball injury while playing with Pittsburgh in 1977: Felix Millan's.

Against the New York Mets, our catcher, Ed Ott, broke up a potential double play by sliding hard into second base. He forced Millan, the Mets second baseman, to hold onto the ball rather than risk an off-balance throw to first.

Ott's slide wasn't dirty or out of line. It was a good, hard, clean baseball play. Nevertheless, Millan took exception. Still holding the baseball in his bare hand, Millan, a native of Puerto Rico and one of the stars of the 1973 National League champion Mets, swung a roundhouse right at Ott's chin. He narrowly missed.

Felix had picked the wrong dude to mess with. Ott, who split time at catcher with Duffy Dyer, had a build like a fireplug. And—this bit of information being crucial to the events that would unfold—Ott happened to be a former high school state wrestling champion in his native Pennsylvania.

Had Felix known what we Pirates knew—that Ott was one mean motorscooter—he would have tossed the ball back to the pitcher and gone quietly about his business. Instead, Millan had committed the mortal sin of trying to take on the baddest Buc.

An instant after ducking Felix's punch, Ott picked up Millan and drove his head and shoulder down into the dirt infield. Just like that: Wham! Bam!

In professional wrestling terms, the particular maneuver Ed Ott executed is known as a pile driver. In pro wrestling, of course, all the moves are choreographed, the ring is padded, and the force of a fall is mitigated. Nobody gets hurt.

This pile driver, however, wasn't phony. Ed Ott didn't pull up and the ground didn't give. In a twinkling, Millan's twelve years in the majors—a creditable dozen years, I might add—were over.

He had suffered a broken collarbone and other shoulder damage. Millan wound up playing professionally in Japan, where he won a batting championship, but he was never the same after taking that ill-advised swing at Ed Ott.

Not only was I reunited with Chuck Tanner in Pittsburgh that year, but I again hooked up with pitching coach Larry Sherry. Sherry had worked with me in the Instructional League in St. Petersburg, Florida, in the winter of 1970–71.

Being back together with Larry, the pitching hero of the 1959 World Series for the Los Angeles Dodgers, gave my career another boost. Larry helped me refine some mechanics, especially with my release point.

Sherry showed me how the power position for pitchers equates to a prizefighter delivering a knockout punch. At the time, I had been getting too much extension with my right arm; under Larry's patient and watchful eye, I adopted a more controlled release point and achieved immediate results.

I soaked up Sherry's advice like a sponge. No one ever has all the answers in baseball—granted, the big leagues have its share of know-it-alls—but I've noticed smart players keep asking questions. My mantra as a pitcher remained: learn and grow.

Other than returning to the bullpen at Chuck Tanner's insistence and refining mechanics under Larry Sherry's direction, my move to the National League in 1977 required little in the way of adjustment.

The rubber was still 60 feet 6 inches away from home plate. The dimensions of the batter's boxes were the same. The baseballs we threw in the National League were stitched at the same sweatshops in Haiti or Jamaica.

About the only difference I noticed was that N.L. umpires tended to have a lower strike zone than their A.L. counterparts. And N.L. umpires seemed to call games more consistently.

The National League in those days was, without question, the superior of the two leagues. Its eleven-game winning streak in All-Star Games during 1972–82 bears that out. The A.L. had a smattering of superstars here and there, but teams in the N.L. were loaded with great athletes.

N.L. teams, for the most part, were built around speed. Many N.L. cities had erected new stadiums in the late 1960s and early 1970s (Three Rivers in Pittsburgh and Riverfront Stadium in Cincinnati, for example), and most, if not all, featured an indoor carpet like Astroturf. That surface puts a premium on team speed.

N.L. teams played a fast, exciting brand of ball, with plenty of steals and hit-and-run plays. A.L. teams, in contrast, played a plodding style. Heavily influenced by the success of Earl Weaver's power-laden Baltimore clubs in the late 1960s and early 1970s, plus the adoption of the designated hitter rule in 1973, A.L. teams played for the big innings; they didn't steal many bases or try to exert much pressure on the defense. Teams sat around and waited for the three-run homer.

I didn't alter my pitching style when I moved over to the National League. I still challenged hitters—Steve Yeager included—with fastballs. I mixed in sliders and an occasional change-up just to keep batters honest.

I didn't try to adjust my stretch position, or shorten my delivery, to counteract all the N.L. speed. I'd never been any good at holding base runners, so why worry now?

Besides, I locked-in on batters, not base runners. They had my undivided attention. They were the ones who could inflict damage. Get them out and you win the war.

One memorable moment that season came early in the year in a game against Montreal at Three Rivers Stadium. Gary Carter, the Expos All-Star catcher, hit a weak grounder his first time up and in disgust flipped his bat.

It rolled into our dugout, where Jim Rooker, one of the Pirate starters who was lounging around on a day off, picked it up. Rooker gave the bat to the batboy, who took it back to the Montreal dugout. No big deal.

By the second time Carter came up, the Expos had mounted a rally, which he promptly ended with a harmless pop-up. In frustration, Carter slammed his bat into the turf. It bounced and rolled and ended up in our dugout again.

Rooker was ready this time. "You big crybaby," he shouted at Carter. "What do you think about this?"

With that, Rooker began to pounding Carter's bat on the turf. He smashed it to pieces.

Seeing what had transpired, Carter ran over in front of our dugout and shook his index finger at Rooker. "I'll get you," he vowed.

A week or so later we went on a road trip that included

beautiful Montreal, one of my favorite cities. As fate would have it, Rooker got one of the starts in the series.

Up came Gary Carter, blood in his eye. Rooker rocked and fired and Carter got all of it. Home run.

The second time through the Expos lineup, here came Carter again. Rooker threw, Carter swung, and—BOOM!— there went another bomb. Touch all the bases, Gary.

When Carter came up again, we had a funny feeling about what would happen. Sure enough, he took Rooker downtown for the third consecutive time.

No sooner had Carter's bat met the ball than Rooker took off his glove and flung it at least forty feet straight up in the air.

Tanner went out to get him, and when Rooker reached the dugout, he announced, "Mark my words. That's the last time I'm breaking anybody's bat."

That remark cracked us up. We hated laughing at Rook after he'd taken such a shelling—each home run had been hit harder and farther than the last—but everyone was howling.

Gary Carter hit three homers in one game. I never hit one in twenty-two years. I used to joke about it, saying, "I'm not going to retire until I hit a home run." That may help explain why I stayed in baseball so long.

Much of my career was spent in the American League, which implemented the designated hitter (DH) rule in 1973. That rule, which took the bat out of pitchers' hands, was, in theory, not a bad idea. (In practice, however, it was something else. What the DH rule costs the game in strategy more than offsets its usefulness.)

Some pitchers wielded a bat as effectively as they would

a toothpick. For exhibit A, take Bob Buhl. In a fifteen-year career in the N.L., Buhl came to the plate 857 times and collected 76 hits, a .089 average. He was at the apex of ineffectiveness in 1962, which he spent primarily with the Chicago Cubs. That season, Buhl stepped into the box 70 times and was retired 70 times.

For exhibit B, take Randy Tate of the New York Mets. In 1975, his one full season in the majors, Tate went up there swinging 41 times. He sat right back down 41 times. He never had to call time and send for his jacket.

For the record, I had 85 official at bats and managed 9 hits, a whopping .106 lifetime average. Sad to say, none of my shots left the yard. But I got to showcase my power for the Pirates—and boost my career slugging percentage—against St. Louis.

We were playing the Cardinals at Busch Stadium. Tanner brought me in late to protect a 2-1 lead. In the top of the ninth, with two men out and a runner at second, I stepped into the batter's box against the St. Louis closer, Al Hrabosky.

Most every baseball fan remembers the colorful Hrabosky, who was nicknamed the Mad Hungarian. He would stomp around the perimeter of the mound, getting himself pumped up, then race up, toe the rubber, and fire.

Hrabosky's first pitch was past me before I blinked. So was his second. I'd never seen anyone throw that hard, so on his third pitch I started the bat early and took a wicked cut.

For one of the few times in my career, I managed to get good wood on the ball. The trouble was, the force of the swing spun me around. I lost sight of the playing field and suddenly had no idea where the ball had gone.

I thought maybe I'd fouled off the pitch up over their dugout. But then I saw our first base coach, Al Monchak, pumping his arms frantically and yelling for me to run. I shot a glance over toward third base and saw a Pirate teammate already halfway home and realized the ball was somewhere in play.

But where?

I took off down the first-base line, accompanied by laughter from both dugouts. I scanned the outfield and noticed that deep in the right-field corner Bake McBride was trying to pick up a ball. The ball wouldn't cooperate.

I turned on the jets, made a sharp turn around first base and cruised into second base well ahead of McBride's throw. The Mad Hungarian was so pissed off at giving up a double—to me of all people—that he came halfway toward second base and shot me a sinister glare.

I just shrugged my shoulders and grinned like the cat who ate the canary. We both knew I'd gotten away with one. I'd been lucky enough to swing where the ball had been pitched.

That season in Pittsburgh proved to be my final one with Terry Forster, my all-time favorite running mate. Before we parted company, though, Forster pulled a good one on me.

The Pirates were playing the Cubs at Wrigley Field. A day game, naturally. To get from the visitors' clubhouse to the field, players traipse along an elevated catwalk. Fans down at street level can look up and see the ballplayers passing by some twelve or fifteen feet overhead.

There was one loud, obnoxious fan standing underneath the catwalk that afternoon, a Cubs fan with a hard-on for the Goose. When he saw a large frame in a Pirate uniform pass overhead, he let loose with a blistering assault.

"Hey, Gossage, you suck!" he bellowed. "You're the worst excuse for a pitcher I've ever seen. The Cubs are going to kick your ass."

Of course the form overhead belonged to Forster, not me. For years, baseball fans had trouble telling us apart, even though he was the one who wore the inner tube around his waist. ("A waist is a terrible thing to mind," Terry once said, a line that got plenty of play.)

Forster saw an opening and seized it. He walked over to the railing on the catwalk, peered down and yelled back:

"You big jerk. Nobody wants to hear your tired bullshit. Either shut the fuck up, or I'll come down there and punch your lights out."

The man below wasn't amused. In fact, he was livid. "I'll kill you, Gossage," he raged. "You're dead."

Forster flipped him the bird, then merrily strolled away. Meanwhile, I dressed in the clubhouse, totally unaware of the wheels Terry had set in motion.

The Gossage-hater spent the afternoon fuming and stewing. He no doubt had a few brewskis to fuel his fury. By the end of the game he lusted for blood. Mine.

It was getaway day for the Pirates, meaning we were going on from Chicago to another city. A bus idled outside Wrigley Field, waiting to whisk us to O'Hare Airport.

Forster dressed quickly after the game. When he came out the side door of the clubhouse, he saw among the well-wishers and autograph-seekers a belligerent fan waiting to pounce.

"Don't worry, Goose will be out in a minute," announced Forster, who climbed aboard the bus and took a window seat, from where he could watch the carnage he had wrought. He clued in the whole team on what was about to happen.

I've neglected to mention that not only did this loud fan hate my guts, he was huge. A beast. I'd conservatively guess that he was six-foot-eight and 350 pounds.

I came walking out as innocently as a lamb being led to the slaughter. Suddenly, from out of the crowd came a giant meat hook, which clamped on my shoulder and spun me around.

"You're dead, Gossage," growled the voice of doom. I took a look at the size of my attacker, who bore a faint resemblance to Andre the Giant, and had one immediate thought:

No shit.

Willie Stargell had come out of the clubhouse right after me. He had seen this monster grab me and immediately attempted to intervene. Keep in mind that Stargell's no small fry either. For his troubles, Pops got swatted like a fly.

Fortunately, three stadium security guards saw the commotion and came over to subdue the beast. They pulled him off me, but not before he'd rearranged my tie and ripped two buttons off my shirt.

I climbed aboard the bus and asked, "What the hell was that all about?" I didn't notice Forster, who was hiding his face and laughing his butt off. He wasn't the only guy roaring, either.

Just when I thought everything was over, the Goose-hater broke free. He began pounding on the windows of the bus, calling me every name in the book and daring me to come off the bus and confront him. He was still pounding when the riot squad arrived. As the bus finally pulled away from Wrigley Field, cops were stuffing his fat ass into a paddy wagon. Forster, meanwhile, was rolling in the aisle.

Late in the 1977 season I got tossed out of a game for the first time in my career. Bruce Froemming, who was working home plate, chased me. The funny thing was, I wasn't even pitching that day. I came out from the clubhouse moments after the first pitch and dawdled in the dugout, waiting to mosey out to the bullpen between half innings.

We were playing Los Angeles. Larry Demery started and got into an immediate jam. The Dodgers loaded the bases in the top of the first and looked like they might blow the game open.

Larry's next pitch split the center of the plate. When Froemming failed to raise his hand, we started razzing him from our bench. Rising to the spirit of the occasion, I went up on the top step of dugout and yelled at Froemming, "You stink!"

Feeling a sudden urge to underscore my point, I held my fingers up to my nose, striking the classic gesture of a foul odor. "That's right," I bellowed for emphasis. "You stink, Froemming."

Bruce immediately called time and summoned Chuck Tanner to home plate. After a brief discussion, Tanner came back to the dugout and informed me my workday was over. I'd been ejected.

"He's throwing me out?" I cried increduously. "For that?"

I went running out to home plate and called Froemming every dirty word I could think of. I even made up a couple new ones. If you're going to the showers, get your money's worth.

After that incident, Chuck issued a new edict. He banished me to the bullpen for good. Tanner wouldn't permit me to sit in the dugout during the early innings because, he insisted, he couldn't afford to have me kicked out of a game.

When baseball's reentry draft took place that fall, I became a hot property. At twenty-six, I had just entered my prime. My fastball, as I continued to grow and mature, consistently registered 98 mph on the radar gun. Clocking 100 mph seemed just a matter of time.

Jerry Kapstein conducted serious discussions with several teams that drafted me, including Atlanta. But when New York Yankee owner George Steinbrenner came to the table and reached for his checkbook, I knew the Big Apple would be my new home.

Having a chance to put on the famed Yankee pinstripes—the greatest uniform in professional team sports—and wear the NY insignia on my cap was too good to resist.

(The uniforms in Pittsburgh, incidentally, were at the other extreme. The Pirates had so many combinations of black and yellow, stripes and solids, checks and patterns, and so many different caps, that seldom were all twenty-five Pittsburgh players in the same attire on the same day. Occasionally, we wore a solid yellow uniform, which made Willie Stargell and Dave Parker look like giant bananas.)

On November 23, 1977, five weeks after New York wrapped up its first world championship since 1962, I signed a six-year contract with the Yankees worth $2.75 million. At the press conference introducing me, I said to the assembled media horde, "This [deal] is what the Yankees need to make a dynasty."

I'm pretty sure either Kapstein, Steinbrenner, or someone in the Yankees PR department put me up to making such a bold declaration. Someone must have figured brashness would play well in the New York press. Bragging has never been my style. I always preferred to let my pitching do the talking.

I had more than a few regrets about leaving Pittsburgh. Chuck Tanner had been like a second father to me. Terry Forster, a brother. Plus Pittsburgh was—and is—a great sports city. Pirate fans are hearty, hardworking folk who bring energy and emotion to the ballpark. They're the kind of fans for whom ballplayers give an extra effort.

Just before the season ended, Corna and I visited Chuck and his wife Babs in Tanner's office at Three Rivers Stadium. Part of him probably wanted to plead with me to stay with the Pirates. He had been after Pete Peterson all spring to sign me to a long-term contract. When Peterson kept telling Tanner to be patient and wait, Tanner would sigh, "Wait? For what?"

Had Tanner tried to talk me into staying that day, I would have listened out of sheer respect for the man. He didn't, though.

"Goose, you're the best reliever in baseball," Chuck told me. "Nobody can touch you. You owe it to Corna, as well as any family the two of you might want to start someday, to get all the money you can. While you can get it."

I knew Chuck hated to have to say those words, but I guess our relationship went beyond the white lines.

———

The day Corna and I turned over the keys to our apartment in Pittsburgh, we stopped by Three Rivers to pick up some of my gear. When we pulled out of the parking lot and began the long drive home to Colorado, I began to cry. They were the kind of tears that flow when you feel a deep sense of loss about something special that likely will never come again.

And 1977, any way you sliced it, had been a special season in my career.

The Pirates were a fun, free-spirited bunch that liked to party. When the guys got down, they liked to break out the wine. I swear I consumed more red wine that one year in Pittsburgh than in all my other major league years combined.

The Pirates were also a closely knit group. The "We Are Family" motto the team adopted for its championship run in 1979—borrowing from a song by Sister Sledge—was genuine. Men can't fake the depth of feeling those guys had for one other. We're too transparent.

I missed out on the Pirates celebration in 1979, having chosen to join a dysfunctional family in New York instead. Against all odds, New York won a second consecutive World Series in 1978, and I played one of the leading roles in the ongoing soap opera.

It's funny how things work out, but there was nothing humorous about my arrival in the Big Apple. In fact, it was brutal. A total and complete nightmare.

CHAPTER 5

1978

REJECTION AND REDEMPTION

My first one-on-one encounter with New York Yankees manager Billy Martin at spring training in 1978 set the tone for my disastrous debut as a Bronx Bomber. When Martin gave me an order that I refused to follow, friction between us surfaced immediately and never went away. After that incident, Billy went out of his way to make me as miserable as possible. He pretty much succeeded.

The Yankees, fresh from defeating the Los Angeles Dodgers in the 1977 World Series, where Reggie Jackson sealed the deal with three home runs off three different pitchers in game six, opened their spring training schedule against the Texas Rangers.

It was another hot and humid day in Fort Lauderdale. The exhibition game figured to be a low-key affair with nothing of consequence at stake. Everyone's immediate goal was to get through the afternoon without pulling a groin muscle or developing a case of jock itch. No one even thought about putting on his game face or taking things seriously.

Before the game I shagged balls in the outfield, minding my own business. From out of nowhere Billy Martin slipped up beside me. He didn't waste time on polite small talk.

"Goose, when you get in the game today, I want you to hit Billy Sample in the head," he said.

"What?" I asked, pretending I hadn't heard him correctly.

"I want you to drill Billy Sample in his fucking head," Martin repeated.

I'd heard him correctly, all right.

I started pawing at the grass. Jeezus, I thought, why should I drill Sample? He'd never done anything to me. And hit him in the head? No way. He could be killed.

I looked straight into Martin's eyes, wondering what kind of twisted sister would give such an order.

"No, I can't hit him in the head," I finally said. "I can't fight your battles for you."

Martin turned beet red and stuck his big nose in my face. "What do you mean you won't hit him?" he shouted. "I tell you to drill a guy and you say you're not going to do it? You worthless piece of crap."

Martin aired me out, but I stood my ground. I had no intention of throwing at Billy Sample's head—not that day or any other.

In Martin's myopic and distorted view, every score—real or imagined—had to be settled. Billy took offense over the most trifling matters, had a memory like an elephant, and was as vindictive as a Mafia don.

He got mad and then he got even.

It's entirely possible that Sample was merely an innocent bystander, a pawn in one of Billy Martin's games. Martin might simply have been administering one of his loyalty tests. In the maladjusted world of the Yankee skipper, people fell into two camps: his allies and his enemies.

You couldn't declare neutrality, like Switzerland. Either

you were with Billy or against him, and if it happened to be the latter, sooner or later there'd be hell to pay.

Martin made sure of that.

That spring in Florida, I developed a staph infection in my right foot, which forced me to spend a week in Imperial Point Hospital in Fort Lauderdale. I hobbled around for the final two weeks of training camp, unable to get in all the work I needed.

When the bell rang for 1978, I knew I wasn't completely ready to compete. Billy, eager to bury me, seized the opening.

He never brought me in to start an inning. When he made the call, runners were already in scoring position, often with less than two outs. Seldom did he hand me the baseball with the opportunity to win a game. His message rang clear: "Let's see you get out of this jam."

If Martin wanted his new high-ticket closer to fail—and it was clear to me he did after I refused to drill Billy Sample during spring training—I tried my best to oblige. In my first few appearances with the Yankees I stunk the joint up.

My own sweet mother would have sent my weak stuff to the outfield wall. Hitters who should have been intimidated by my fastball stepped into the batter's box drooling like beggars at a feast.

New York opened the 1978 season on the road, against Texas, and in my first appearance as a Yankee I surrendered a game-winning home run in the tenth inning to Richie Zisk (who had stayed with the Chicago White Sox only one season). Zisk got a hanging slider and hit a bullet through a 25 mph headwind into the left-field seats.

In Milwaukee, I blew a save by first surrendering a homer

113

to Larry Hisle and then later giving up a game-winning hit to Don Money. Hisle's shot had been a great piece of hitting; I nearly decapitated him on a 2-2 pitch and then on 3-2 threw a real bastard pitch—a fastball at the knees on the outside corner—which he sent into the bullpen beyond the right-field wall. Yankee catcher Thurman Munson was amazed. "How in the hell did he hit that pitch?" he asked after the game. I shrugged.

By the time the Yankees came home from that first road trip, I sported a matched set of two losses and two blown saves. Adding to the uneasiness created by my big contract, the run-in with Martin, and my atrocious start, I felt immense pressure trying to replace as Yankee closer one of the team's most popular players, Albert "Sparky" Lyle.

My arrival in New York had pretty much put the winner of the 1977 American League Cy Young Award on the shelf. As Graig Nettles would later say, in one of baseball's most memorable lines, "Sparky went from Cy Young to sayonara."

When I signed with the Yankees, I figured Sparky and I could become a dominating duo. The sort of one-two, lefty-righty combination that Terry Forster and I provided for Chuck Tanner in Chicago and Pittsburgh. Over time, though, it began to dawn on me that one of us would have to emerge as the Yankees dominant closer.

Sparky knew right away who that person would be. He tried to tell me by saying, "What do you think they're going to want for an out-pitch, Goose, my slider or your fastball?" He made the statement without a trace of bitterness.

I finally realized Sparky knew best: No team in baseball succeeds in the long run with a closers-by-committee approach. One person has to be entrusted with the job of being the balls-to-the-wall stopper.

Much of the supreme confidence a closer needs to succeed comes from knowing he can handle the paralyzing pressure of a ninth inning. You can't really become *The Man*, in other words, until over and over you've proven yourself as the man.

The situation is comparable to what occurs when a pro football team tries to rotate two quarterbacks. Neither will develop enough confidence in himself, or inspire enough confidence in his teammates, to drive the team the length of the field in the waning seconds with no timeouts. As the saying goes in football, if a team has two quarterbacks, it doesn't have any. The same holds true in baseball: If a team has two closers, it doesn't have any.

Sparky Lyle was a terrific competitor with a wicked slider pretty much on a par with Steve Carlton's. Which is to say Sparky's out-pitch at times could be unhittable. It would leave his hand looking like a strike and then the bottom would fall out. He also had the ice-water veins a closer needs to deal with all the heat.

Off the mound, Sparky took a lighthearted, loosey-goosey approach and employed an overdeveloped sense of mischief and impishness. He was a prankster and natural leader. A free spirit. In short, his teammates admired him and Yankee fans adored him.

I learned how much New Yorkers loved Sparky Lyle when we came back to Yankee Stadium for the home opener against the White Sox. It being our first appearance at home since Reggie Jackson's heroics in the World Series the previous fall, Yankee Stadium sold out. To commemorate the 1977 world championship, Yankee greats Mickey Mantle and Roger Maris raised a banner in the outfield.

Each of the 1978 Yankees received an introduction before the start of the season's first home game. We were announced in numerical order and trotted out to a spot down the first base line. Being number 54, I was the last player introduced.

I followed Ken Holtzman, who was no fan favorite in the Bronx. Yankee fans were already busy booing Holtzman, who would be traded to Chicago that June, when p.a. announcer Bob Sheppard called out my name.

Boos began to cascade down from the upper deck and rumble around in the lower deck. As they reached a crescendo, Holtzman playfully jabbed me in the ribs. "That's not 'Goose' they're saying, buddy boy."

I didn't even bother to reply. I seethed so much I couldn't utter a single word. Hearing Yankee fans jeer and heckle me made my blood boil. Standing there in the face of such derision, I promised myself that, no matter how long it took, one day I would turn the fans' boos into cheers.

That I did, but by no means overnight. My troubles continued throughout the first home stand. I committed the cardinal sin of trying too hard. Instead of relaxing and staying within myself and allowing my natural ability to take over, I began to press.

Instead of throwing with freedom and fluidity—just cutting loose—I tried to force good pitches. I overthrew, which only made matters worse.

It's hard to say which was more unruly during my first six weeks in New York—my pitching or the New York fans' behavior. While I was being chauffeured in from the bullpen in a Toyota Celica, fans would pelt the car with beer, peanuts, and hot dogs. Nobody bothered to hold the mustard or mayo.

By the time the car reached the dugout area, the windshield would be plastered with condiments. When I stepped out, I needed an umbrella, or poncho, to keep dry. (Granted, it's ludicrous to think a major league pitcher would have to be driven in from the bullpen. How long does it take to jog a few hundred feet—maybe twenty or thirty seconds? It's not like that would wear out anyone. Nevertheless, during my career I was driven to the mound in Chevrolets, Cadillacs, Toyotas, golf carts—practically every kind of vehicle except a go-cart.)

If seeing me summoned from the bullpen made Yankee fans surly, it had an opposite effect on my teammates. They thought my trials and tribulations were hilarious. Munson, the great Yankee catcher who perished in a plane crash the following year, once came out to the mound, slapped the ball in my glove, and asked, "Okay, Goose, how you going to lose this one?"

"Just get your ass back behind the plate and we'll find out, won't we?" I joked.

Munson and the other Yankee veterans had a way of staying loose by making light of game situations and playing like they were on a sandlot, not in front of 50,000 fans. The Yankees always put a premium on having fun, which freed them up to play at a high level. They didn't treat baseball like it was life-or-death.

In another game during my miserable start, I worked into a jam by loading the bases. I looked in to get a sign and saw Thurman squatting back there, laughing. He finally called time out and ran out to the mound.

"What the hell are you doing?" I asked.

Thurman stood transfixed by a strange sight beyond the infield. Finally, he said, "Check Rivers out."

Mickey Rivers, the Yankees swift center fielder, had turned to face the outfield wall and assumed a sprinter's stance. He was making an editorial comment about the likelihood of having to chase down another rocket. Munson thought that was hilarious; I couldn't keep from cracking up either.

The most unforgettable moment from a month I would have liked to forget came the night that Rivers threw himself on the hood of the Toyota as I was about to be brought in. He refused to let the driver proceed, unless it was over his dead body.

The driver, Danny Colletti, couldn't budge with Rivers draped across the hood. I rolled down the window and yelled at Mickey to get off, but he refused. One of the umpires came running out from the infield to see what was happening.

"What the hell is going on here?" he snapped.

Mickey appealed to his higher authority.

"Pleeeaassse, Mr. Umpire," Rivers begged. "We don't wants Goose to come in. We wants to win this ball game. We don't wants to lose."

The people in the outfield seats, reading Rivers's body language and gestures, began cracking up.

"Mickey, get off the car," the ump told him. "We gotta get this game going."

Mickey picked himself up off the hood. "We're gonna lose," he said, shaking his head. "Sure as hell, Mr. Umpire, we're going to lose this game."

When Rivers finally got out of the way, I glared at him and growled, "Get ready to run down the next line drive."

Sure enough, the first batter I faced ripped one toward the alley in right. Rivers raced over, laid out in a horizontal dive worthy of an Olympic diver or World Cup goalie, and made one of his all-time best catches. He received a standing ovation from the home crowd.

Mickey came running in toward the dugout, searching me out. He stopped at the top step and, for everyone's benefit, hollered, "Hey, where's the Goose? You know, he told me to be ready to run one down. That motherfucker wasn't kidding, was he?"

Everyone in the dugout, me included, doubled over in laughter.

The Rivers bullpen fiasco, embarrassing as it was, didn't come close to being the worst I endured. Shortly thereafter, I hit rock-bottom one night in Toronto.

Billy brought me in during the ninth inning of a tied game—with runners on first and second, naturally, and no outs. A sacrifice was in order and everyone in the stadium knew it.

When the next Blue Jay batter bunted down the third-base line, I fielded the ball cleanly but, in my heightened state of anxiety, failed to set myself properly for the throw. My peg got caught up in the jet stream and sailed way over the head of Willie Randolph, who was covering first.

It must have landed in the fifteenth or twentieth row. The runner from second trotted home. Ball game.

I went into the visitors' clubhouse and had a nervous breakdown. I crawled into my locker, curled up in a fetal position and bawled like a baby. For the first (and only) time in my career, I felt ready to pack up and head home to Colorado Springs.

There I was, being paid millions of dollars to be the Yankees closer, and all I had accomplished in my first month in pinstripes was to put the defending world champions in a deep hole. And, no matter how hard I tried to work through all the funk, things only seemed to get worse.

I had no one to blame but myself for the whole stinking situation. I certainly didn't blame Yankee fans, who booed me unmercifully and kept crying out for their darling Sparky. Heck, I'd have booed me too. I deserved to hear it from the New York fans.

I don't know how long I stayed down on the floor blubbering. The pity party must have lasted five or ten minutes at least. I finally felt someone's hand touch me on the shoulder. I looked up and saw Catfish Hunter. Gathered around him were Munson, Jackson, Piniella, and Nettles.

"Get up, Goose," Catfish said. "Get dressed. We're all going out to dinner and you're going with us. You're down now, but you're going to come out of it. We all know that, buddy. Now pull yourself together and let's go. C'mon."

Catfish and the other guys picked me up that night in Toronto—literally and in spirit. Thanks to them, I began turning things around shortly thereafter.

Flash forward five months. What began as a dreadful and humiliating season transformed itself into one of the best of my career and without question the most memorable.

I regrouped after that tortuous beginning, won 10 games (with 11 losses, many early in the year) and posted a 2.01 ERA. I led the American League with 27 saves and gradually won over the hearts of Yankee fans. The boos that had ruined my debut at Yankee Stadium gradually gave way to cheers. By the end of the year thunderous choruses of "GOOOOOOOOSE" greeted me upon my arrival from the bullpen. The windshield of the Toyota remained dry and spotless. The only thing fans were throwing at me was praise.

After that dismal beginning, a strong performance in May and June earned me a spot on the All-Star team. My midseason miseries, which had become as annual as a flu shot, continued in San Diego on July 11.

I entered the game in the bottom of the eighth inning with the score tied 3-3. By the time the N.L. finished working me over, the senior circuit had its 14th win in 15 games and 20th in the past 25. Anyone see a trend there?

Steve Garvey started the barrage with a triple. Next I threw a wild pitch to Dave Concepcion, which allowed Garvey to score and break the tie. Steaming, I walked Concepcion. Dave Winfield followed with a sharp single, and when Chet Lemon bobbled the ball, both runners took an extra base.

I wasn't finished screwing up. Bob Boone touched me for a two-run double, pushing the score to 6-3. To top it off,

Dave Lopes singled home Boone. Final score: N.L. 7, A.L. 3. I've seen less carnage and bloodshed in a Freddy Kreuger movie.

A week or so later Billy Martin was replaced as Yankee manager by Bob Lemon after Billy made his infamous crack about Reggie Jackson and George Steinbrenner: "One's a born liar and the other's convicted." Billy popped off to reporters a few days after suspending Reggie for disobeying his orders.

In the bottom of the tenth inning against Kansas City, Billy had given Reggie a bunt sign but took it off with two strikes. Reggie, though, went ahead and attempted a two-strike bunt. He struck out. The Royals won in the eleventh inning, and Billy, to no one's surprise, was pissed. He immediately notified Reggie that he was being suspended five days for insubordination.

Yankee management backed Martin up on Jackson's suspension, and we actually won five games straight while Reggie sat, but by then Billy's nerves were shot, and his self-destructive streak surfaced. He backed himself into a corner by popping off about George and Reggie, and tearfully submitted his resignation.

Then things got even weirder. The following week, at Old-Timers Day, who should come trotting out on to the field—the last Yankee legend introduced—but old number one?

Billy the Kid.

The Yankee Stadium crowd went ballistic hearing Bob Sheppard state that Billy would return as Yankee skipper—

in *1980*. Seems Billy had gone to Steinbrenner shortly after resigning and expressed sincere remorse for his actions. George embraced Billy, forgave him, and promised him another job eighteen months out.

And I thought only Rod Serling could dream up stuff like this.

Under Bob Lemon's steady hand, as opposed to Billy Martin's erratic one, the Yankees came together. When Lem took over, he called a team meeting and said, "Hey, boys, the talent to win is here. You guys won it last year, and the same group, basically, is still here. I'm going to give you the bats and balls, go get 'em. I'll handle the pitching staff and hopefully I'll make the right moves. Let's have some fun."

That's how long the meeting took. Lemon had said all that he needed to. We went to work.

Throughout August, New York whittled away at Boston's big lead in the A.L. standings, which on July 20 had been 14 games. In September we swept a four-game series—subsequently dubbed the Boston Massacre—at Fenway Park. The Yankees outscored the Red Sox 42-9 in the series, outhit them 67-21, and committed 5 errors to Boston's 12.

Ron Guidry, a lefty from Louisiana with a live fastball and a heart as big as an alligator's mouth, won a team record thirteen straight games at the start of the season. Guidry, who didn't lose a decision until July 7, maintained his brilliant form all season. Meanwhile, Ed Figueroa became the first native of Puerto Rico to win twenty games in a season, and Catfish Hunter overcame season-long shoulder problems to pitch masterfully down the stretch.

It didn't hurt any that the big New York newspapers had gone on strike in early August. Distractions caused by incendiary and inflammatory headlines were conspicuously absent as the Yankees made their charge, the biggest comeback in team history.

In one of the most thrilling races in baseball history, we caught up with Boston, pulled ahead for a few days, and wound up tied with the Red Sox with identical 99-63 records. We had a chance to clinch the A.L. pennant on the final day, but Cleveland and Rick Waits smoked us, 9-2. Boston showed its class that afternoon by winning its eighth straight game, as Luis Tiant shut out Toronto.

That set up a one-game playoff at Fenway Park on October 2. Both the Red Sox and Yankees had put together great seasons in 1978, and it didn't seem fair that one wouldn't advance to postseason play. But six months of hard work suddenly came down to nine innings, and one team was headed home.

Fenway Park may be the most difficult place in baseball to play a road game. It's got the Green Monster in left, of course, and the short porch in right and a bunch of asymmetrical lines and strange angles.

What really gives Boston a home field advantage, though, is the home crowd. With the configuration of the grandstand, it feels as if Boston fans are sitting right on top of the players. New Englanders are intense, nasty, and they can ride you like cheap underwear.

I remember Chris Chambliss telling the story about how he rounded third base at Fenway Park one day when he suddenly felt a sharp pain and realized he'd been hit with a dart. I can recall stories of Yankee base runners being pelted with

AA batteries. Nothing that happens at Fenway would ever surprise me.

The good news for Yankee fans was that we had our ace, Guidry, ready to pitch after three days of rest. The man some fans called Louisiana Lightning had locked up the 1978 A.L. Cy Young Award. His 25-3 record that year still represents the highest winning percentage (.893) ever for any pitcher who won at least twenty games.

The bad news for Yankee fans, especially superstitious types, was that each of Guidry's three losses that season had been to a guys named Mike—Mike Flanagan of Baltimore, Mike Caldwell of Milwaukee, and Mike Willis of Toronto.

Guess who Boston had ready to pitch in the playoff game? Mike Torrez.

We took the shuttle to Logan Airport immediately after losing to Cleveland on October 1, checked into the downtown Sheraton Hotel, and began the tortuous wait for tomorrow. I felt too jacked-up to lollygag around, so I left the hotel and made the short walk to Daisy Buchanan's, my favorite Boston saloon. Before long most of the Yankees would congregate there.

As we whiled away the hours that evening, I began to daydream about the playoff: It seemed all but inevitable that the game would come down to a matchup between Carl Yastrzemski and me. I went to bed that night thinking the same thing. I didn't count sheep—I counted fastballs to Yaz.

The great Yastrzemski staked Boston to a 1-0 lead in the second inning, pulling a Guidry fastball just inside the right-field foul pole. The margin remained until the bottom of the sixth inning, when Jim Rice followed a Rick Burleson double with an RBI single. Boston, 2-0.

Mike Torrez, meanwhile, shut New York down on two hits through six innings. In the seventh Torrez surrendered singles to Chris Chambliss and Roy White. With two out, up came shortstop Bucky Dent, the number nine hitter.

What happened next became the stuff of legend. Bucky fouled a pitch off his foot, and while he was hobbling about, Mickey Rivers instructed our batboy to give Dent a different bat. Rivers claimed the bat was "lucky."

After a delay of several minutes during which Dent tried to walk off the injury, Bucky got back in the box and, on Torrez's next pitch, lifted a fly ball to left field. Yastrzemski looked like he had a play in front of the giant wall, but Bucky's ball kept carrying and carrying. The next thing we knew, the ball rested in the netting above the Green Monster and the Yankees were ahead, 3-2. Mickey's bat had been lucky, after all.

Talk about the sounds of silence. As Bucky ducked down into our dugout, Fenway Park was as quiet as an ICU. I had the feeling that a giant Hoover vacuum cleaner had sucked the life out of New England.

I relieved Guidry in the bottom of the seventh inning and worked out of a jam, striking out Bob Bailey (his last major league at bat) for the final out. We padded our lead to 5-2 in the eighth on a RBI double by Thurman and a solo homer by Reggie.

Boston wouldn't give up, however. They were too proud a team to roll over and die. Jerry Remy ripped a double off me and was singled home by Yastrzemski. Carlton Fisk and Fred Lynn followed with singles, and the Red Sox had closed to 5-4.

We carried that precarious lead into the bottom of the ninth. After getting a quick out, I fell behind in the count to Rick Burleson and walked him. Then came the game's pivotal play: Jerry Remy hit a liner to right field that Lou Piniella momentarily lost in the late afternoon glare.

Showing both great reflexes and athleticism, Piniella sensed where the ball would land in front of him and, miraculously, managed to snare it on the first bounce. Lou's split-second reaction kept Burleson from going to third base.

Burleson's failure to advance became significant when the next hitter, league MVP Jim Rice, flied out to right. If Burleson had been parked at third base, he could have trotted home easily to tie the score. He wasn't. He didn't.

Instead, Burleson moved up to third base on Rice's out. Jerry Remy stayed at first. Up came Yastrzemski, Boston's best clutch hitter and its best player, period, since Ted Williams.

Yaz, the Red Sox captain then in his eighteenth season, was a mortal lock for the Hall of Fame in Cooperstown. In 1967, the year he carried Boston to the A.L. pennant, Yastrzemski won the coveted Triple Crown—batting average, home runs, and RBIs—and was a runaway choice as the league's MVP. The following season, Yaz managed to become the only player in the American League to hit .300. His .301 average earned him his third batting title.

In 1978, having turned thirty-nine in August, Yaz hit .277 with 17 home runs. His bat may have been slower than in his prime, but he was still a helluva tough out.

It was the poetic justice I'd been thinking about for the past twenty-four hours—a confrontation between power pitcher and power hitter. The kind of one-on-one matchup that makes baseball so exciting.

I could say I felt calm and composed facing Yaz in that situation, with the A.L. East and a World Series shot riding on the line and so much electricity flying around in Fenway Park that I felt as if the whole city of Boston might combust.

I could, but I'd be lying.

My knees shook. My palms sweated. I couldn't get enough air in my lungs. As Yaz headed toward the batter's box, I stepped off the mound and gave myself a much-needed pep talk:

"Relax, Rick. You've always played the game for fun, so enjoy the moment. This is why you play the game. You've been playing all your life for a moment like this."

I took a deep breath—my very first of the day—and amid all the noise and nervous energy in Fenway Park experienced a moment of total clarity. In that one instant, I asked: "What's the worst thing that can happen? That Yaz beats me?"

Even if he did, the sun would come up tomorrow. I'd be headed back home to Colorado to hunt elk. Life would go on.

The awareness that the universe wasn't going to collapse, whatever the outcome of my battle with Yastrzemski, had a calming effect. It felt like the weight of the world had been lifted off my shoulders. Nervous butterflies fluttered away and I became my normal, focused self.

I missed badly with the first pitch to Yaz. Then I locked in on Munson's mitt, reached back, and found my best fastball. The pitch came in like a low missile and exploded at the plate, forcing Yastrzemski to lift a weak pop-up down the third base line.

Nettles, at third base, had been in his crouch, muttering under his breath, "Pop it up. Pop it up. Pop it up." When

Graig saw the ball leave Yaz's bat and head in his direction, he started saying, "Not me. Not me."

The sure-handed Nettles drifted underneath the pop-up, which was a couple of feet in foul territory, and clutched it. I raced over and lifted Nettles in my arms.

Later, in the clubhouse, Munson asked me where I'd found that extra foot on my fastball to Yaz.

"That's all I've been thinking about since last night at Daisy Buchanan's," I replied.

Eighteen years later Yankee closer John Wetteland coaxed a similar pop-up from Atlanta's Mark Lemke to record the final out in the 1996 World Series. In my mind, Wetteland and I are joined in a time-and-space continuum, as are Nettles and Charlie Hayes (and, for that matter, Yaz and Lemke).

I listened to the broadcast of that Yankees vs. Atlanta game on a little transistor radio while on a hunting trip with my sons, Jeff, Keith, and Todd, and my cousins Rod, Chad, Josh, and Janie. The eight of us were camped at about 9,000 feet in the middle of the Rockies.

A light snow began falling that evening, the flakes as big as silver dollars. I paid the weather conditions no mind. I was too busy thinking about all the tension and drama in the 1978 playoff with Boston and the showdown with Yaz.

When Wetteland came in to close, I knew he was experiencing the same awesome feelings and the same rush of adrenaline that I'd had eighteen seasons earlier. When I heard the announcer say that Wetteland had just stepped off the mound and taken a deep breath, I smiled at the memory of the deep breath I'd taken before facing Yaz.

I knew in that moment that John Wetteland had calmed and composed himself, and that the Yankees would win. It was déjà vu.

One of the most beautiful aspects of baseball is how memories accumulate over years and decades. How, for example, the acrobatic defense of a Ken Griffey Jr. harkens back to the amazing Willie Mays; how a Randy Johnson fastball is compared with the heat of Nolan Ryan, Sandy Koufax, and Bob Feller; how Mark McGwire's and Sammy Sosa's homers evoke memories of Mickey Mantle and Roger Maris, Eddie Mathews and Ralph Kiner, Jimmie Foxx and Mel Ott, and ultimately, of course, Babe Ruth.

I'm sure that in the past two decades somebody watching a ball game come down to the final out—with a power pitcher facing a power hitter—has leaned over to the person sitting next to him and said, "Hey, this is like when Goose Gossage faced Carl Yastrzemski back in 1978. Remember?"

After the madcap season we experienced in New York—which Sparky Lyle captured so richly in his book with Peter Golenbock, *The Bronx Zoo*—the American League Championship Series against Kansas City seemed an anticlimax.

It's not that the Royals weren't a talented team. They were. Whitey Herzog's squad had All-Star George Brett to begin with, as well as a lineup dotted with proven veterans like Amos Otis, Hal McRae, Frank White, and Darrell Porter. Herzog had Dennis Leonard, Paul Splittorff, and Larry Gura for starting pitching, and Al Hrabosky as his closer.

It's just that beating the Red Sox in the playoff at Fenway

Park gave the Yankees a feeling that we were a team of destiny in 1978. To paraphrase Tug McGraw, after beating Boston we *believed*.

We dispatched the Royals three games to one. I got the win in game three, a seesaw affair in which we survived three George Brett homers off Catfish Hunter, and I got a save in game four, in which Ron Guidry outdueled Dennis Leonard.

The 1978 World Series pitted New York against Los Angeles for the second straight year. Again, we put a cork in Tommy Lasorda's bluster about Dodger Blue.

It wasn't easy. We lost the first two games in L.A. before sweeping four straight. The swing game was the fourth, when we rallied from a 3-0 deficit to force extra innings and then won in the bottom of the tenth inning on a Lou Piniella single that drove home Roy White.

It was a World Series for the unsung. Brian Doyle, a utility infielder who hit .192 that season, replaced the injured Willie Randolph at second base and batted .438. Bucky Dent, still in the zone after his homer at Fenway Park, hit .417 and was voted MVP of the Fall Classic. Rookie Jim Beattie, who had been shipped down to Columbus a couple times during the season, pitched a complete-game victory in game five. Doyle and Dent had three hits apiece in that game and three more in game six.

Graig Nettles kept Los Angeles at bay by playing spectacular defense, particularly in game three. Diving, twisting, and turning to corral some wicked smashes—two with the bases loaded—Nettles singlehandedly kept the Dodgers from going up three games to none.

Anyone could see how Nettles had set a major league record for assists by a third baseman in 1971. There wasn't anybody in baseball who played the position as well. Graig made cleaner scoops than an experienced soda jerk. He was the kind of big-game performer teams need to progress from good to great.

So was Reggie Jackson. Put Reggie in a pressure situation, and like Dick Allen, he would take his focus and intensity to a higher level. You might handle Jackson in a meaningless at bat, but at money time he turned into a different creature.

You could see it in his body language as he walked to the plate. You could see it in his deliberate practice swings. You could see his level of concentration increase before the first pitch.

Reggie added two homers in the 1978 World Series to the five he'd hit the year before. He also kept us alive in game four with some heads-up running on the basepaths.

I also learned in 1978 that playing with a size XXXL personality like Reggie took a lot of outside pressure off ordinary Joes like me. Reggie was a veritable quote machine, and the media, consequently, sought him out like bees seek honey. Outspoken and opinionated, Reggie never found himself at a loss for words.

Jackson could talk about the backdoor curveball in one breath, how to play the outfield carom in the next. You could ask him anything—"Are we close to a cure for cancer?" or "What's the outlook for Middle East peace talks?"—and Reggie would weigh in on the matter.

At the 1978 World Series, all the microphones and mini-cams belonged to Reggie. I learned that if a reporter stopped by your locker in the clubhouse, he had rookie jitters or was lost. Everyone else hovered around Reggie.

———

About the only Yankee player left out of the spotlight in 1978 was Sparky Lyle, who handled his demotion from closer with as much class and as little disruption as possible. Sparky pitched solidly when called upon that season—posting a 9-3 record with a 3.47 ERA—but in the World Series the phone never rang for him.

Sparky marched to his own beat. One of his great joys was smashing his music machine (a forerunner of the boom box) at the end of the season. He'd take out a Louisville Slugger, put the box on one of the picnic tables in the Yankee clubhouse, and hammer it to bits.

Another Sparky Lyle ritual was desecrating birthday cakes. On days when the clubhouse staff would put out a cake in honor of a Yankee player's birthday, Sparky would drop his trousers, dash over and jump butt-first into the cake.

Then he'd ask if anyone wanted to lick off the frosting. He'd get no takers.

Sparky made an emphatic statement that summer when, for the first time, female reporters were admitted to major league clubhouses after games. This milestone event in sports journalism made many ballplayers uncomfortable, and didn't sit too well with their wives and girlfriends either.

Sparky didn't pitch a fit, he pitched a tent. The first night the clubhouse door opened and a woman reporter came in, Sparky covered his member with one of his sanitary socks and marched across the clubhouse, the sock dragging on the floor.

Everybody got his point.

One of the legendary Lyle stories that helped elevate Sparky to cult-hero status concerns the breezy afternoon when the Yankees organization, as a gesture of goodwill, invited physically challenged youngsters to be special guests at the stadium.

Sparky, who for once was awake early in a game—Lyle liked to take little catnaps in the Toyota Celica, reclining in the passenger-side front seat—looked around the outfield and realized a large group of these youngsters sat near the bullpen.

Sparky summoned one of the stadium attendants and started an animated conversation. Those of us in the bullpen thought nothing of it and went back to watching the game.

Between innings, here came a couple of hot dog vendors down to the rows where the kids were. The vendors started handing out franks, courtesy of Sparky, to the kids. The vendors must have revealed the identity of their benefactor, because the kids started waving toward the bullpen in appreciation. Eager to share in the glory, we waved back.

The kicker was that Sparky, being the scamp he was, had given special instructions that the hot dogs be served with mustard. Lots o' mustard.

We looked up in a few minutes and the bleachers resembled a sea of yellow. All these challenged children had mustard everywhere—in their hair, on their clothes, dripping on the seats and in the aisles.

I must say, though, those kids seemed to be having the time of their lives. I'm sure it made a memory for them.

Sparky's mustard prank gave me a bright idea several years later when the Yankees were in New Orleans for an exhibition game at the Superdome. Several of us were walking down Bourbon Street, checking out that lively scene, when we stopped to buy hot dogs from a street vendor.

Guys were busy putting condiments on their franks when I took one of the handheld dispensers and squirted mustard all over the back and shoulders of first baseman Jim Spencer.

He didn't realize what I'd done, and we continued walking down Bourbon Street, laughing among ourselves. Then Spencer's nose began working like a beagle at a fox hunt. "Any of you guys smell mustard?" he asked. We poked each other in the ribs. The jig was up.

Spencer craned his neck around and saw the yellow sea on his shirt. He hopped around like someone being attacked by bees. "Why you son of a buck," he said, pointing at me. "I'll get you for this."

Spencer happened to be one of my favorite foils. We had a team party at his house outside Baltimore one night, during a series with the Orioles, and Jim and I engaged in a typically intense game of pool. For once, he held the upper hand.

On this one particular rack, Spencer had an easy shot left on the eight-ball to win. The eight-ball stood directly in front of a corner pocket, no more than a foot away. The cue ball stood directly behind the eight-ball. It was, in other words, a dead-on, can't-miss shot.

Just as Spencer bent over and drew a bead on the eight-ball, however, I tossed my wallet directly under his nose. When our teammates watching the game saw this, they began oohing and aahing at Jim to answer my challenge.

He reached into his pocket and pulled out his money clip. When he threw it on the table next to my wallet, the clip broke into two pieces. I interpreted that as a favorable omen for what would unfold.

Perhaps I should mention here that the Yankees had just begun a fourteen-day road trip, which meant that all the players had received $500 or $600 in meal money. And that Spencer threw nickels around like they were manhole covers. I mean, he had shorter arms than a crocodile; he was as tight-fisted as a heavyweight boxer.

Spencer sized up the winning shot again and suddenly broke out in a sweat. He needed a handkerchief to wipe off his brow. He finally pulled back his stick and proceeded to miscue so badly he nearly ripped the felt on the table. His shot didn't even come close.

I picked up my wallet and his money clip and thanked him for the game. On my way out I confessed to Spencer that my wallet, other than containing a couple of moths, had been empty. He begged to see for himself, but I wouldn't show him. After we got to the next city, I returned his money clip. The thought of him squirming and stewing for three days made the whole trip.

On another occasion in Baltimore, I spent the evening at the home of Oriole reliever Tim Stoddard, who introduced me to darts. Stoddard and I had become friends when he came up to the Chicago White Sox at the end of the 1975 season. We relievers like to stick together.

Stoddard was a terrific all-around athlete. In 1973–74 he started at power forward for the North Carolina State Wolfpack, the David Thompson-led team that ended UCLA's amazing streak of seven consecutive NCAA basketball championships.

I got carried away that evening at Tim's and threw darts in his basement until two or three in the morning. The next afternoon I sheepishly realized what a toll the exercise had taken on my arm.

While doing my pregame running in the outfield, I saw Stoddard loosening up across the way. I yelled over at him: "What the hell did you do to me last night? I can't even play catch."

Stoddard relayed that bit of information to the Orioles clubhouse. "Don't worry about the Goose," he crowed. "I took care of him last night."

Never underestimate the recuperative power of adrenaline, however. When I got the call with the game on the line that night, I had a live fastball. I struck out the side with fastballs. Baltimore players jumped all over Stoddard for that; some saboteur he turned out to be.

Actually, my arm did remain sore for a few days. I put darts on the back burner of favorite bar games and stuck with shooting pool.

I incorrectly assumed that the World Series ring from 1978 would be one of many for me. It wasn't. I never again played on a championship team.

The "dynasty" prediction I'd made for the Yankees didn't materialize. After the championship run in 1977–78, New York's fortunes tacked a bizarre course for the next few years. George Steinbrenner and Billy Martin went back and forth like a tennis rally. George fired Billy and rehired Billy four more times before all the fussing and fighting ended.

Over the next few seasons, the Yankees had some good teams that came close to winning championships. Close, however, only counts in horseshoes, hand grenades, and slow dancing.

I wore the pinstripes another five seasons. I had more

problems with Billy Martin, good rapport with my teammates (except, notably, Cliff Johnson), a reasonably good relationship with George Steinbrenner (until I came to the
conclusion his actions compromised our chances to win),
and great support from Yankee fans.

My emotions were never again as raw and chafed as they
had been at the beginning of 1978. A season that began with
rejection and scorn had ended with redemption and glory.

The battle with Yastrzemski became perhaps the defining
moment of my entire career. Had I not gotten Yaz out, had
he delivered the winning hit in the one-game playoff, it's
quite possible that I would have had only a mediocre-to-
good career.

Who knows? Careers in baseball are that fragile. There's
always a fine line between success and failure. A pitch here, a
pitch there, or an out here, an out there—the margin between
hero and goat is narrow. A player would go crazy if he sat
around and thought about it for too long.

I do know this: When I faced Yaz in the bottom of the
ninth at Fenway Park, the Yankees had Sparky Lyle warming
up in the bullpen. Bob Lemon could easily have gone to a
lefty vs. lefty matchup by bringing in Sparky and no one
would have raised a peep. Instead Bob Lemon stuck with
me—something the Yankees had done all season and which I
deeply appreciated. After my awful start, New York would
have been justified in putting me in mothballs. But that
didn't happen.

Given a second chance, I made the most of it. I battled
back. Had I reacted differently during the summer of 1978,
had I tucked my tail, I wouldn't have been standing on the

mound at Fenway Park on that crisp autumn afternoon, facing the great Carl Yastrzemski. But I'd demonstrated enough heart, guts, and determination to make Bob Lemon believe I could deal with the situation.

The trial by fire I endured in 1978, which culminated with the playoff game in Boston, showed everyone in New York that I had the right stuff. Even if I wouldn't follow orders and hit someone in the bleeping head.

CHAPTER 6

1979–83

NEW YORK, NEW YORK

Timing, as the saying goes, is everything. My arrival in New York in 1978 was fortunate not only because the New York Yankees won the second of back-to-back world championships, but because relief pitching had become such hot stuff.

The trend began early in the 1970s. Rollie Fingers closed brilliantly for the great Oakland teams that won three straight series from 1972 to 1974. Relievers Will McEnaney and Rawly Eastwick played vital roles in Cincinnati's consecutive championships in 1975 and 1976. Sparky Lyle turned out the lights for the Yankees in 1977. I did the honors in 1978.

Baseball's conventional wisdom had considered pitching to be ninety percent of the game. Now insiders started to say that relieving represented sixty percent of pitching. And that the paper-thin margin between world champions and contenders could be found in the bullpen.

The closer-or-no-cigars theory gained credence in 1979, after relief pitching haunted the Yankees for the entire season, costing us a chance at a third straight championship.

I had a big hand in the Yankees problems. A big right hand. A big right hand mending in a cast for two months, during which time New York went through closers like Mickey Rooney went through wives.

I was injured, unable to perform. Sparky Lyle was gone—traded to the Texas Rangers at the end of 1978 in a deal that brought New York a terrific prospect named Dave Righetti. A cattle call of relievers who auditioned for the role of stopper blew their lines.

At one point early in the season, the Yankee bullpen failed to complete any of eight straight save opportunities. We went more than two months and registered a mere three saves. Things grew so desperate that Ron Guidry, the ace of the staff, volunteered for bullpen duty to stop the bleeding.

Such extreme measures would not have been necessary but for a clubhouse fracas on April 19. We had just lost a home game to Baltimore. I sat in front of my locker, undressing, and casually wadded up the tape that held up my socks. I winged the tape across the clubhouse at a teammate, something I did after every game. It was one of those little nonsensical rituals ballplayers have.

That particular day, I chose Cliff Johnson, a sturdy and somber reserve catcher/DH, as my target to drill. I missed, though, the tape buzzing over Cliff's head and winding up in his locker. Seeing this transpire, Reggie Jackson casually inquired, "Say, Goose, how did Cliff do against you in the National League?"

I had faced Johnson maybe once or twice when he played for the Houston Astros and I was pitching for the Pittsburgh Pirates. If memory served, I'd handled him well.

Meaning no disrespect to Cliff, I responded to Reggie with my usual bluntness: "He couldn't hit what he couldn't see."

Teammates who heard the exchange laughed at my bluster. It was just typical locker-room banter.

Cliff apparently didn't think so. No sooner had I headed for the shower, stopping off at a urinal, than Johnson, still in uniform and wearing shoes with rubber cleats, approached. In a menacing tone he said, "Do you think you can back that shit up?"

He had to be kidding, right? There was no reason to get bent out of shape over some throwaway remark I'd made to Reggie. But, no, Cliff was really pissed. He glared at me with cold fury.

Johnson suddenly slapped me with his open palm. I responded by punching him in the face a couple of times. We grappled, both getting in our licks, and fell heavily against a bathroom stall.

Imagine the look on Chris Chambliss's face: He was sitting on the can, doing his thing, when the wall crashed in on him, along with two thrashing hulks.

Brian Doyle arrived on the scene and tried to break up the fight. Poor Brian. He went about 160 pounds soaking wet. Johnson was 240 pounds and built like a linebacker. I was 225 pounds and built like a tight end. When Brian tried to separate us, we tossed him like a salad. He went running for help.

Several guys, including Reggie Jackson, came in and pulled us apart. I had to get in the last word, so I told Cliff that he was a "lazy and worthless piece of crap."

(Which I believe to be a fair and accurate assessment, one not without justification or basis in fact; Johnson was notorious for moping around in the bullpen, refusing to help warm up relievers.)

The melee might have been over had I not shot off my mouth. Now it was Cliff's turn to have the final say. He broke free from the guys restraining him and came at me again. Wearing only shower shoes and a smile, I had little traction on the wet shower floor. When Johnson knocked me against a wall, I lost my balance and started to fall. Just as I put out my right hand to brace myself for the impact, Cliff crashed down on top of me.

Four-hundred-fifty-plus pounds versus one right hand constituted a total mismatch. Game over, man. Game over.

Within a half hour of the altercation my thumb began to swell and throb. The Yankee medical staff determined I had torn—or Johnson had torn—the ulnar collateral ligament. I had to undergo immediate surgery to repair the damage. The preliminary diagnosis: out ninety days.

I got word from Yankee GM Cedric Tallis that George Steinbrenner intended to dock me for the entire time I spent on the disabled list. But I pled my case: "Look, what would you have done if someone had punched you in the face? Wouldn't you have tried to defend yourself?"

Justice prevailed. I received my full salary for the twelve weeks I rode the pine. Within sixty days Cliff Johnson was shipped to Cleveland, presumably because the Yankees could find no baseball franchise operating in Siberia.

I don't sit well. I like to stay active and keep busy. Having to park my butt for the first half of the '79 season was like being in purgatory. Watching the Yankee bullpen struggle intensified the inferno.

By the time I came off the disabled list in mid-July, the

Yankee season qualified for disaster relief. We had fallen deep in the A.L. East standings, trailing Baltimore, Boston, and an emerging Milwaukee team loaded with big bats.

Expecting us to perform another miracle like our amazing run in 1978 was like expecting to win the Powerball lottery. The odds against our coming back again were astronomical. Forget about it.

Not even a change in managers in mid-June could right the Yankee ship. Out was Bob Lemon. Back in was Billy Martin.

Much of the joy in Lem's life had been snuffed out the previous fall. Just a few days after we wrapped up the World Series over Los Angeles, his son Jerry had been killed in an automobile accident. The tragedy leveled Lem.

When Bob came back to the Yankee bench in 1979, he lacked the same spark. Never a demonstrative guy to begin with, he'd grown distant and withdrawn. Grief consumed him to the point that his head was no longer in the game.

Not surprisingly, the team's whole atmosphere changed. During our 1978 surge, we had been so inspired by Bob's leadership that we'd sit at the back of the bus and sing "When Lemon Strikes Up the Band," a takeoff on a tune by Warren Zevon.

No one was singing in 1979—except the blues.

I'd been back on the active roster for less than a month when we took the biggest hit of all. Our captain, Thurman Munson, perished in a plane crash on August 2.

It was an off-day for the Yankees. That meant Thurman was back home in Ohio with his family and his newest toy— a $1.2 million Cessna Citation jet. He'd sold his home in

Wyckoff, New Jersey, moved Diane and his children back to Canton, and commuted to see them every chance he could. Thurman stayed with Corna and me at our home in Wyckoff when the Yankees played an extended home stand, but at every opportunity he flew to Ohio to be with his family.

Munson constantly begged me to fly with him. Some of the Yankees, like Nettles and Reggie, had gone up with him, but I steadfastly refused.

"Remember, I'm from Colorado," I'd tell Thurman. "I've seen planes fall out of the sky my whole life."

"Goose, you're just a big sissy, aren't you?" Munson would tease.

"You're damn right I am," I would agree.

Munson had bought the Cessna, moving up from the Piper Cubs he'd been flying, to reduce his commute time. Some of us worried that he bought too powerful a plane and that he'd been trying to absorb too much new information too quickly. Then again, Thurm always did things full-bore.

I learned about the accident from George Steinbrenner. When I picked up a ringing telephone about four-thirty that afternoon, he said, "Goose, this is George. I've got bad news. Terrible news. Thurman was killed today in a plane crash. I'll know more tomorrow. We'll have a team meeting. That's all I can say."

After George hung up, I spent the rest of the day in a daze. Corna and I had tickets that night for a Waylon Jennings concert off-Broadway, but I have no recollection of the performance other than that we went with the Ken Clays. If you've ever been bowled over by the unexpected death of a best friend, you know what kind of fog I was in. Or perhaps I spent that evening in denial.

The next day, when I walked into the clubhouse and saw

Munson's locker, empty except for his catching gear, I completely broke down. I sobbed inconsolably.

Reports from Ohio indicated Thurm had been practicing touch-and-go landings with his new jet when the accident occurred. His plane clipped some treetops and crashed several hundred feet short of the runway at the Canton airport. The two passengers aboard managed to scramble to safety, but Thurm had been pinned in the wreckage, which burst into flames. The official cause of death was asphyxiation. Thurman Munson was thirty-two years old.

The Yankee family flew to Canton for the funeral, as sad a scene as I've ever witnessed. Several players tried to eulogize Thurman but discovered they couldn't talk. I vividly remember Lou Piniella vainly attempting to offer words of consolation but getting so choked up he couldn't go on.

We returned to Yankee Stadium to play Baltimore. Cardinal Cooke delivered a eulogy for Thurman before the game; when the Yankees took the field at the top of the first inning, no one went to home plate. New Yorkers gave Munson a ten minute standing ovation before Jerry Narron finally went out to the catcher's spot. I doubt if there were any dry eyes in the entire stadium. There certainly were none in the Yankee bullpen, on the bench, or up in the owner's box. It ranks as my worst baseball memory.

In 1976, Munson had been named the Yankees first team captain since Lou Gehrig in the 1930s, which shows the respect Thurm commanded; the team didn't toss the honor out lightly. Munson, like Gehrig, led by example. As one Yankee said, "Thurman exemplified a leader and that's why he was our captain. He played hard, he played tough, and he played hurt."

Munson in 1979, however, clearly had changed from the good-time guy I'd grown to know so well after the "White Gorilla" incident. Instead of hanging out with the guys, he started keeping to himself. On the road, instead of having a few beers at the hotel bar, he stayed in his room studying aviation manuals.

I believe that Thurman had grown tired of playing baseball. He'd had his fill of the circus atmosphere inside the Yankee clubhouse and the pressure of dealing with the insatiable New York media. I remember reading a quote of Munson's in which he said one of the reasons he enjoyed flying so much was because "when you get up there no one asks you any questions."

Munson felt he'd done enough explaining. Besides, his family was the most important thing in his life. Thurman was so committed to Diane and his kids that he would have preferred to have been traded to Cleveland before the '79 season began.

Imagine, a big-leaguer who *wished* to be traded to Cleveland. That seemed a contradiction in terms. No one of sound mind wanted to play in that cavernous stadium in Cleveland. Graig Nettles joked that Munson should have sewn up Comeback Player of the Year honors in 1979 just for coming back to the Yankees.

What can I tell you about Thurman Munson, other than I loved him like a brother? No teammate of mine ever played with more enthusiasm or joy. If you ever got your dobber down, hanging out with Thurman would lift your spirits. Even when the game was on the line, Munson would always try to make light of the situation, no matter how critical. That's what made him so special.

Munson might have been the Lee Trevino of baseball. On the surface Thurm seemed like a fun-loving, jovial guy, but underneath he was a fierce competitor with the heart of a lion.

I once gave up a homer on an 0-2 curveball—after smoking two fastballs by an overmatched hitter, I had the brilliant idea of trying to fool him off-speed—and Munson came to the mound and said, "Boy, did he ever put a charge into that one!"

We were going out to start the ninth inning one game and Munson told me to throw my first warm-up pitch all the way back to the screen. He said there was a blonde in the third row he wanted to check out. I obliged.

He spent a few extra seconds retrieving the ball, inspecting the seams and wiping off a smudge. What he was really doing was getting an eyeful of row three. When he came back and squatted for the second warm-up pitch, I made a gesture to ask if he wanted another wild one. He shook his head.

"She was a dog," he told me later in the clubhouse.

Once, Thurman got down in his crouch, held up his mitt and motioned for me to pitch. I kept waiting for him to flash a sign, but he never did. I finally called time out.

When he waddled out toward the mound, I met him halfway and demanded, "What's the sign?"

Thurman started laughing. "What the hell do you need with a sign? Who are you going to trick? Everyone knows what's coming next."

One time Munson's clowning around on a plane got him in trouble with Billy Martin. We were on a commercial flight back to New York, and Thurm was playing Neil Diamond on his portable tape deck. He had on his headset and sang along in his off-key fashion (Thurm sounded like a cow in heat). Every so often he'd pull out the earphone jack, and blaring through the cabin would be "Crackling Rose" or "Solitary Man" or "Sweet Caroline."

After a few minutes, Martin came back to check on the commotion. Billy, who had been in the sauce, apparently didn't have the same appreciation for Neil Diamond.

Martin told Munson to can the music. Thurman suggested that Billy perform a sex act on himself. Martin flew into a rage, calling Thurman some uncomplimentary names and accusing him of being less than an ideal leader for his teammates. Munson went back to listening to Neil Diamond, ignoring the expletives.

After the plane landed and we checked into our hotel, I went to hang out in Munson's room. We were lounging around when Billy called from the lobby to say he was coming up to settle the matter. I volunteered to leave so they could work out their differences in private, but Munson told me to stay put. "Billy's not coming up here," he assured me. "If he does, I'm going to kick his ass."

Thurman was right—Billy never showed.

One thing baseball fans should remember about Thurman is that in addition to being a true leader in every sense of the word, he was a tremendous athlete. Despite his short and stocky build, he had excellent speed. He could steal a base or stretch singles into doubles. Behind the plate, Thurman had amazing quickness. His style may have been a bit unorthodox—he lacked the textbook mechanics of a Carlton Fisk or Johnny Bench—but he could catch anything pitched and throw out base runners from any position. He was marvelous to behold.

Munson's death in early August removed what little fight the 1979 Yankees had left. We went through the motions the final seven weeks of the season.

Not that the remainder of the year proved uneventful. When the team arrived in Boston for a series in September, rookie pitcher Roger Slagle and I went to watch "Monday Night Football" at Charlie's, a bar near the downtown Sheraton.

No sooner had we stepped into Charlie's than we ran into Yankee pitching coach Art Fowler, who was Billy Martin's best friend. Fowler already had several pops under his belt, which loosened his tongue.

He started in on me at once, saying I'd let the team down by getting hurt in the fight with Cliff Johnson back in April and that I'd been a pain in the ass for his buddy Billy. I listened to Fowler rant for a few seconds and then told him, as politely as possible, "Do me a big favor and go fuck yourself."

With that, I told Slagle we could watch the football game back at the hotel room. Which we did. I stretched out on the bed and Slagle took the chair.

Within minutes the phone rang. I heard a slurred voice screaming, "You no good motherfucker. You piece of shit."

"Who is this?" I asked.

"Billy."

"Billy who?"

"Billy Martin, you prick. Give me your room number so I can come up there and kick your ass."

I gave Billy the information he wanted, hung up the phone, and walked over to open the door.

Roger Slagle sensed something out of whack.

"Who was that?" he asked.

"Billy," I said nonchalantly. "He's drunk and he's coming up."

Slagle started for the door. "I better get out of here," he said, sounding worried.

"Stay here. You don't have to leave," I said. "I may need a witness."

My room was directly across from the elevators. When we heard a "ding," we knew Billy had arrived on the floor.

Martin found the door ajar and wobbled in drunker than ten sailors. He took off his glasses, set them on a nightstand by the bed, and pulled the sweater he was wearing over his head. He took off his shirt, ripping a couple of buttons in the process. Meanwhile, I lay on the bed, one eye on the football game, the other on Billy. You couldn't ever let him out of your sight in a situation like that, or the next thing you knew he would have thrown a sucker punch.

Seeing Slagle in the room, Billy told him to get lost. He took Roger by the arm and tried to lead him to the door.

"Stay right where you are," I told Roger. "I want you to see this."

Slagle pulled away from Martin, and I got up and looked Billy straight in the eye. "Hit me," he dared.

"If we're going to fight, you're going to have to throw the first punch," I replied.

But Billy was too drunk to throw any punches. Instead, in his anger, he tried to pull the mattress off the bed and throw it at me. Not a bad concept, but he lacked the strength to do it. He had to settle for ripping off the sheets and bedspread and trying to heave them at me.

"Get the hell out of here," I finally said.

We helped Billy get his shirt on and he stumbled out the

door, still calling me every name in the book. He made a wrong turn and walked the length of the corridor before realizing his mistake. He had to walk all the way back, bouncing off the walls, to get to the bank of elevators.

When he went by, I said, "Get your ass on that elevator."

"Fuck you," he snarled.

Roger Slagle came up for a cup of coffee in the major leagues in 1979. He appeared in one game for New York that September, pitching two innings. He gave up no hits and fanned two batters. His career ERA was a spotless 0.00.

I hope my encounter with Billy in that Boston hotel room didn't dampen Slagle's enthusiasm for the game. How surreal must it have seemed to a guy getting his first shot at the majors to witness the manager of the Yankees wanting to punch out his relief ace?

As Graig Nettles once said: "When I was little boy, I wanted to either play baseball or join the circus. I'm doubly blessed. With the Yankees, I get to do both."

The next day, as we boarded the team bus for the ride to Fenway Park, I returned Billy's glasses, which he had left in my room. He refused to look me in the eye when I handed them over, turning his head away. At the ballpark, Martin sent Fowler out to the outfield to offer an apology.

"He's really sorry about what happened last night," Fowler said.

"Tell Billy if he wants to apologize, he should be man enough to say it to my face," I told Art. "That goes for you too. You owe me an apology for what you said at Charlie's."

Neither one ever did apologize, of course.

———

It didn't take 20-20 vision to see that Billy Martin was out of control. He had a habit of drinking excessively, and when he got boozed up, he did stupid things. I wasn't the least bit surprised when, in late October, a week after the 1979 World Series, Billy got into a fight with a marshmallow salesman in Minnesota.

Martin apparently took exception to something the man said about his managerial abilities and smashed the guy in the face. The wounds required seventeen stitches.

Billy's behavior forced the Yankees to act. Steinbrenner had no choice but to let him go. Dick Howser replaced Billy for the 1980 season.

Pittsburgh won the 1979 World Series, and I was overjoyed for my ex-teammates. To celebrate, I invited two Pirate pitchers, Bruce Kison and Jim Rooker, to come visit me in Colorado.

We had a great time catching up on old times. Kison had to leave early, but Rooker stayed for several extra days of elk and deer hunting. One of the last nights Rook remained, we drove to the town of Buena Vista to watch an NFL game between San Diego and Oakland.

What is it about pro football and bars that promotes rowdiness? I've never understood it. We were watching the game, having a few cold beers, just kicking back and relaxing. We struck up a friendly conversation with some ladies sitting nearby.

A few of the locals took exception. They appeared less than pleased to see outsiders on their turf, talking to their women. The next thing I knew, words were exchanged, tempers rose, and fists filled the air.

It looked like a scene out of a cowboy movie. Chairs and people started flying around the room.

Rooker, looking for someone to pound, pulled one guy out of a booth by his long hair and was doing some serious damage when the guy's buddy, a giant mountain man, intervened.

Rook said later he thought Paul Bunyan had grabbed hold of him. This giant applied a choke hold to his windpipe. Rook's face turned purple, then blue, and his arms began to flap like chicken wings. He thought he was about to meet his maker.

Right then Rooker heard an angel. An angel with a deep voice. Summoning up something straight out of *The Exorcist*, I bellowed: "LET HIM GO! RIGHT NOW!"

I must have sounded like the devil incarnate, because Paul Bunyan relaxed his grip. Just as he did, the local cops charged into the bar and broke things up. We had some explaining to do, but we managed to get out of town without having to see a judge or the chief of police.

I didn't throw a single punch that night. I had no intention of returning to the disabled list, so I'd begun treating my hands like a concert pianist's. Besides, after the shower room brawl with Cliff Johnson and the near-fight at the Sheraton with Billy Martin, a melee at the Lariat Lounge in Buena Vista was about the last thing I needed.

I'd done enough tangling for one season.

Under Dick Howser, New York rebounded with a strong showing in 1980. The Yankees won 103 games—the most of any New York team I played on—and finished three games ahead of Baltimore in the A.L. East. Tommy John won 22 games. Ron Guidry chipped in with 17. Rudy May, a third left-hander in the rotation, posted a sterling 15-5 mark.

For the second time, I was named the American League's Fireman of the Year, after leading the league with 33 saves. My ERA was 2.27 with a record of 6-2. Howser began using me almost exclusively in short relief (no more of those two- or three-inning jobs), and in 64 games I pitched 99 innings. I struck out 103.

I responded to the new workload with some of the best pitching in my career. For a stretch in August and September, I may have hit my peak. I retired 31 consecutive batters—the equivalent of a perfect game plus four outs. I finished third in the A.L. Cy Young award balloting, behind Steve Stone of Baltimore, who won 25 games, and Mike Norris of Oakland, who won 22.

I also came in third in the A.L. MVP vote. Reggie Jackson, who had his greatest season in New York in 1980, finished second. Mr. October hit 41 homers and drove in 111 runs. Like Dick Allen in 1972, Reggie did damage. All his hits seemed to be big ones that won games.

But even Reggie had to take a back seat in 1980 to Kansas City's George Brett. Brett flirted with the magical .400 plateau—last achieved by Ted Williams in 1941—and wound up hitting .390. Brett made a spirited bid, staying above .400 well into August.

Many experts consider Brett's offensive performance that year the best ever by a third baseman. Limited by injury to 117 games, Brett, in addition to his remarkable batting average, hit 24 homers and drove in 118 runs. Project an RBI a game over a full season and you can see the numbers he put up. Brett carried the Royals to 97 wins and a comfortable fourteen-game margin over runner-up Oakland.

Kansas City had consistently contended for an A.L. pennant in the mid-1970s, after Whitey Herzog took over as manager, but they just as consistently failed to get over the hump. The Yankees ended the Royals season a step short of the World Series in three straight years (1976–78), no defeat more painful than in 1976, when Chris Chambliss hit his memorable bottom-of-the-ninth home run.

All of which set up a fateful encounter when New York and Kansas City squared off for the best-of-five American League Championship Series. The Royals won the first two games at home, the first a relative laugher, the second a pitching duel in which Dennis Leonard nipped Rudy May.

We came home to the Bronx still expecting to prevail. Tommy John kept the Royals in check through six innings of game three, and we took a 2-1 lead. In the top of the seventh inning, though, two Royals reached base off Tommy. With two out and Brett coming to the plate, I got the call from Howser.

New Yorkers appreciate their drama, of course, and what could possibly have been more dramatic at that moment than Brett against Gossage? It represented a classic showdown. Get George out and we would likely win game three and regain momentum in the series. Lose the battle to George and . . .

As I stepped on the mound, "GOOOOOOSE" calls rumbled out of Yankee Stadium and floated across the river into Manhattan. The moment couldn't quite match the intensity of facing Carl Yastrzemski in that playoff game at Fenway Park two seasons earlier, but believe me it came damn close.

There may have been suspense about what would happen next, but no mystery. I intended to challenge Brett, George knew I would challenge him—and each of us knew what the other knew. As he said later, "Once I saw Rich Gossage coming in, I was relieved because I knew exactly what he was going to do. He had one thing in mind, to blow it right by me."

Correcto-mundo. I planned to blow Brett away with my fastball. I wound up, cut loose, and watched—in disbelief—as Brett sent an absolute rocket to the far reaches of Yankee Stadium.

It was a massive home run, probably the hardest and farthest ball ever hit off me. A Royals executive said later he thought Brett's blast had a chance to carry all the way to Coney Island. His direction was off, but the ball had been hit that hard.

Three runs crossed and Kansas City led 4-2. Nine outs later they completed the series sweep.

I got the last out of the seventh inning, then went into the clubhouse and wept. I cried not because I was embarrassed to have been beaten by Brett, but because I'd let down my Yankee teammates. I failed to do my job.

What I cared about most in baseball was winning. Not celebrity. Not wealth. Not awards and accolades. Winning. I could cope with giving up a homer—even a humongous one—to Brett. There was no disgrace in that. As his manager, Jim Frey, once said, George Brett could have made solid contact on an aspirin.

What I had difficulty coping with was losing. New York is a city of winners. The Yankees were a group of players who played to win. Anything less left everyone devastated.

I went home to Colorado. George Brett and the Kansas City Royals went on to the 1980 World Series against Philadelphia. That was the Series, you may recall, when Brett suffered through his hemorrhoid problem. Which, to every pitcher in the American League, especially me, seemed like poetic justice. He'd been a pain in the butt for all of us. (I like to tell people, incidentally, that if George hadn't swung so hard hitting that home run off of me, he probably never would have had hemorrhoid problems.)

That was also the Series in which, after the Phillies won in six games, Tug McGraw was asked what he intended to do with his winner's share. In the great tradition of flaky relievers, McGraw replied, "Ninety percent I'll spend on women, whiskey, and good times. The other ten percent I'll probably waste."

George Brett didn't just beat the Yankees with his bat in the 1980 playoffs. An outstanding defensive play of his set in motion a series of events that would affect the New York organization for several years to come.

In game two at Kansas City, the Leonard-May battle, the Royals held a slim 3-2 lead in the eighth inning when Bob Watson rifled a Leonard pitch into the gap. Randolph had been on first base, and when third base coach Mike Ferraro saw Willie Wilson overthrow his cutoff man, he waved Randolph home. What Ferraro didn't see was Brett, backing up the play. To a heads-up play Brett tacked on a perfect peg that gunned down Randolph at home plate.

George Steinbrenner went ballistic. He blamed Ferraro for putting us in a two-game deficit. Steinbrenner ran into Mrs. Ferraro after the game and made a derogatory remark about her husband. Then he went in front of the national media and ripped Mike into little pieces.

Steinbrenner announced he would fire Ferraro—had Mike held up Randolph, Reggie Jackson would have batted next, and with Reggie's flair for the dramatic, anything could have happened. But Dick Howser stood up for Ferraro. Howser in effect told George, "If Mike goes, I go"—and he meant it.

That would be the beginning of the end for Howser. After the season ended, Steinbrenner hatched a story about how Howser had been offered a lucrative real estate opportunity in Florida that was too good to resist. But everyone knew the real reason Howser would not be back: He'd stood up to Steinbrenner.

That amounted to a major mistake, like pulling on Superman's cape or tearing the mask off the Lone Ranger. Jim Croce could have told Dick—you don't mess around with George.

The Howser incident began a dark period for the proud New York franchise, which retained enough veteran talent—Reggie, Nettles, Randolph, Piniella, Guidry, John, to name a few—to win more world championships in the early 1980s. Sadly, a new World Series banner did not fly at Yankee Stadium until 1996.

I'm no scholar, but I remember enough about Shakespeare from high school to know the next few years in New York had all his touches. The jealousy, rivalry, envy, intrigue, duplicity, and deceit within the organization could easily have come from his quill.

At the center of all the controversy, of course, was the owner. After running off Dick Howser in 1980 (Howser later returned from the real estate world to manage Kansas City), George tapped Gene "Stick" Michael as Yankee manager for the 1981 season. Then Steinbrenner proceeded to exasperate Stick by questioning his every move.

Stick took as much of George's carping as he could, but

in late August he went public, more or less demanding that George quit criticizing and second-guessing him. Which was sort of like a wife asking her husband not to snore: It ain't gonna happen.

During the strike-shortened 1981 season, I added another element to my intimidation factor: a Fu Manchu mustache. I had reported to Fort Lauderdale that spring with a full beard, which made Yogi Berra, the Yankees designated hair coach, flip out.

Don't worry, I told Berra, I plan to shave the beard. Which I did. But to aggravate Yogi, I left the mustache flowing out from both sides of my mouth.

"No, no, no," Berra shouted when he saw me again. "You gotta shave dat thing. You can't have no hair below da corner of da lip."

I would have done anything for Berra—including pick up a razor and raise the mustache, which I did. He's about as great a guy as I've ever met in baseball. A gem.

As for all the Yogi stories you've probably heard, I'd have to say that the vast majority of them are true. Yogi has an amazing way with words.

One of Corna's and my favorite stories about Berra, incidentally, concerns the time Yogi's wife, Carmen, called him at Yankee Stadium to say she was taking the Berra children to see *Doctor Zhivago*.

"Aw, what's wrong with dem kids now?" Yogi asked.

When the strike occurred in early June—this was the owners' major push to put a stop to free agency—I went home to

Colorado Springs and kicked back. I did some fishing in the mountains and threw batting practice to my nephews, Scott and Steve, aspiring high school ballplayers. I grew facial hair.

The Fu Manchu filled in while we were idle for nearly two months that summer. When play resumed in August, I had acquired the menacing look of a Conrad Dobler.

There was no beef from the Yankee hair police when they saw the Fu Manchu. Yogi shrugged it off. I was in the middle of a remarkable season—my ERA was a microscopic 0.77, a career low—and everyone adopted the attitude "If Goose wants to grow a Fu Manchu, then let him." Had my ERA been 4.00 or higher, I'm sure Yogi would have come around with a razor.

The mustache made me even more imposing on the mound. Batters who had been on the fence about my sanity now were convinced I was half crazy and mean as hell.

Between my size, windup, fastball, and mustache, no one wanted to dig in. Some batters didn't want to step in the box. Teammate Catfish Hunter once told me I was the only pitcher in the major leagues he would flat refuse to bat against. "If I had to face you, I'd just forfeit my at bat," he said.

I soon realized batters were intimidated by the new look, so I let it grow thicker and fuller. (Nearly twenty years later, I still wear the Fu Manchu; only now I intimidate travel agents, bank tellers, and checkout clerks.)

By then I had also developed a controlled rage on the mound. I'd work myself into a lather entering the game. Just to get on my game face, I'd cuss out Danny Colletti, the Yankee Stadium attendant who drove me in from the bullpen. If I didn't feel mad enough warming up, I'd call out the catcher and verbally abuse him.

Ron Guidry still laughs at the memory of the time I came in from the bullpen and Graig Nettles walked over from third base to remind me of the game situation—runners on base, the number of outs, and my responsibilities on a sacrifice bunt.

I got in Graig's face and shouted, "I don't tell you how to do your fucking job! Don't try to tell me how to do mine!" Nettles, keep in mind, was one of my closest pals. Guidry's recollection shows the over-the-top intensity I had on the mound.

The Goose had become a loose cannon. I was off the charts in intensity. As a result, it often took me several hours after a game to wind down. I usually was the last Yankee out of the clubhouse at the end of the night.

Steinbrenner had just begun warming up the carousel of Yankee managers. He dumped Gene Michael late in the '81 season. Replacement Bob Lemon led us through our 1981 World Series loss. The next season, Lem sat on our bench for all of fourteen games, at which point Steinbrenner sacked him and brought back—who else?—Gene Michael.

Stick's second tenure stretched eighty-six games. He was axed again in early August after we dropped a doubleheader to Chicago. Clyde King replaced Michael and finished the 1982 season, only to be replaced in 1983 by—drumroll, please—Billy Martin.

More than one New York skipper from that era commented that the minute Steinbrenner named you Yankee manager, he lost all respect for your opinion and capacity to make decisions. As Bill Madden and Moss Klein wrote in their best-selling *Damned Yankees*, Steinbrenner asked Stick Michael, after firing him the first time, "Why would you stay manager and be second-guessed by me when you can come up into the front office and be one of the second-guessers?"

Why, indeed?

Steinbrenner, in addition to being a millionaire in the ship-building business and a powerful, pugnacious baseball owner, did a short stint as a football coach. That experience apparently convinced George that motivational speeches have a place in sports.

Granted, they probably do serve a purpose in athletics at the high school and collegiate level. They register with impressionable young minds. But not with adults, certainly not a team of veterans like the Yankees. As I said earlier, in pro sports actions speak louder than words.

Shortly after I arrived in New York in 1978, Steinbrenner came into the Yankee clubhouse to deliver one of this patented "pep" talks, which more aptly could be called a tirade. George addressed the entire squad, but every Yankee knew the target for his rant about the team's slow start. *I* was the guy blowing saves, losing leads, and getting George's bowels in an uproar.

As Steinbrenner paced back and forth directly in front of my locker, making sure I got his message, I looked directly across the clubhouse and realized Thurman Munson was mocking George behind his back.

When Steinbrenner turned to address the guys on the other side of the room, Munson would sit there with a stone face, nodding in agreement with everything the Boss said.

But as soon as George looked back at us, Munson would either put a thumb in each ear and wiggle his fingers or he'd stick out his tongue and make funny faces. Finally, Munson puffed up his cheeks like a squirrel, making fun of Steinbrenner's considerable girth.

As George rambled on and Thurman kept cutting up, I began to panic. I could feel tiny beads of sweat popping out on my forehead. It took all my powers of concentration just to keep a straight face. I knew that if I let out one little peep of laughter, Steinbrenner would have my ass.

Fortunately, I managed to keep a stiff upper lip until George finished his rant and stormed out of the clubhouse. Then I, along with every other Yankee, roared with laughter at Munson's antics. It was typical Thurman—he always played the role of class clown.

George's motivational techniques—if that's the proper term—had a darker side. In the first round of the 1981 playoffs, the Yankees faced the Milwaukee Brewers in a best-of-five series. After we won the first two games at their place, everyone figured we were a lock to advance to the ACLS. Everyone but the Brew Crew, that is. Robin Yount, Paul Molitor, Ted Simmons, Cecil Cooper, and all their guys envisioned a different outcome.

Milwaukee stormed back to win games three and four at Yankee Stadium, the latter a pitching gem by my old pal Pete Vuckovich. Vukey-baby had been a teammate and playmate with the White Sox. I remember a flight to the West Coast where Vukey and I kept ordering beers and naively forgot to dispense of the empties. More than a case of them was stacked between us when who should come sauntering down the aisle but Chuck Tanner. The skipper took one look at us, one look at the pile of dead soldiers, and said, "You two sons of bitches better get somebody out tomorrow."

The home losses unsettled Steinbrenner. He stormed into our clubhouse after game four and raked us over. No one was spared his wrath. Players were demeaned, belittled, and called every name in the book. "We'll see who deserves to be in the playoffs and which of these players don't deserve to be Yankees," Steinbrenner spewed to the press.

Our experience in pressure situations made the difference in game five. Powered by home runs by Reggie, Oscar Gamble, and Rick Cerone, we prevailed 12-5. Dave Righetti, who came in to relieve Ron Guidry, got the win. I earned a save. Milwaukee remained a year away. (The Brewers, under Harvey Kuenn, won their first A.L. pennant the following year.)

Steinbrenner's dressing-down simmered while we swept Oakland in three games to win the A.L. pennant. But the after-effects hung over us as we faced our old pals from the West Coast, the Dodgers, in the 1981 World Series.

The Fall Classic, played with a two-three-two format, opened with two games in New York. We won both, on the strength of solid starting pitching by Ron Guidry and Tommy John and timely hitting by, principally, Bob Watson. I earned a save in each game.

The series shifted to Los Angeles. Right before game three, Steinbrenner came into the clubhouse and told starter Dave Righetti, scheduled to face fellow rookie sensation Fernando Valenzuela: "This is the biggest game of your life, kid. Don't blow it!"

What a load to dump on any pitcher, much less a rookie like Righetti. Instead of taking a positive approach, or zipping his lip, Steinbrenner said something totally out of line.

In Los Angeles, George got into a fight in an elevator with a couple of abusive Dodgers fans who popped off. It wasn't exactly the kind of behavior you might expect from a team owner. George climbed aboard the team bus the next day with bruises on his face and his arm in a sling.

"Where were you guys when I needed you last night?" he asked.

"We went to bed early like you told us," Nettles shot back.

After we lost the series in six games, dropping the final four in a row, Steinbrenner felt compelled to issue a public apology to "the city of New York and to Yankee fans everywhere." I thought that was bush. We had nothing to be ashamed of; we'd fought hard and had a terrific season.

The 1981 Series turned on game five, a classic pitchers' duel between Guidry and Jerry Reuss. Gator shut out Los Angeles for six innings, but in the bottom of the seventh he surrendered back-to-back homers to Pedro Guerrero and Steve Yeager, and Reuss, a tough left-hander, made them stand up in a 2-1 complete-game win.

Guerrero returned to center stage the next evening, driving in five runs as Los Angeles ran us out of town, 9-2. Luckless reliever George Frazier lost his third decision of the series. He shared the goat's horns with Dave Winfield, who had only one hit (in 22 at bats) during the Series.

Winfield's underachievement in the Fall Classic incurred the derision of Steinbrenner, who began referring to Dave as "Mr. May." That started a feud between them that had a longer run than most Broadway plays.

George Steinbrenner's behavior during the Milwaukee series and World Series began to dampen my enthusiasm for playing in New York. Ask yourself: How much fun would you have working for a boss who demeans your efforts? Besides, the way George played musical chairs with managers like Martin, Lemon, and Michael made a mockery of the game.

After the 1981 season, I silently vowed that if things didn't improve—if playing for the Yankees remained such a hassle—I would move on after my six-year contract expired. I'd be gone.

In the fifth game of the 1981 World Series, relieving Ron Guidry in the bottom of the eighth, I hit Dodger third baseman Ron (the Penguin) Cey in the head with a 96 mph fastball that tailed in. The ball hit precisely at the base of his batting helmet. The impact sounded like a rifle shot.

Cey crumpled in the batter's box and lay motionless for several minutes. A hush came over the entire stadium. People held their collective breath to see if Cey would be all right.

I stood out on the mound thinking, "Get up, Ronnie. Get up." I repeated those words to myself over and over, fearful that I might have maimed him. Or worse.

But I didn't allow myself to show any emotion or concern. I remained stoic. I knew that if I went to home plate to check on Cey's condition—our catcher, Rick Cerone, later told me Ron's eyes rolled back in his head—I might lose my competitive edge. I couldn't afford that with the World Series on the line. I still had a job to do.

Doctors later determined that the helmet had absorbed most of the impact. Had my fastball hit Cey an inch lower, he might never have played baseball again.

I received mountains of hate mail for weeks after beaning the Penguin. People couldn't understand my seeming callousness, my emotionless response to seeing Cey laying in the batter's box. They called me, among the nicer things, a cold-hearted bastard.

What can I say? I hated the Dodgers. I considered our World Series battles with them to be war. Yes, hitting Cey upset me. No, I would never let the enemy see me drop my guard.

If I'm not mistaken, after I beaned Ron Cey the lords of baseball instituted a new rule requiring all hitters to have ear flaps on their batting helmets. Some people refer to it as the Goose Gossage rule. If it prevents a serious injury—or saves someone's life—I'm all for it.

By the way, Cey and I appeared together the following spring on "Good Morning America." There were no hard feelings on his part. He knew that pitch had been an accident, one of those inexplicable things. For a keepsake, Ron gave me the batting helmet he'd been wearing.

Graig Nettles recently told me that he came over to the mound right after the beaning. To lighten the mood, Nettles said, "I think [Cey's] still waiting for that ball to break." It's good that we can joke about those things now.

On those occasions when my mechanics were slightly off, my body had a tendency to get too far ahead, and my arm couldn't quite catch up. When that happened, my pitches had a tendency to sail away from left-handers and in on right-handers, like Ron Cey.

When I pitched for the Pirates in 1977, I threw a fastball that sailed in on Phillies slugger Greg Luzinski and clipped his chin. He went into the clubhouse afterward, looked in a mirror and saw a little knick like you'd get from shaving. In the missing piece of skin were seam marks, where the ball had grazed him. Talk about the proverbial close shave.

That same season, another fastball got away when I faced Mike Schmidt. The Phillies star froze and barely managed to pull in his neck, like a turtle. The ball skimmed off the top of his helmet.

I had to bat the next inning and knew what to expect. Ron Reed undressed me. He aimed his first pitch right between my eyes and I went flying to get out of the way. I picked myself up, dusted off, and told Philadelphia catcher Bob Boone, "Go out there and tell that miserable son of a bitch that if I ever face him, I'm not going to miss him." I never did get the chance to make good on my threat.

Seldom—a handful of times, tops—did I ever hit a batter intentionally. And then only when I believed circumstances demanded some form of retaliation.

In a spring training game against Baltimore in the early 1980s, I drilled Al Bumbry on the hipbone. Earlier that same spring, Oriole left-hander Mike Flanagan smoked Graig Nettles in the rib cage. Earlier that same day an Oriole runner took Willie Randolph into left field on a double-play ball. He cleaned Willie's clock.

Nothing was said in the dugout, but I felt obligated to stand up for our team. So when Al Bumbry came to the plate, I burned a pitch right on his hipbone. Branded him like a dogie. Al spun around in the batter's box and collapsed. When the inning was over, several of our guys came over to me in the dugout and thanked me. They knew what was up.

Steinbrenner ran amok second-guessing his managers, but he's the one who should have been second-guessed for allowing Reggie Jackson to get away after the 1981 season. George felt Jackson's skills had slipped, and he made no effort to re-sign Reggie, who subsequently went to the California Angels and—oh, by the way—hit 39 homers in 1982. Some slippage.

That set up a memorable occasion in early 1982 when Jackson made his first return visit to Yankee Stadium. Reggie crushed a three-run homer to beat us, and Yankee fans, still outraged at the owner because Jackson was no longer wearing pinstripes, began a rhythmical chant: "Steinbrenner sucks, Steinbrenner sucks."

In a season of unrelenting disappointments—the Yankees finished 79-83, in fifth place in the A.L. East—that was one of the few moments to file away.

I played to win. I couldn't swallow the fact the '82 Yankees were not a factor in the pennant chase. Fed up with all the nonsense, I vented my frustration after we won a doubleheader against Kansas City in August. Reaching a new high in profanity, I unleashed a blistering attack that included, among an avalanche of earthy phrases, a reference to Steinbrenner as "the fat man upstairs."

That remark received plenty of ink in the New York papers. It also prompted a reply from George. "Tell Goose I've been on a diet and lost eleven pounds," Steinbrenner shot back.

In 1983, Billy Martin returned for his third stint as Yankee skipper. Our relationship had thawed somewhat from the cold war of the late 1970s. We practiced a form of peaceful coexistence, keeping a respectful distance from each other.

New York returned to its winning ways, but our 91-71 record left us seven games behind Baltimore at season's end. The Orioles subsequently beat Philadelphia in five games to win the World Series.

I had a good year overall but had to endure a rough patch in which I blew several save opportunities, causing the hypercritical New York newspapers to speculate that the Goose was turning into a turkey. My record of 13-5, with a 2.27 ERA, could have been better, but batters wore me out in 1983 with bloops and bleeders.

In July we faced Kansas City in a series in New York that would produce a game that would live in infamy: the Pine Tar Incident. Before we get to George Brett's home run and a ridiculous American League ruling that would ultimately cost us a game we needed, a little background is necessary.

A few weeks earlier I faced Brett in Kansas City in a save situation and got him out. Before I did, Graig Nettles called time and came in from third base.

"Hey, Goose," Nettles told me, "Brett's got pine tar way too high on his bat. If he gets a hit, let's grab his bat and have it checked. It looks illegal."

Nettles drew on experience. In a game against Minnesota in 1975, Thurman Munson singled home a run, after which Twins manager Frank Quilici came out and protested to the umpires that pine tar was too high on the barrel. The rule book said that pine tar, which many major league batters use to get a better grip, could be no higher than eighteen inches up from the handle. The umps measured Munson's bat, found the pine tar higher than eighteen inches, called Thurm out and took the run off the books. Nettles remembered.

On July 24, Billy brought me in for the ninth inning to protect a 4-3 lead over the Royals. I got the first two outs, then U. L. Washington beat out an infield chopper over my head. Here came Brett to the plate. And here came Nettles to the mound. Brett's bat still looked illegal, Graig reminded me.

My first pitch was a fastball, high and away. Brett reached out and slapped a wicked shot down the left-field line. It sliced foul just before disappearing into the seats.

Damn, I thought. That was close. Better try him inside.

So I came inside with a fastball on the second pitch, and George promptly tomahawked the ball into the right-field stands, putting Kansas City ahead, temporarily, 5-4.

The Royals lead lasted less than five minutes. No sooner had Brett crossed home plate and returned to the dugout than Nettles motioned to Billy Martin, who came running out of our dugout, demanding that the bat be inspected.

The Kansas City batboy had already picked up Brett's bat, but several stadium security guards helped us get it back. Meanwhile, Martin gave the umpires an earful about the eighteen-inch rule.

None of the umps carried a tape measure, but someone had the bright idea of laying Brett's bat across home plate, which is seventeen inches wide. When they put it down, anyone could see the pine tar extended well up the barrel of the bat. Maybe twenty-five inches or so.

At which point crew chief Joe Brinkman ruled that Brett's home run didn't count and signaled that the ball game was over. Yankees win, 4-3.

Brett went bonkers. He came charging out of the Royals dugout and headed straight for the umpires with blood in his eye. I've never seen a ballplayer come as unglued as Brett did that day. I've never seen a human being that irate.

George later said that was the maddest he's ever been in his life; I believe him. The only surprise is he didn't maul anyone.

The replay of the Pine Tar Incident has to rank as one of the all-time highlights on "Sports Center." ESPN must have shown it a million times by now. The replay has given me a great deal of extra exposure, although not necessarily the kind a relief pitcher wants. We'd rather see ourselves punching out some hitter in the bottom of the ninth than serving up a tater.

When I went into the clubhouse after the game, Nettles ragged me about getting a save for giving up a home run. "Believe me, I'll take them any way I can get them," I laughed. It had been that kind of year.

But wait! The game wasn't over after all!

Kansas City manager Dick Howser protested the umpire's decision to negate Brett's home run and took his case to the American League. Four days later, in an unprecedented decision that ignored the rule book and usurped the authority of the umpires, A.L. President Lee McPhail ruled that Brett's home run should be allowed to stand.

McPhail acknowledged that while the pine tar on Brett's bat was clearly illegal, the pine tar itself had nothing to do with propelling the ball into the seats. Therefore, McPhail concluded, in the "spirit of the rule" the home run should be allowed to stand. McPhail ordered that the game be restarted from the point of the contested homer. Kansas City had its 5-4 lead back.

Basically, McPhail had figured out a way to put the shaft to George and Billy. American League officials hated those two for the way Steinbrenner and Martin always bad-mouthed the league and acted like the Yankees were bigger than baseball.

We were in Chicago when we got the news of McPhail's decision. It was a day off for the Yankees, and several players had made plans to go swimming at the beach along Michigan Avenue. When we came down to meet in the lobby of the Westin Hotel, several TV crews waited for us.

We told the media we had no comment and headed out. Undeterred, reporters and cameramen followed us for several city blocks, sticking microphones under our noses and trying their best to get some kind of reaction.

We kept saying "No comment" as politely as we could, but the media's persistence quickly grew tiresome. Finally, out of utter frustration, I hocked a big loogie on one reporter's microphone. That did the trick; the media dispersed and we were free to go about our business.

That day in Chicago was a scorcher. The sand on the beach must have been close to 150 degrees. It gave new meaning to the term "hot foot." People would sprint to the water and, after their swim, race back to stand on blankets. Otherwise, the sand would sear the soles of their feet.

We played a prank on Dom Scala, our bullpen catcher, late that afternoon. When Dom went in for a dip, we took his clothes and disappeared. He had to walk back to the Westin during rush hour, wearing only his swimming trunks. People stared and pointed, and buses and cabs honked their horns at him. When he got back to the hotel, Dom found his clothes in a pile outside his room with a friendly note—"What an asshole!"—attached.

If I'm not mistaken, that same day Yankee slugger Steve "Bye-Bye" Balboni got so much sun on the top of his (balding) dome that by the time we got back to the hotel his head had started turning purple. I spent several hours that night putting cold washcloths on Balboni's scalp. He kept saying his head felt like it was going to explode.

The American League ordered that the pine-tar game be resumed at a later date. The Royals couldn't fit it into the schedule until mid-August. Still incensed by the ruling, Yankee players talked things over and we voted not to play. We decided that rather than play a game we'd been cheated out of, we'd forfeit.

Then reality set in. We were still trying to win a pennant. What if at the end of the season we were one game back? We'd look like some kind of dummies for forfeiting a game we could have won.

In the meantime, our team lawyers had been appealing the American League's ruling. We were hopeful that a judge would uphold our position, but the ruling never came down. We were forced to troop back into Yankee Stadium on August 18 and play a four-out game.

The stadium was almost empty. No more than a thousand people showed up. Those who stayed away must have known what was coming.

Never one to go down without a fight, Billy Martin went

out and protested that George Brett had missed a base. The umpire crew pulled out an affadavit from the July 24 crew, stating that Brett had touched 'em all.

That protest over, the game began. Hal McRae struck out for the Royals third out, and in the bottom of the ninth the Yankees quickly went down 1-2-3. The four-out game had lasted less than ten minutes. We left the field without breaking a sweat.

Win or lose, Corna and I had planned a pool party that evening. A lot of the Yankee players showed up, but no one particularly felt like partying. Besides the painful resolution to the Pine Tar Incident, our mood had been darkened by an automobile accident involving teammate Andre Robertson, who was in critical condition. He recovered, but his career was never the same.

Between the massive home run Brett hit off me in the 1980 playoffs—which Catfish Hunter claimed traveled as far as the three homers Brett hit off him in one 1978 playoff game—and the Pine Tar Incident in 1983, George and I became linked in baseball history.

Napoleon had Wellington. Hamilton had Burr. Al Capone had Eliot Ness. I had George Brett.

It's tempting to regard Brett as my nemesis. On the other hand, we had many duels during the bitter years of the Yankees-Royals rivalry, and I probably won the vast majority. Pitchers always do.

"There's no one else who can come in and get out of a bases-loaded jam with K's like Gossage can," Brett had said on the eve of our 1980 showdown. "When I face him, we match power against power. I win once in a while, but he wins most of the time."

It's just that Brett possessed a flair for the dramatic, and in a few of our battles that he won, his histrionics left as lasting an impression as any by Al Pacino or Jack Nicholson.

Besides, let's give the devil his due: I never saw Ted Williams hit, but I can't imagine that he could have been any better than George Brett.

In my opinion, Brett has been the best hitter of the past three decades. He hit for average. He hit for power. He hit in the clutch. He used the whole field and could handle any type of pitch. His hits did damage.

I played with, and pitched against, some excellent hitters—Dick Allen, Dave Parker, Rod Carew, Tony Gwynn, Ken Griffey Jr.—but for my money, Brett is the best of the whole bunch.

During the period when we were waiting for resolution on the pine tar matter, another bizarre episode occurred. We were in Toronto in early August when Dave Winfield killed a seagull in the outfield. It immediately brought back memories of my own experience in Chicago as the Sparrow Killer.

Several things should be said in Winfield's defense. First, there were flocks of seagulls swooping and soaring around Exhibition Stadium that night and, for that matter, every other night. The Toronto franchise might have been nicknamed the Seagulls as easily as the Blue Jays.

Second, Dave wasn't the first major league player to throw at a seagull in Toronto. Guys did it all the time. Part of the bargain, though, was that the birds were supposed to fly away. That's why God gave them wings.

This dumb cluck didn't even try to get out of the way. (Nettles claimed that the same bird was acting peculiarly in the infield moments before the fatal throw; I suppose that's possible, although Graig may have been helping Winfield construct a defense.)

Winfield was loosening his arm between innings, throwing to a teammate in the bullpen. He saw the seagull. He aimed and threw. The ball hit the bird in the neck. Rest in peace.

Time was called, and the Toronto batboy ran out and covered the corpse with a towel. In what his Yankee teammates considered a touching gesture, Winfield doffed his cap and held it over his heart while the body was removed.

The good citizens of Toronto had a different interpretation: They felt Winfield was mocking the dead seagull. The Canadians began hurling insults at Winnie and peppering right field with debris.

What none of us Americans knew was that seagulls were on the endangered species list in Canada. For committing this fowl, er, foul deed, Winfield was looking at hard time.

Holy Jonathan Livingston Seagull!

Toronto plainclothes detectives came into our clubhouse after the game and arrested Dave. They took him downtown and grilled him about being a seagull assassin. For the cruelty-to-animals charge they waved in his face, Dave could be fined $500 and sentenced to six months in jail.

After several hours of questioning, Winfield was released on $500 bond and allowed to accompany the Yankees to Detroit. The next night, the first time Dave came up to bat everyone at Tiger Stadium stood and flapped their arms like bird wings. Cute.

Meanwhile, law enforcement officials in Toronto came to their collective senses and decided that Dave Winfield wasn't such a bad guy. Charges against him were dismissed. Case closed.

Before leaving New York, I had one other memorable caper in Boston and pulled off a few pretty decent pranks in the bullpen.

Whoever made out the A.L. schedule always brought the Yankees into Boston—the scene of the Boston Massacre in 1978, the impromptu visit by Billy Martin to my hotel room in 1979—in September. Fans at Fenway Park, if they didn't hate us so much, could have chosen to serenade the Yankee players with "See You in September" or "September Song."

They knew we showed up as regularly as Labor Day.

One of our relievers, Jay Howell, had fashioned a giant slingshot out of rubber tubing and a four-foot-long funnel. Field tests showed that Howell's invention could propel water balloons enormous distances. Arriving in Boston and ascertaining that next to the Sheraton Hotel stood a multistory bank building with a flat roof, a small band of Yankees proceeded to put Howell's slingshot to the ultimate test: live rounds.

We gained access to the roof, assembled the contraption, and started flinging water balloons far into the night. They hit buildings and windows two blocks away. Good citizens of Boston walking down the street saw a cloudless sky one moment and found themselves drenched by a cloudburst the next. But where were the clouds?

Meanwhile, we were up on the roof laughing like six-year-olds at recess. What we didn't know was that a silent alarm had sounded and the jig was almost up.

Here came a bunch of Boston's finest creeping onto the roof, pistols drawn. Rather than finding a nefarious gang of bank robbers, they found a sheepish bunch of ballplayers. They caught us wet-handed.

The evidence was overwhelming. We were sloshed (in more ways than one). The police, determining we weren't latter-day Daltons, or the James Gang, let us go with a simple warning to take our hijinks back to the hotel.

The incident would have ended there if George Frazier hadn't decided to reassemble Howell's slingshot out in front of Daisy Buchanan's. From close range, Frazier hurled a water balloon into the plate-glass window of my favorite saloon, and glass shattered like the lights in the chandelier Bill Veeck had kicked with his peg leg.

Like Veeck, Frazier had the decency to pay for the damages. He slapped $300 on the bar and then walked out.

On a trip to Milwaukee, we played a trick on bullpen coach Jeff Torborg. Before the game began, Bob Shirley removed a piece of wire from the telephone in the bullpen and put lamp-black on the receiver. Every time pitching coach Art Fowler would call from the dugout to tell Torborg to get a reliever up, Jeff would put the phone up to his ear and hear nothing but static.

Torborg didn't know what was going on. Nor did he know he was getting lampblack all over his ears, neck, and hand. He looked like a coal miner. Everyone in the bullpen managed to keep a straight face, but we were howling inside.

While the Yankees batted in the top of an inning, I sneaked over and repaired the phone. The next time it rang,

Torborg picked it up and got reamed out by Billy Martin for not having any relief pitchers ready. When the game ended, Jeff came into the clubhouse looking as dark-faced as Al Jolson.

Some of my fondest memories of New York center on the Yankee bullpen and the guys who hung around there. There was one stadium attendant named Frankie, memorable principally because the fingers on his right hand were missing. "C'mon, Frankie," I used to joke with him. "Teach me how to throw your palm ball."

There was a little Italian guy, Marinacchio, always buzzing around. One night I waited until he went into the tiny makeshift bathroom near the bullpen and then locked the door from the outside. I ran a hose underneath the door and soaked him. Marinacchio started banging on the door and crying out for help, but I kept the hose going. When I finally opened the door, he stumbled out along with a wall of water. From then on Marinacchio held his bladder during Yankee games. He didn't go near the bathroom.

My favorite bullpen sidekick, though, was Dom Scala. "Disco Dom" we called him—a reference to his sensational moves on the dance floor, which brought to mind John Travolta in *Saturday Night Fever*.

Dom had been a collegiate baseball star at St. John's and a draft choice of the Oakland A's. When his career didn't pan out, he joined the Yankees in 1978 as full-time bullpen coach. He later became a coach and advance scout, and he also made a small fortune designing sports-themed jewelry with NFL, NBA, and MLB logos. I remember buying some Yankee jewelry for Corna.

Dom and I became fast friends, even though we were

total opposites. He was city and I was country. He liked disco, I liked country-and-western. He liked to dress up, I liked to dress down. He liked fine cuisine, I liked cheeseburgers and pizza.

After the 1981 World Series, Corna and I invited Dom and his wife, Yolanda, to join us in Colorado for a New Year's celebration. Dom arrived in Colorado Springs wearing a floor-length leather coat and looking totally like a fish out of water. When we went to one of the local hangouts, I had to call the rednecks off before they beat him up just on general principle.

During Dom's visit we went snowmobiling up near Aspen. He had never been on a snowmobile before, and even though I showed him how to steer and tried to keep him on the best-marked trails, Dom managed to plow into a snowdrift. We spent at least an hour dragging that machine (which weighed a couple hundred pounds) out of chest-deep snow. The exertion nearly killed us both.

I swore I'd get even with Dom—and I did. At the end of the day, I was standing in the middle of a road, waving for him to join me. Here he came hurtling down the mountain, going 35 or 40, when he ran into an embankment and got airborne like an Olympic ski jumper. I'll never forget the look on Dom's face as he went flying by.

"Gotcha, motherfucker," I waved to him.

One of Dom's favorite stories about the Yankee bullpen concerns Sparky Lyle's dining habits. Seems Sparky, when he wasn't asleep early in the game, liked to chow down on a pastrami sandwich. One evening he had just polished off his sandwich when a surprise call came from Billy Martin to get Lyle ready.

Sparky felt too bloated to pitch, so he stuck two fingers down his craw and forced himself to throw up. As Dom tells it, I turned the color of split-pea soup at the sight of Sparky retching. I'd never seen anything like it—before or since.

Late in the 1980 season one of the newspaper guys on the Yankees beat took a break from writing about turmoil and infighting and wrote a feature about the favorite musicians of Yankee players. I told him my taste ran toward country-and-western music and my favorite artist was Willie Nelson.

A few weeks later, after the season ended, I received a big box at our home in Colorado Springs. Opening it, I found every album and tape Willie Nelson had ever recorded. Enclosed was a personal letter in which Willie said he was a big baseball fan who enjoyed the way I pitched.

That was the beginning of a long friendship. During the strike in 1981, Corna and I and a group of friends in Colorado Springs drove up to Denver and saw Willie perform at the Red Rocks amphitheater. We were invited backstage after the show and got to meet the man himself.

Other visits with Willie and Connie Nelson followed. Corna and I went to see them in Las Vegas a couple of times and greatly enjoyed the experience. They've since been divorced, but Willie and Connie Nelson are still good friends of ours. They're among the nicest, kindest souls you'll ever meet.

I became close buds with several members of Willie's band and crew, especially Poodie Locke, the stage manager. A few years after that first meeting at Red Rocks, I went back up to Denver to catch another of Willie's performances. That night, the guys talked me into tagging along to the next show, in Casper, Wyoming.

It was great fun to be traveling with the band; sort of reminded me of bus travel in the minor leagues, although smokier.

I needed to get back to Colorado Springs after that, but the band had adopted me as an unofficial tour mascot. Willie's two buses were getting ready to leave Casper after the show that evening, and I went out to say good-bye.

"Come on," said Poodie Locke, who was standing on the steps of the first bus. "We're leaving and you're going with us."

"Can't," I shrugged. "I've got to get back to Colorado," Poodie held up a garment bag. "Does this look familiar?" he asked, and laughed.

He had packed my bag and checked me out of the hotel.

"You're going with us, chicken dick," Poodie said. "Get on."

Willie's entourage rolled through Wyoming holding me hostage. After we got to Salt Lake City, I headed straight for the airport and flew back home. Life on the road ain't easy, brother.

During the 1983 season, Willie Nelson held his Fourth of July weekend celebration at The Meadowlands in New Jersey and performed before a sellout crowd of 90,000 on July 3. That night, Billy Martin, Bobby Murcer, and I went out on stage during the encore and sang along to "Whiskey River." Granted, it was a bit ironic to be singing that particular song with Billy.

New York Yankee fans in the audience started shouting "GOOOOOOOSE," but with the acoustics and all, it sounded like they were shouting "BRRRUUUUUCE." For a moment there I thought I was Springsteen.

Before the concert, I'd been hanging around backstage with Billy Martin, Graig Nettles, Sparky Lyle, and Dave Righetti. Willie, Waylon Jennings, and Merle Haggard were busy rehearsing a new song—something about two guys named Pancho and Lefty. They asked us what we thought about the song (which later became a hit on the pop and country charts). We liked it.

Billy was hassling Righetti about even being at Willie's concert, because Dave was scheduled to pitch for us the next day. Martin thought Righetti should be at home, getting his rest. "I don't ever go to bed before ten o'clock on the night before a game," Righetti said. "I'm going to hang around for a while and watch the show."

"Well, you'd better pitch good tomorrow," Billy chided.

The next day, of course, Dave Righetti threw a no-hitter against Boston, striking out Wade Boggs for the final out.

When Billy Martin came running out to join in the celebration near the mound, Righetti looked at him and said, "Was that good enough for you?"

The date was July 4. In addition to being America's birthday, it was George Steinbrenner's. Also of note: Yankee third baseman Bert Campaneris set a major league record by appearing in his eleventh no-hitter.

Righetti, whom everyone called Rags, was a great kid. In addition to being a terrific pitcher, he could do the best imitation of Elvis Presley I've ever seen.

Rags remembers me and Jim Spencer giving him a lecture during spring training in 1981 at a club in Fort Lauderdale. We got in Righetti's face and challenged him to win the final spot in the Yankees starting rotation. Rags later said our remarks helped him realize he might be a better pitcher than he'd thought, that he actually had a chance to help the team. Otherwise, he knew, Spencer and I wouldn't have wasted our breath.

Rags also remembers that I picked up the tab. That was something I did all the time. What mattered more to me than money was enjoying myself and having a good time. I was notorious for having to go to Nick Priore, the team's equipment manager, and get an extension of a few extra hundred to make it through a road trip. I needed the cash because I had drinks, beer, and pizza to buy—especially for pitchers and youngsters on the Yankee roster.

One night Corna and I were driving home after a game and we recognized Righetti's car getting ready to enter the tunnel that leads to the George Washington Bridge. I sped up alongside him and Corna pulled down her pants and mooned Rags and his passenger, Yankee pitcher Mike Morgan.

The next day in the clubhouse, Righetti shouted over at me, "Tell Corna she has a zit on her butt." I immediately called home to relay the news.

"No! Really?" Corna said, sounding mortified. She should have known Rags was just jerking her chain.

By the end of 1983, I had reached the end of the six-year contract I signed with New York back in 1978. It was time to test the free-agent market again. I was thirty-two years old and in good health. I still possessed a live fastball and a nasty streak. That combination of factors figured to make me an attractive catch for some club.

After surviving six years with the Yankees, I remained confident I could compete at the highest level. My experience in New York had taught me that if I could make it there, I'd make it anywhere.

CHAPTER 7

1984

NIGHT AND DAY

My six years wearing the classic New York Yankee pinstripes constituted the highlight of my career—no ifs, ands, or buts.

We had great teams, including a world championship in 1978 and an awesome outfit in 1981 that might have won the World Series had someone been able to slip George Steinbrenner a sedative or had Dave Winfield had a halfway-decent performance. We had a roster full of great players—Thurman Munson, Reggie Jackson, Ron Guidry, Graig Nettles, Willie Randolph, Lou Piniella—guys with uncommon amounts of resiliency and grit.

We also had great fans. Those same leather lungs that dog-cussed me during our 1978 home opener became my greatest allies. They fired me up every time I took the mound, showering me with cries of "GOOOOOOOSE" the way Yankee fans in the 1950s and 1960s greeted first baseman Bill Skowron with cries of "MOOOOOOOSE."

As much as I loved playing for the Yankees (remember, this was my family's favorite team), I hated the constant bickering between George and his managers. After weighing all the pros and cons, I decided to leave. Six seasons on a Tilt-A-Whirl were enough.

I became eligible for free agency in November 1984. My agent, Jerry Kapstein, sent out feelers to several teams but at first met with indifference. That seemed a strange reaction to the possibility of acquiring one of the best relievers in baseball, still at the peak of his game.

The pose major league teams struck made me seriously consider, for the first time, whether baseball's owners actually were in collusion to hold down players' salaries. In retrospect, though, other teams probably believed Kapstein and I were trying to use any interest they expressed in my services to create leverage in our talks with New York. Most baseball executives expected me to re-sign with the Yankees. No one was eager to get into a bidding war for my services with Steinbrenner. Whatever else he was, the Yankees owner couldn't be considered miserly. George never hesitated to meet a large payroll if he believed paying big bucks would bring a big return.

That month, I traveled to San Diego for a meeting with Kapstein and my personal attorney, Robert Teaff. Two members of the Yankees front office, Jeff Torborg and Stick Michael, called and asked if they could fly out from New York and visit with us. Having great respect for both of them, I said okay.

It was, as we say in baseball, a long run for a short slide. The meeting lasted no more than fifteen minutes. I'm not sure we even got around to having a second cup of coffee. I reiterated that I had no interest in a contract offer from the Yankees. I told Jeff and Gene I'd had enough; things had grown stagnant for me in the Bronx, and I felt a change of scenery would be good.

That evening, Kapstein arranged a press conference and I announced that I would not be returning to the Yankees in

1984. Going public with such an emphatic statement broke the logjam and started negotiations rolling with other clubs.

Kapstein began having serious conversations with the Atlanta Braves, San Diego Padres, and California Angels. For a while it looked like I might wind up in Anaheim, but that scenario failed to materialize. I would have enjoyed playing for Angels owner Gene Autry, who, along with Mickey Mantle and Roy Rogers, was one of the heroes of my youth.

I finally signed with the San Diego Padres on January 12, 1984. Before the ink had dried on the contract—roughly $5 million for five years, with additional money deferred— Padres executives whisked me to a local hospital and introduced me to owner Ray Kroc, the man who had made the McDonald's arch into a worldwide icon.

As someone once said about Ray Kroc, he was a man who could cut the mustard.

Mr. Kroc was in serious condition, as sick as anyone could be (he died two days later). He had tubes and lines running into all parts of his body, but his spirits rose when they brought me into his private room. In our few moments together I could sense his warmth as a human being and his zest for life. I'll always treasure the memory of getting to shake the hand of such a great man.

Moving my office from New York to San Diego represented a change as radical as night and day. The two cities and franchises were polar opposites in virtually every respect:

New York was noisy, congested, anxious, and always in a hurry. They don't call it a "New York minute" for nothing.

San Diego was mellow, easygoing, and laid-back. Its residents constantly talked about spending "another perfect day in paradise."

Yankee fans were loud, smart, aggressive, abusive, and in-your-face. They were also masters, as I discovered during my first appearance at Yankee Stadium, of the "Bronx cheer."

Padres fans liked to sit on their hands. They were about as animated as mannequins—until we turned them on during the second half of the 1984 season. Then they went crazy.

In New York the commute to the ballpark from our home in New Jersey was a twenty-two-mile headache. In San Diego the commute one exit down a freeway was a five-minute breeze.

In New York the weather could be freeze-your-tush cold in the spring and fall, hot as a jalapeño pepper in the summer. And humid too. In San Diego the weather was gorgeous and temperate year-round.

The pressure to win in New York was enormous and un-relenting. Fans analyzed and criticized Yankee players to the nth degree; every move you made was examined carefully under a microscope.

In San Diego in the early 1980s the pressure to win was nonexistent. Because the Padres had experienced no previous success to speak of, expectations were as low as sea level.

Finally, the New York media kept the kettle boiling at all times. Being able to manipulate such fly-off-the-handle types as Billy and George, the press in New York had no trouble creating constant turmoil in our clubhouse.

In San Diego the media were as mellow as their viewers and readers. Beat writers covered the club like they'd rather be surfing than digging up dirt. Their whole attitude could be summed up with the words "Later, dude." Baseball seemed like no big deal.

One of the principal reasons I signed with San Diego was because the Padres appeared on the verge of winning an N.L. pennant. The biggest holes the team needed to fill were in the bullpen and at third base. By filling the former, I knew I could make a difference in San Diego, the guy to get the team over the hump. As I said, winning motivated me.

My initial impression about the Padres potential proved to be correct. A team that previously had never sniffed the playoffs went 92-70 in 1984, won the N.L. West, and dusted the Chicago Cubs in the championship series before losing to Detroit in a five-game World Series.

I began having good feelings about the club at spring training in Yuma, Arizona. After six years at the Yankees camp in Fort Lauderdale, where the city overflowed with lifelong baseball fans and college students on spring break, I discovered Yuma represented another radical change. I went through culture shock of the highest order.

A town of 50,000 or so tucked away in the far western corner of Arizona near the top of Baja California, Yuma was arid, desolate, and remote. The Caballeros, a local civic group, did their best to welcome and entertain Padres players and make our six-week stay in the desert enjoyable. But the truth is there wasn't a whole lot to do, other than drink at a bar called Johnny's or hang out at Lutz's, a casino that had been in operation since the mid-1800s.

I also remember there was a Marine Corps detachment in Yuma, and a lot of guys in uniform showed up at our practices and games. When someone asked me the difference between the Padres camp and the Yankees camp, I replied,

"Down there in Florida, you get to see a bunch of beautiful young girls in bikinis. Out here we get to see jarheads."

The limited number of entertainment options in Yuma, though, helped create camaraderie and team chemistry. The Padres ate together, drank beer together (except for the tee-totalers), shot pool together, and hung out together.

When we weren't working out or playing intrasquad games, we also played a lot of golf. One of our favorite venues was Yuma Country Club, a lovely course in the middle of town.

Unfortunately, my foul mouth got our playing privileges at YCC revoked. Believe me, it wasn't the sort of first impression I wanted to make on my new teammates.

What happened was, several of us were sitting in the nineteenth hole, reliving some of the highlights of the day's round and having a few drinks. Okay, more than a few.

We started telling some jokes, and I chimed in with a few off-color ones. The female bartender, who was talking and laughing right along with us, didn't seem to mind.

One of the club's members, however, chose to make an issue of my lack of propriety (and sobriety) in the presence of a lady. He walked over to our table, looked me straight in the eye, and said, "Why don't you watch what you say, buddy. You've got a bad case of trash mouth."

At which point I suggested that he take his putter, or pitching wedge, and perform an amazing anatomical feat with it.

My new teammates laughed, but this guy didn't crack a smile. Evidently, he carried some serious weight at the club. The next day, we got a call at training camp informing us the San Diego Padres were no longer welcome at Yuma Country Club.

Fortunately, there were two other golf courses around Yuma, so we didn't miss a beat, or a tee time. But my teammates told me if I got us kicked off another golf course, there'd be hell to pay.

The annual highlight of the Padres spring training camp, though, was a St. Patty's Day Fun Run in Phoenix. Terry Kennedy and Tim Flannery, two good Irish lads, served as organizers for the event.

After a few weeks of intrasquad games in late February, the Padres headed out on a two-week trip to the Phoenix area, where we played exhibition games against the Giants, Cubs, Angels, A's, and Indians (who trained in Tucson). The Cactus League, as it's known.

On March 17 we would rent a Winnebago, hire a designated driver, and make the St. Patty's Day Fun Run. We'd generally start the festivities at a Mexican restaurant, swilling down margaritas, but after dinner we'd make an all-night tour of the city's finest saloons and watering holes.

We were a menagerie of characters riding around on a bus seeking out adventure and mischief. Believe me, when the Padres hit the road in that Winnebago, it was time to lock up the women and children.

As I said, my plan in San Diego was to be the kind of player who elevates a contender to a pennant or world championship. Then the Padres filled their one remaining hole, at third base, by hiring another difference maker.

On March 30 the Padres acquired my pal Graig Nettles

from the Yankees for pitcher Dennis Rasmussen. Almost forty years old, Nettles had plenty left to contribute. He still possessed a great glove and a quick bat. And, as he had proven all those years in New York, Nettles was a leader, a winner, someone who knew how to play the game the right way.

Playing the game correctly, like Graig Nettles did, was something Padres manager Dick Williams demanded. Williams was a stickler for doing all the little things—throwing to the proper base, hitting the cutoff man, laying down bunts, seeing (and following) signs—that win ball games.

Dick had developed a reputation in baseball for mistrusting rookies, but what he really mistrusted was inexperience. The kind of inexperience, or unfamiliarity with game situations, that causes players to make poor decisions. A physical mistake Dick could tolerate; a mental mistake he wouldn't abide.

A former big-leaguer who came up through the Los Angeles Dodgers organization, and the man who guided Oakland to two world championships in the early 1970s, Williams didn't waste any of his precious time with on-the-job training. Dick believed that if you wore a major league uniform, you should know how to play the game properly. Play hard every night, and play the game right, and you'd get no quarrel from him. Take a lacksidasical approach or fail to execute basic assignments, however, and he'd be on your ass like diaper rash.

One of Dick's favorite whipping boys that season was pitcher Andy Hawkins, a tall (six-foot-four) and rangy young Texan. Much to Andy's dismay, Dick started referring to Hawkins as the Timid Texan, primarily because Andy wouldn't challenge hitters or throw inside. Because Hawkins lacked toughness on the mound, and Williams possessed as much sarcasm as Don Rickles on his best night, their relationship was bumpier than twenty miles of gravel road.

Hawkins finally went to Williams's office and begged Dick to stop calling him such a demeaning nickname. Williams agreed, with one caveat: that Hawkins start busting hitters inside. Their pact would lead to some outstanding performances by Hawkins down the stretch and in the playoffs.

Dick Williams was another main reason I signed with San Diego after New York. I knew his record for putting together great teams. Not only did the Padres have rising talent, but at the helm they had a tough, focused leader who understood the demands of winning a championship.

Before Dick took over the club in 1982—only in San Diego would a team owner celebrate coming to terms with a new manager by serving cheeseburgers, fries, and shakes— the Padres had been perennial patsies. They were so overshadowed by the powerful Los Angeles Dodgers it's like they were barely a blip on the radar screen. San Diego led the league in empty seats. They had also set a precedent in 1980 by hiring Jerry Coleman as manager. The year before, Coleman, a former New York Yankee infielder, had been one of the team's broadcasters on TV and radio.

To the surprise of no one, Dick Williams turned things around in San Diego. His teams in 1982 and 1983 finished 81-81—which may not sound like much, but from the depths of the .373 winning percentage in 1981, .500 ball represented a quantum leap. Then came 1984, when the Padres broke through.

Dick was all business. He didn't waste time on pleasantries. My first season in San Diego, more than one young player came up to me and asked, "Jeez, what am I doing wrong? The skipper doesn't say one word to me."

"Don't feel like the Lone Ranger," I'd reply. "He doesn't talk to me either."

Which was true. The first time I encountered Dick on the runway between the clubhouse and dugout before a game, I said hello. No answer. The second time it happened, the same thing occurred: I spoke and he didn't.

I thought he might be blowing me off, but before I took offense, I realized Dick was already focused on the day's game.

One quality the Padres exhibited throughout the 1984 season was the ability to get their opponents down early. It seemed like Alan Wiggins always reached base on his first at bat. Then either Wiggins would steal second or Dick Williams would call for a hit-and-run and Tony Gwynn would move Wiggins to third with a base hit. Gwynn, who possessed one of the best strokes in the game, hit .351 in 1984 and won the first of his eight N.L. batting crowns.

What Wiggins and Gwynn would initiate at the top of the order, guys like Steve Garvey, Kevin McReynolds, and Nettles would consummate. Before they knew it, opposing teams found themselves in a 2-0 or 3-0 hole against us.

Those holes helped buffer a San Diego pitching staff that was solid, if unspectacular. What we lacked in a true ace, a starter who could win 20 games, we made up for with depth. Five pitchers (including me) reached double figures in victories, led by Eric Show with 15, and Ed Whitson and Mark Thurmond with 14.

Ten wins as the team's primary closer were a few more than I would have liked. Early in the year, though, I blew several save opportunities, allowing the tying run or runs to score in the top of the ninth. Then the Padres would rally to win in the bottom of the ninth and I'd pick up a victory.

This resulted in some good-natured ribbing in the club-house. Several of the starting pitchers pooled their resources and bought me a T-shirt that showed a big black bird picking over an animal carcass. The T-shirt read: "The Vulture."

In baseball lingo, a reliever vultures a starting pitcher if he gets a win instead of a save. My blown saves early that year became a running joke, but as I told the starters, "All you have to do is go nine [innings]. Finish the sumbitch yourself and you won't have to worry about me."

It was all said in jest.

A number of Padres had outstanding years, but the team's MVP in 1984, for my money, was shortstop Garry Templeton. His defense was textbook. He made tough plays look routine. He made sensational plays on balls no other short-stop could have put a glove on. Templeton had incredible range and a cannon for an arm. He could throw out runners from so deep in the hole at short you'd have sworn he was playing a short left field.

One of the little things that can make a pitching staff look good is the range of its fielders. Templeton kept Padres pitchers out of trouble by taking away a wheelbarrow full of potential hits. Garry robbed more batters than a pickpocket.

San Diego coasted to the '84 N.L. West title. No other team in the division could manage a .500 record. The Atlanta Braves and Houston Astros each finished 80-82, twelve games back.

On September 20 the Padres beat San Francisco 5-4 in a day game to clinch a tie for the championship. The magic number was down to one: either our next win or Houston's next loss (the Astros were playing in L.A. that night and wound up losing) would uncork our champagne.

Corna and I had decided to host a team celebration at our home in Tierrasanta. Spirits flowed freely that evening, and it being another day in paradise, many of the guys and their wives romped in the pool.

After sundown more and more Padres showed up. Finally, in came the immaculately groomed Steve Garvey. Garvey had played in Los Angeles long enough to have mastered the image game. He was one of those guys, like Lakers coach Pat Riley, who dressed impeccably and never had a hair out of place.

To say Steve Garvey cared about his appearance is like saying Colonel Sanders cared about his fried chicken. Or Orville Redenbacher cared about his popcorn.

On this particular evening, Garvey's teammates decided Steve looked a little too suave for his own good. As he walked past the swimming pool, several guys tossed him into the shallow end. Head first. When Garvey came up for air, every hair was still in place. He stepped out of the pool looking as composed and unruffled as James Bond.

"Perfect," I muttered. "Steve Garvey has to be the only guy in the world who could get tossed in a swimming pool and come out looking the same way he did going in."

Super Steve wasn't the only one who took a surprise dip that night. Padres owner Joan Kroc did too. I'd seen Joan arrive with her son-in-law, Ballard Smith, the team president.

Joan Kroc looked fabulous. She was wearing an evening dress, and her hair—to quote from the Warren Zevon songbook—was perfect. Joan looked like she had stepped out of the pages of the Neiman-Marcus catalog.

As news of the Astros' impending loss began to spread, Joan and Ballard worked the crowd, congratulating players. They had moved over near the swimming pool when Joan noticed me, half in the water and half out, resting with my arm on the side of the pool.

"Goose, congratulations," Joan said, extending a hand downward. "It's been a great year. Way to go."

"You're welcome," I replied, reaching up to shake her hand. At which point I jerked Joan Kroc into the deep end.

When she came up for air, Joan was dripping more than diamonds; her coiffure was matted to her scalp.

Nobody could believe what they'd just witnessed. For that matter, neither could I. Pulling the Padres owner into the pool had been a spur of the moment thing; it happened to feel right.

Maybe on other teams such a brazen act would have cost a ballplayer his job. But Joan Kroc was such a classy lady she probably saw my stunt as just the right touch for the evening.

After toweling off, Joan stayed for the rest of the party, swapping stories. Of course, no story tops the one about Joan's reaction when Ray Kroc came home one day in the early 1970s and told her he'd bought the team:

"The San Diego Padres?" Joan replied. "What is that, a monastery?"

Padres president Ballard Smith, Gucci loafers and all,

also got pulled in the pool that night. No one was spared. Corna and I had spent $800 for a case of champagne, but rather than drink it, people got so busy pouring it all over each other that the next morning the water in our pool had a golden hue.

If there was one event that brought the 1984 team close together and lit the competitive fire Dick Williams desperately sought, it was a basebrawl game in Atlanta in August.

We were busy administering the Braves last rites. We beat them in a Saturday night game, stretching our lead to 10½ games, and then faced them again in a Sunday afternoon affair. Wiggins led off, as usual, and Pascual Perez immediately drilled him in the rib cage.

Perez, who wore as much gold jewelry as anyone this side of Mister T, was a total flake. After he was traded to Atlanta from Pittsburgh, he was scheduled to start a game for the Braves, but he couldn't find his way to the ballpark.

Perez spent hours driving on the freeway, unable to determine which exit or access road to take. By the time he arrived at the stadium, the game was already in the second inning. That incident earned Pascual the nickname Perimeter Perez.

Our pitcher that day, Ed Whitson, was a country boy who knew the difference between come here and sic 'em. Dick Williams didn't have to tell Eddie Lee what to do next. The first time Perez came up, Whitson threw at his back. Perez bailed out of the box so fast, the pitch missed.

That brought out home plate umpire John McSherry, who summoned Dick Williams and Braves manager Joe Torre and told them the next brushback pitch would result in immediate ejections. Whitson, who had a mulish streak, was undeterred. He aimed his next offering directly at Perez, who once again danced out of harm's way.

That pitch got both Whitson and Williams sent to the showers. They were gone but not forgotten. The matter of getting revenge for Perez hitting Wiggins, however, remained unresolved.

When Perez batted again in the middle innings, Padre reliever Greg Booker took his shot. Like Whitson before him, Booker missed. For his troubles, Greg and acting manager Ozzie Virgil were both tossed out by McSherry. The showers had begun loading up so fast, someone needed to check for enough clean towels.

Perez pitched a solid game that day (the Braves won 5-3). He made one final plate appearance late in the game, and this time Craig Lefferts nailed him. Lefferts, a lefty, threw an overhand curve that kept breaking toward Perez even as Perimeter Pascual scooted toward the Braves on-deck circle.

The donnybrook that followed was the best, most intense baseball fight I've ever seen or been involved with. I realize it was the Sabbath, but guys were taking the Lord's name in vain. Fists flew and skulls rattled. Unlike most baseball fights, which are more like hugging contests than real fisticuffs, guys on both teams got pasted. Ed Whitson came running out from the clubhouse completely deranged. He and Kurt Bevacqua went into the stands and duked it out with some hecklers. Stadium officials had to send out for the riot squad to settle things down.

Things went so well in 1984 that I even had success in the All-Star Game. I got credit for a save in the National League's 3-1 victory at Candlestick Park on July 10. To accommodate the large TV audience back East, the game began a little after five o'clock Pacific Daylight Time. It was a typically cool afternoon in San Francisco, with strong gusts swirling around the stadium.

Conditions played hell with hitting, and the game produced a record 21 strikeouts. Dwight Gooden of the Mets, at nineteen the youngest participant in All-Star Game history, combined with Fernando Valenzuela of the Dodgers to post a record 6 straight strikeouts.

In the top of the fourth inning Valenzuela successively fanned Dave Winfield, Reggie Jackson, and George Brett. Then in the top of the fifth, Gooden cut down Lance Parrish, Chet Lemon, and Alvin Davis.

Exactly fifty years to the day earlier, in the second All-Star Game ever played, Carl Hubbell of the New York Giants had consecutively whiffed the mighty American League array of Babe Ruth, Lou Gehrig, Jimmie Foxx, Al Simmons, and Joe Cronin.

I came in and worked the ninth inning and protected the N.L.'s winning margin. I struck out Eddie Murray and got Don Mattingly to fly out. After Dave Winfield touched me for a double, I struck out Rickey Henderson to end the game.

In the 1984 National League Championship Series, we tangled with Chicago, which was making its first postseason appearance in nearly forty years. For once, the Cubbies weren't playing like lovable losers. Under manager Jim Frey, Chicago had won an impressive 96 games. Solid hitters dotted the lineup from top to bottom, guys like Ryne Sandberg, Leon "Bull" Durham, Keith Moreland, and Ron Cey.

Chicago's rotation also included Steve Trout and Dennis Eckersley, who had yet to make the transition to closer. Especially imposing was six-foot-six right-hander Rick Sutcliffe, who posted a 16-1 record (.941 winning percentage) after coming over in a trade with Cleveland. That was good enough to earn Sutcliffe the N.L. Cy Young Award. In the bullpen, meanwhile, the Cubs had hard-throwing Lee Smith, who saved 33 games.

Hitting, defense, starting pitching, relief—there was no denying the Cubs had the total package.

On the eve of our playoff series with Chicago, the major league umpires went on strike, seeking more pay for postseason work. They stayed out a week before agreeing to binding arbitration. In hindsight, I'll say this: Major league players should have supported them.

I believe you can trace the deteriorating relationship between players and umpires—which may have bottomed out with the Roberto Alomar spitting incident in 1996—back to that strike. Instead of refusing to play unless the umpires were reinstated, the Players Association allowed the 1984 playoffs to start with high school and college officials.

As players, we should never have allowed that to happen. I sincerely regret that, as a veteran player with possibly some influence, I didn't stand up and say, "Wait a minute! These games are too important to be called by inexperienced umps. What if a game is decided on a close play or bad call?"

Instead of helping the umpires gain extra leverage at the bargaining table, major league players allowed the issue to get swept under the carpet. Shame on us.

———

The Padres first-ever foray into postseason play triggered an unprecedented wave of excitement throughout the city. Our laid-back fans became frenzied and vocal. For once, San Diegans dropped their typical reserve and cool and went crazy over the Padres.

Even losses in the first two games in Chicago didn't cool the ardor of our fans. We got hammered 13-0 in the opener, as Sutcliffe dominated us. Then we lost a well-played game two, 4-2.

Two quick wins were enough to convince long-suffering Cubs fans their team was World Series–bound. The whole Windy City began to party after the final out. As our team bus pulled away from Wrigley Field, we could see Chicagoans dancing in the streets. Several waved brooms at us, indicating a you-know-what.

We could understand the delirium of Cubs fans. The team hadn't won a World Series since 1908, but now it appeared they might have another chance.

On the plane trip back to California, however, I started talking up a Padres comeback. "All we have to do is win game three," I told Dave Dravecky, Mark Thurmond, and some of the other pitchers who gathered around. "One win turns this whole series around. Believe me."

Here's why, I explained: The Cubs wanted the series over as soon as possible. They couldn't afford for us to gain any momentum. To avoid having to play games four or five in San Diego, Chicago would feel enormous pressure to win game three.

I told my teammates, "If we take game three, we'll gain a huge psychological advantage. Believe me, we'll win this series because momentum will have shifted to our side, big-time."

By the time our plane touched down around midnight, I had the guys starting to think that a win in game three at Jack Murphy Stadium would set off a chain reaction. We'd be harder to stop than a runaway freight train.

Waiting for us at the airport, incidentally, were thousands of Padre fans. We had an impromptu pep rally there, with Dick Williams and me leading cheers, and another one at the ballpark before we ever made it home that night. Like it or not, the Cubs were heading to a city suddenly on fire with baseball fever.

We quickly rediscovered the joy of home cooking. Ed Whitson silenced the Cubs in game three, 7-1, before an SRO crowd that roared like cannons on a pirate ship with every pitch. I worked the ninth inning just to stay sharp.

Game four turned into a nail-biter. We took an early 2-0 lead, promptly fell behind 3-2, then rallied to go ahead 5-3 after seven innings. Dick Williams brought me in for the eighth inning, but I was unable to hold the lead.

In true Hollywood fashion, though, Steve Garvey took Lee Smith deep in the bottom of the ninth. With a gut-wrenching 7-5 win, keyed by Garvey's four RBIs, we squared the series at two apiece.

In game five we fell behind 3-0 early. Once again we had trouble with Sutcliffe's overpowering stuff. But we finally touched him for two runs in the sixth inning, and broke the game open with a four-run rally in the seventh.

Tim Flannery's routine grounder somehow went right through the legs of first baseman Leon Durham, opening the floodgates. Two batters later, a Tony Gwynn grounder took a bad hop over the glove of sure-handed Ryne Sandberg. All the breaks went our way as we cruised 6-3. I came in for the ninth inning and got my only save of the NLCS.

In the World Series, though, we were overmatched against Detroit, which enjoyed one of the best seasons ever in baseball history.

The 1984 Tigers led the American League from wire to wire. They won something like 35 of their first 40 games and finished with a record of 104-58. They kicked Kansas City's butt in the ALCS, then abused us in the series.

If manager Sparky Anderson's team had a weakness, no one ever got around to exposing it. The Tigers had great pitching, hitting, fielding, team speed—you name it. Shortstop Alan Trammell and second baseman Lou Whitaker were the premier infield combination in baseball. Lance Parrish was by far the best catcher that year. Parrish, like outfielder Kirk Gibson, exuded star quality. Those two guys were studs.

The Tigers also had Jack Morris, a take-no-prisoners stopper, the kind of pitcher who can stand up to the heat of pressure-packed games without soiling his britches. Morris, as he proved against us in the 1984 series—and vividly demonstrated again in the 1991 World Series pitching for Minnesota—was a consummate clutch performer.

If that weren't enough, the Tigers had Guillermo "Willie" Hernandez in the bullpen. All the left-handed Hernandez did in 1984 was make 80 appearances, save 32 games, and win both the A.L. Cy Young and MVP awards.

We split the first two games at San Diego, but when the Series shifted to Tiger Stadium, Detroit won three straight to end our season. The Tigers jumped out to a quick lead in each game (which was supposed to be our specialty) and refused to surrender.

In truth, some of the Padres were just happy to be playing in a World Series—win or lose. Also, having to go to war without Kevin McReynolds, one of our top run producers, who had been injured in the Chicago series, meant we weren't sending out our best lineup against Detroit.

While we were tentative, the Tigers played like famished beasts starved for victory. They had a delightful time picking us apart and chewing us into little pieces. The 1984 World Series ended almost before it began. No question, the better team won.

Two memories from that series stand out. In the first inning of game five I was sitting on the dugout steps next to pitcher Tim Lollar. When Kirk Gibson came up, Lollar asked, "How did you do against him when you were in the American League?"

"I think he has one hit off me lifetime," I crowed. "He's lucky to have that one. It was a broken-bat single. I own the guy."

Oops. Big mistake. My mouthing off turned out to be the kiss of death.

Gibson had a career evening. He hit a two-run homer in the first inning off Mark Thurmond to stake the Tigers to a 2-0 lead. In a fabulous bit of baserunning, he broke a 3-3 tie in the fifth inning by scoring on a sacrifice pop fly just behind second base. Alan Wiggins had to race out to catch the ball with his back turned to the infield, and Gibson, whose great speed made him an All-America wide receiver at Michigan State, beat the throw home.

In the bottom of the eighth the Padres trailed 5-4 when Gibson came up with two runners aboard. If we were going to keep the Series alive, it meant getting out of the inning and staging a rally in the top of the ninth.

First base was open, and Dick Williams signaled from the dugout that he wanted me to walk Gibson intentionally. I didn't like the idea at all. I yelled to Dick that I didn't agree with his strategy. I had a great record of success against this guy.

Williams came out to the mound to pursue the point. "Let me pitch to this guy," I pleaded. "I can get him out. I know I can."

Dick mulled the situation over for a few seconds. "All right, go after him," he said.

On the second pitch—WHAM!—Gibson made a liar out of me. Seems I didn't own him, after all.

Reminiscent of Brett's shot in the 1980 playoffs, Gibson sent a thunderous blast into the upper deck at Tiger Stadium. The Tigers went ahead 8-4. When the Padres went down meekly in the top of the ninth, the World Series was history.

Graig Nettles looked at the loss philosophically: "You may have won the the World Series," he said to the Detroit media, "but we get to go back to San Diego." As for Dick Williams, I don't think he's said another word to me since. Well, maybe a few.

I jinxed myself by bragging to Tim Lollar about how well I had handled Gibson in the past. That kind of talk can backfire on a player big-time, which is why it's always a good idea for a ballplayer to keep his mouth shut and his focus on the moment.

Talking to Lollar, I convinced myself I owned Kirk Gibson, and—BOOM!—he took me deep. I had committed the cardinal sin of getting gay.

My other vivid memory is of barely getting out of Tiger Stadium alive. The aftermath of game five was as scary a situation as I'd encountered in baseball: mass hysteria in the streets of Detroit.

The Tigers victory touched off a wild celebration in the downtown area that turned violent and ugly. Revelry was quickly replaced by looting, rioting, and the ever-popular arson.

My teammates and I had showered, packed our bags, and loaded up our gear for the ride to the airport, when Tiger fans, still hanging around to soak up thrills, came over and began shaking our bus. Gently at first, then harder.

It might have started as harmless fun, like tearing down the goalposts after a football game, but insanity took over. When Tiger fans began rocking our bus back and forth more belligerently, it became obvious they intended to tip us over.

Just then, here came the cavalry. Detroit police officers, mounted on horseback, formed a single line and began moving toward our bus. The horses were trained to kick out their front legs—like the goose step of Nazi soldiers—and the way the Tiger fans were all crammed together in the street, the horse's hooves inflicted serious pain.

It was sickening to watch those horses disperse the crowd. But I also knew that if the cavalry hadn't gotten there quickly, we would have been trapped on an upside-down bus. And who knows what might have happened after that? Maybe someone would have lit a match and tossed it into the gasoline tank.

All I can say is that the entire scene in downtown Detroit seemed surreal. Seeing all those thousands of Tiger fans getting crunched and pummeled by mounted police reminded me of a Godzilla movie.

That night, I saw a taxicab flattened and a police car set on fire. I saw people with whacked-out expressions on their faces and terror in their eyes. All this mayhem because of a baseball game? Amazing.

After such a fantastic and wholly satisfying first season in San Diego, things slowly began to unravel. We had the nucleus in place to become a perennial contender in the N.L. West, but the front office allowed the team to grow stale.

We failed to make any more significant acquisitions in subsequent years and drifted back to the middle of the pack. Dick Williams, one of the best managers in the history of the game, was fired at the beginning of spring training camp in 1986. That was a huge mistake.

Friction developed between factions on the team. A pious, archconservative clique on the Padres (the Birchers) voiced their displeasure and disapproval of the lifestyle of some of the team's freer spirits (the Bingers).

The Birchers vs. the Bingers—sounds like one of those hillbilly feuds in Appalachia, doesn't it? It was heated and bitter, but thankfully, without any real violence.

I got singled out as one of the ringleaders of the Bingers and was accused of being a bad influence on some of our younger, more impressionable players. I would later find myself embroiled in several unpleasant scenes, not the least of which was a nasty showdown with Joan Kroc and Ballard Smith after I made pointed remarks about the nutritional value of McDonald's hamburgers.

I never thought I'd see a baseball team implode because of off-the-field matters like religion and drinking, but that's precisely what happened with the Padres.

CHAPTER 8

1985–87

BIRCHERS AND BINGERS

High hopes raised by the Padres banner season in 1984 subsequently wilted like crops during a summer drought. Dreams of a world championship went unfulfilled. Instead of remaining near the top of baseball during the mid-1980s, as our roster suggested we might, San Diego reverted to form and plunged in the standings.

Padre fans went back to surfing, sunbathing, and visiting the San Diego Zoo. Baseball fervor that peaked in the fall of 1984 rolled back like the tide. It became business as usual.

In 1986, two years after winning its first pennant, San Diego slid back to its comfort zone, sub-.500. In 1987 the Padres plummeted to 65 wins, only one more than the crack 1976 Chicago White Sox squad of Bill Veeck and Paul Richards.

Life between the lines became the pits. What might have been a three- or four-year waltz through the N.L. West instead became a mad dash for the men's room. We threw up all over ourselves. Not even the gentle breezes blowing off Coronado Island could carry away the stench.

Our downturn began in 1985. The Padres remained competitive through the All-Star break (where I made my ninth and final appearance in the mid-season classic), during which we stood only a game and a half behind the resurgent Los Angeles Dodgers.

San Diego seemed poised to make a run. LaMarr Hoyt, who had come over from the Chicago White Sox, gave our starting pitching a big boost. Andy Hawkins started the season by stringing together victories like rainbow trout, eleven all together. Tony Gwynn continued to display his genius at the plate.

In the second half of the '85 season, though, San Diego spit the bit. We fell off the pace and wound up twelve games behind the Dodgers. Near the trading deadline at the end of July, we failed to secure any help for our starting rotation.

GM "Trader" Jack McKeon couldn't squeeze off another of his patented deals. We thought we had a shot at acquiring John Candelaria, my old Pirate buddy, but the Candy Man escaped upstate to Anaheim and the California Angels.

The Padres stayed pat—and sank in the West. We always seemed to be one pitcher short.

If there's an apt symbol for San Diego's descent, it occurred in a game in September 1985 in Cincinnati, when the Reds Pete Rose finally fulfilled his long quest to replace Ty Cobb as baseball's career leader in hits.

Rose, at the age of forty-four, was in his twenty-third year in the majors. He'd gone back to Cincinnati, with which he broke into the big leagues in 1963, as player/manager near the end of the 1984 season.

A sellout crowd of nearly 50,000 assembled at Riverfront Stadium to watch their favorite son (Rose grew up near the ballpark) make history. Cobb's heretofore unassailable record had been on the books since 1928.

Being at Riverfront that night to see Rose supplant Cobb

must have been something like being at Atlanta Stadium in April 1974, when Hank Aaron wiped Babe Ruth's record for career home runs off the books. Baseball fans lucky enough to attend either game would revel in the electricity and relive the experience for decades to come.

In the first inning, batting from the left side, the switch-hitting Rose stepped in against Padre starter Eric Show and assumed his familiar crouch. Flashbulbs popped like at a rock concert. The count stood at 2-1 when Rose hit a sharp liner into left field for career hit number 4,192.

Rose's single triggered a prolonged standing ovation. As his teammates mobbed Pete, streamers and confetti poured down from the upper deck. Fireworks flashed above the scoreboard. Rose's teenage son Petey, wearing a Reds uniform and his dad's number 14, came out and gave the old man a hug. So did Cincinnati owner Marge Schott, who also handed Rose the keys to a red Corvette.

What did Eric Show do during all this? He parked himself on the pitching rubber.

Apparently, Eric didn't have any respect for baseball's grand history. Or he lacked an appreciation for what Pete Rose had accomplished. Or, knowing Eric, he might have been off in his own world. Whatever, sitting down on the mound during one of baseball's greatest moments showed a total lack of class.

It was, in a word, disgraceful.

But then so were the Padres. While other major league teams busted their humps like Charlie Hustle, the Padres, like Show, sat down on the job. Not all the guys—but we did have enough deadbeats to pull us down from the lofty heights we scaled the year before. The competitive spirit we'd shown in that brawl with Atlanta had gone with the wind.

215

———

The poster boy for indifference and nonchalance was out-fielder Kevin McReynolds. A collegiate star at the University of Arkansas, McReynolds was a good-looking kid with an athletic body and enough power and speed to ensure a bright future. Who knows, had he played with any passion, by now McReynolds might be chasing some records of his own.

Kevin had been named the minor league Player of the Year after putting up massive numbers at Class AAA in Las Vegas. Unfortunately, once McReynolds made it to the majors he stopped trying to excel. He seemed as contented as a pig in slop. Kevin's idea of a tough workout was having to reach for the remote control.

I pulled McReynolds aside one day and tried to push his hot button. I encouraged him to try to improve his work habits, which were largely nonexistent. "Look, all you have to do is play hard for three hours a day," I told him. "Three hours. That's not going to kill you. Play 162 games to the best of your ability, then you can go back to Arkansas and relax all you want."

I had about as much luck motivating McReynolds as Dick Williams did. Which is to say, none.

Kevin wouldn't argue with any criticism of his performance. He wouldn't brush you off or dismiss your suggestions about how he could improve. In fact, he'd nod his head like he understood everything you said. Then he'd immediately revert to his old work habits. He remained the quintessential couch potato.

———

The 1985 season would prove to be the last of my blue-chip years. I posted a 1.82 ERA and had 26 saves to go along with a 5-3 record. I pitched the final inning of the All-Star Game at Minneapolis and recorded the last out.

That season, though, I began to suffer some of the physical problems that would hound me for the rest of the 1980s. Stiffness developed in my right shoulder. My left knee had to be scoped.

The downtime I spent on the disabled list limited my workload to 79 innings in 50 games. My strikeouts-to-innings-pitched fell well below one per inning.

Turning thirty-four that summer, I showed some signs of wear and tear. That generally goes with the territory, though. It's difficult to throw that hard for that long without body parts beginning to break down.

Still, the achievement in my career that gives me the most satisfaction is knowing that from 1975, when I came of age as a closer in Chicago, until 1985 in San Diego, when my body started sending out distress signals, I was on everyone's A-list of top relief pitchers.

To borrow what Houston Oilers coach Bum Phillips once said about his star running back Earl Campbell, I may not have been in a class by myself, but it didn't take long to call the roll.

Consistency represents the true mark of excellence in any sport. Whether it's baseball or badminton, bowling or billiards, few athletes are able to maintain a standard of excellence for ten or fifteen years. Consistency sets apart the Pete Roses of the world, athletes who accomplish lofty goals year after year after year.

The relief pitchers I've admired most in the past two

decades are guys like Rollie Fingers, Bruce Sutter, Dan Quisenberry, Lee Smith, Kent Tekulve, Jeff Reardon, Dennis Eckersley, Tom Henke, Rod Beck—all of whom performed their craft brilliantly and consistently. Year after year.

There's a high burnout factor in relief pitching. The stress associated with coming in night after night with the game on the line, as well as the thin margin between success and failure, can wear away at a reliever. It often becomes too big a burden to bear.

Because of the intense pressure, many of baseball's top relief pitchers pack their career highlights into a burst of five years or less. A few are one-season wonders.

At times, I found pressure getting to me. I constantly had to remind myself to back away and realize I wasn't facing a life-threatening situation, I was playing a game. As important as it was, as much as the outcome mattered, when all was said and done, what we were doing was just playing a game.

Another reason many closers burn out is because they don't listen to their own bodies. They try to pitch when their arm is hanging or they're out of gas.

Granted, it can be a difficult balancing act, especially for a young pitcher who's trying to carve out a reputation as someone who wants the ball in his hand. But closers have to respect their bodies and give it the proper rest. Otherwise, they're liable to wind up on injured reserve—and then what good are they to their team?

Every pitcher has to realize that a baseball season is a marathon, not a sprint.

San Diego's unraveling in the mid-1980s stemmed from two primary sources. One, after taking us to the World Series in

1984, manager Dick Williams became embroiled in a running battle with general manager Jack McKeon. (And I'd thought only the Yankees engaged in such skirmishes.)

McKeon, who coveted Dick's job, began to undermine Williams, hiring and firing coaches without Dick's knowledge or approval. He began suggesting to Ballard Smith that Dick's fondness for a nip of whiskey might be impairing his ability to lead.

Which was nonsense. What was impairing Williams most was Trader Jack's inability to solve our shortage of starting pitching, by signing free agents like Rick Sutcliffe.

All this infighting went on behind owner Joan Kroc's back. Joan freely admitted she knew nothing about baseball and probably cared the same amount.

Joan did have enough savvy, however, to know that it was Dick Williams who had lifted the Padres out of baseball's sewers. Had she known that Dick was being given the shiv by his bosses, she might have intervened. But she was clueless in La Jolla.

While Williams fought with the front office, a civil war between the Birchers and Bingers broke out in the clubhouse. Led by the enigmatic Eric Show, several Padres became card-carrying members of the John Birch Society and joined Eric in passing out pamphlets at local shopping malls. They'd even leave copies of their Birch Society literature on players' chairs in the clubhouse, hoping more Padres would enlist in the cause.

The Bingers, by contrast, were less concerned with the threat of communism and protecting the U.S. Constitution and the American way than planning their next party.

Guess to which group I belonged?

At the risk of oversimplifying, the Birchers disapproved of the Bingers' lifestyle. They believed ballplayers should behave like Eagle Scouts. The Bingers, by contrast, believed all that really matters in baseball occurs between the white lines.

We also considered the Birchers' conservative views a bunch of baloney. We were suspicious about any lifestyle that made ballplayers so clean they squeaked.

A clubhouse divided—not unlike a family divided—can only harm everyone. Differences between the two factions festered like open sores.

I have always tried to follow a live-and-let-live credo. To each his own. You do your thing and I'll do mine. Consequently, I was prepared to tolerate the Birchers as long as they tolerated the Bingers. But the Birchers made it a clubhouse issue by confronting us and challenging us— to paraphrase the rock group Santana—to change our evil ways. They insisted we cut down on our beer drinking and carousing. They went so far as to accuse me of being a ringleader for the Bingers, the guy having a negative effect on impressionable young players.

Me? A ringleader? If someone wanted to hang out with me, fine. But I didn't go recruiting ballplayers to keep me company.

The kind of frontal attack being made by the Birchers required a response. So I asked them why they were so hung up on pregame prayer. One day in the clubhouse I said, "What are you guys doing praying before you go out to pitch? Don't you think that God has more important things to worry about than whether you paint your next pitch on the outside corner?"

"We've put our trust and faith entirely in his plan," they said.

"All I know is that the plan better be to keep the fastball down in the strike zone," I sniffed, unimpressed with their piety.

Baseball and religion don't mix, unless perhaps your name is Billy Sunday. Sunday, a star in the 1880s and reportedly one of the game's fastest runners ever, later became a renowned evangelist. He was the Billy Graham of his time.

I had no quarrel with baseball's chapel service program, which in those days was growing in influence around the major leagues. If chapel fit into a player's belief system, fine. But I didn't expect chapelgoers to turn around and hassle me for having a few beers after a ball game, something that fit into my belief system.

I'd never seen religion drive a wedge through a club before, but that's what happened in San Diego. Team chemistry vaporized.

Before the 1986 season began, we lost our boss. Some of the pitchers had already shown up in Yuma for spring training in February when Joan Kroc summoned Dick Williams to her home in Palm Springs and dropped the pilot.

Joan bought out the last year of Dick's contract, and with it, a year's silence. You didn't have to hear Williams's side of the story, though, to figure out he'd been sabotaged by Jack McKeon and Ballard Smith. Why anyone would run off the man who had lifted the San Diego Padres up from mediocrity is something I'll never understand.

We went from having one of baseball's most experienced managers in Williams—who had managed 44 postseason games, 26 of them in the World Series—to one of the least experienced in Steve Boros. In two undistinguished seasons as the Oakland skipper (1982-83), Boros had failed to reach .500. He couldn't have found the postseason for the 1986 Padres if someone had given him a road map.

Boros lasted one year and was replaced in 1987 by Larry Bowa, the longtime Phillies shortstop. San Diego would become Bowa's first and last managerial gig. His tenure lasted 208 games. Let's just say that Larry, too, was overmatched.

Some cynics might suggest that by ousting Williams and replacing him with Boros and Bowa, two inexperienced field bosses, Trader Jack was positioning himself to ultimately take over. McKeon had managed Kansas City and Oakland in the 1970s; he probably felt the urge to scratch a familiar itch.

In fact, McKeon fired Larry Bowa early in the 1988 season and hired himself. Draw your own conclusion.

Games stopped being much fun my last two years in San Diego. We got folded, stapled, and stuffed as regularly as the phone bill. So we had to look for other diversions to amuse ourselves—like spitting.

Two of baseball's greatest traditions are chewing and spitting. Any fan who watched Mark McGwire chase the ghosts of Roger Maris and Babe Ruth during the summer of 1998 saw that Big Mac gives his gum quite a workout.

Anyone tuning into a World Series telecast and seeing all the tight shots network TV directors love, quickly realizes that ballplayers have mouths like magpies: They're busy all the time.

Seeds, gum, nicotine—there's always something going on between a player's molars and bicuspids. It's almost as if one prerequisite for making the major leagues is having an oral fixation. As long as it's not sucking your thumb.

On a personal note, I often chewed sticks of gum sitting in the bullpen. I occasionally chewed while loosening up. But once the call came from the dugout, I'd spit it out.

It wasn't, as some of my teammates thought, because I couldn't walk and chew gum at the same time. As I've mentioned, more than once, I built my approach to pitching around intimidation. How intimidating can a pitcher be if he's busy smacking his lips or, heaven forbid, blowing bubbles?

The Padres had a tradition in spring training that involved spitting tobacco juice on the prospects in camp awaiting assignment to the minor league. I can't recall offhand who started the tradition, it predated my arrival, but it was priceless.

Here were these fresh-faced youngsters, jacked up at being able to work out with the big-leaguers. They were so awed and excited they would run around for a couple weeks without their feet touching the ground. I know, I had felt the same way in Sarasota, with the White Sox, in 1971.

Some of the crusty veterans on the Padres would get a big chew of tobacco working, then spit the juice on the back of the kids' uniform pants. That way, it looked like the kids had taken a dump and forgotten to wipe.

You would see one of these kids pop out of the dugout and dash to the on-deck circle, confident that some organizational bigwig was watching. The kid was busy telling himself that one good at bat could earn him a promotion to a higher level.

The kid would be out there loosening up with the doughnut or heavy bat when some snowbird in the stands would notice his stained uniform and a nervous titter suddenly broke out. Fans would begin pointing at the youngster and laughing. The kid wouldn't know what was up, but he'd correctly assume someone had played a prank. He'd go to the plate distracted and make a quick out. Then he'd come back into the dugout, inspect his britches and be mortified.

It happened every spring.

I seldom chewed tobacco, but I was exposed to nicotine products in 1978, my first year with the Yankees. On a day in Fort Lauderdale when Billy Martin didn't ask me to hit anyone in the head, Don Gullett introduced me to smokeless tobacco. Snuff.

It was a typical South Florida morning, which is to say hot and humid. The air felt sticky and close. Gullett pulled a small cylinder out of his hip pocket, and when he opened the can, an exotic aroma—wintergreen, as I recall—came wafting out.

I'd been around dipping pitchers (and some dippy ones too) for years, but at that moment I became intrigued.

"What you got there, hoss?"

"Copenhagen. Want to try some?"

"Never have."

"Never too late to start, bud."

"Oh, what the hell? Sure, gimme some."

With that, Gullett reached up with one hand and grabbed my lower lip, pulling it out. With the other hand, he took a pinch of Copenhagen and poked it down to the base of my gum line. Hmmmm. Not bad, I thought, as I resumed working out. Not bad at all.

A few minutes later, during pitchers' fielding practice, I broke out in a cold sweat. My head felt like a roulette wheel. I fell to all fours and started retching with dry heaves.

I don't know if I swallowed some of that wad of Copenhagen, but I knew my day's work was over. I went into the
clubhouse, laid down on a training table, and didn't move for
several hours, until the earth stopped spinning.

After the 1986 season I invited several Padre teammates to
join me for an elk hunt on our 10,000 acre ranch in central Colorado, near Canon City. Among the six or seven
rowdies on hand was pitcher Ed Whitson, known to his pals
as Eddie Lee.

Whitson, who in 1984 had persisted in his attempt to
plunk Pascual Perez and then pitched splendidly in the playoffs against Chicago, signed a big free-agent contract with
the Yankees after that season.

I knew that a thin-skinned, excitable boy like Eddie Lee
would never last in New York. I knew the media would have
Whitson sliced, diced, and served on a platter by Easter Sunday.
He was too nice and too naive to survive in that tough environment. Eddie Lee couldn't swim with the sharks; he was chum.

The sharks circled after Whitson dropped his guard and
admitted to a reporter that the pressure of pitching in New
York and before the Yankee fans—who derisively chanted
"Eddie, Eddie" whenever he took the mound—had been
getting to him. It became such a feeding frenzy that Whitson
developed a phobia about pitching home games. He hyper-
ventilated on the sidelines one night at Yankee Stadium and
had to scratch his start.

Adding to Whitson's problems in New York in 1985 was
his intense dislike for Billy Martin. The two were like a cobra
and mongoose—natural enemies. Martin and Whitson engaged in one memorable bar fight in Baltimore, in which

the wild-eyed Whitson planted his cowboy boots squarely in Billy's package. The kick was as pure as any of Jan Stenerud's.

Early in 1986, Steinbrenner shipped Whitson back to San Diego, in exchange for Tim Stoddard. We welcomed Eddie Lee back like the Prodigal Binger and were happy to have him along on our postseason hunting trip.

I'd bought the ranch, which included another 35,000 contiguous acres that were under lease, after signing with San Diego in 1984. The spread, which encompasses gorgeous prairie, runs up to 9,000 feet and is set against the beautiful backdrop of Rocky Mountain peaks. The land, while mostly open, does have several timber groves.

We set out on the hunt before daybreak in groups of two and three. The temperature must have been in the high twenties or low thirties. A couple feet of snow blanketed the ground.

Louie Coszalter, the ranch foreman, drove Eddie Lee and one other guy to the east side of the ranch. When they started their stalk, Whitson somehow got separated. It's pretty difficult to get lost on such an open range, but Whitson somehow managed the trick. He wandered away to the east, exactly the opposite direction in which he should have been tracking.

I spent that day hunting with Padre teammates Bruce Bochy and Andy Hawkins. Around four o'clock we returned to the ranch house. As we drove up in my Suburban, a two-wheel-drive Pinto was pulling away. We figured the driver was someone seeking permission to hunt on the property. That happens all the time.

The driver of the Pinto, however, had been a delivery

boy, not a hunter. The package he delivered was Whitson. When we went inside, we found Eddie Lee taking off his wet clothing, shivering to the bone.

"Who was that?" I said, gesturing to the Pinto driving off over the snow-covered road.

"That g-g-guy? He g-gave me a ride back fr-fr-from, hell, I don't know where he br-br-brought me back from," shouted Whitston, his teeth still chattering. "I've b-b-been lost out there ALL FUCKING DAY LONG!"

Eddie Lee was still shaking from having been lost in such—as he put it—intimidating country.

"I g-gave that boy a hundred dollars to bring me back here," Whitson said. "I f-f-flagged him down on the highway."

"The highway?" I said. "Are you talking about the blacktop road?"

"That's right," Whitson said. "The b-b-blacktop."

A Colorado state highway runs about ten miles east of the ranch, as the crow flies. Whitson must have been humping his way through snow for hours. I felt sorry for him.

At dinner that night everybody started getting on Eddie Lee about his misadventure. We ragged him so hard, he pushed away from the table and went to bed early.

Later that evening, while we were shooting pool, we talked it over and decided to lighten up on Eddie Lee. He'd had an ordeal, no doubt. None of us would have liked to walk a mile—or a dozen—in his shoes.

When Whitson came down to breakfast the next morning, no one said a word. All you could hear was the sound of forks against plates. Finally, though, Bruce Bochy started up again: "Eddie Lee, got your cab fare ready for today?"

Whitson erupted like a volcano. "Screw all you motherfuckers," he said. "I've had enough of your bullshit. Goose, take me to the airport. Right now. I mean it."

It took me a while, but I finally settled Whitson down and talked him into staying another couple of days. The incident blew over. But during the 1987 season, whenever we were on a road trip, nobody bothered to ask Eddie Lee for directions for fear that we'd all get lost.

The first year catcher Bruce Bochy came to hunt at the ranch, he spent several days without any kills. You could tell that Bochy—who was born in France, where they probably know more about wine and cheese than hunting—had become frustrated by his lack of success.

The guys decided to have a little fun at Bochy's expense. Louie Coszalter owned a deer head that he'd mounted back in high school. So Louie drove out on the property after supper and tacked the head to an aspen. The tree stood off from the road a bit, creating the illusion of a deer peering out from the woods. It looked like the real thing—if you didn't get too close.

The next morning we left the house just before first light. When we arrived at the designated spot, Louie blurted out:

"Big buck, Bochy. Big buck."

Bochy got out of the truck hurriedly and reached into his pockets for shells. Bruce had big, gnarled hands from catching, and in his excitement to get the gun loaded and the trigger pulled he became fumble-fingered. More shells were landing on the ground than going into his rifle.

Finally, Bochy took aim and fired. BOOM! The report echoed off the trees. The deer didn't fall.

Bochy had contracted a bad case of buck fever. He hurriedly fired a second round. Missed again. He was taking aim for a third shot when a light went off in his head: He'd been set up.

"Damn, that's not a fucking deer," he said disgustedly.

We died laughing at the would-be deer killer. For a long time after that, we called him Big Buck Bochy.

Bochy, like a lot of veteran catchers, developed a habit of kicking his legs out to the side when he walked. That comes from spending so many years wearing shin guards. An occupational hazard, I suppose.

The Padres would be going through an airport and Graig Nettles would point at Bochy's peculiar walk and shout out, "Hey, Boche, you can take your shin guards off now. The ball game is over."

Bochy's leg action inadvertently played a role when a brawl broke out one day when we were playing the Phillies. Philadelphia pitcher John Denny knocked down Tim Flannery, who hit a gapper on the next pitch and slid into third base ahead of the relay.

Flannery came up from his slide pointing at Denny and barking about the previous inside pitch. Denny went over to third base to see if he'd heard Tim correctly. He had. The fight was on.

I immediately jumped up in the bullpen and took off running toward the field. In my peripheral vision I could see my bullpen buddies Bochy, Tim Stoddard, and Greg Booker getting up and starting to run too. Between the four of us, we represented some serious poundage: about a half ton or so.

"Wait for the cavalry!" I shouted to my teammates. The Padres could use four big meats like us in any fight.

I raced toward the infield, but I arrived there alone. I looked back toward our bullpen and saw Bochy, Stoddard, and Booker all tangled up, a cloud of dust billowing over them.

The Denny/Flannery skirmish ended without serious damage. Finally, here came Bruce, Tim, and Greg, absolutely covered in dirt. Nettles looked at them and broke out laughing.

"What the hell happened to you guys?" Graig said. "Did you stop in the bullpen and have your own fight?"

Stoddard and Booker had tripped on Bochy's legs, which started going sideways and brought them all down in a heap. They looked as foolish as Moe, Larry, and Curly.

The only thing remotely as funny as Bochy's legs was Whitson's toupee. Eddie Lee, not a bad-looking guy at all, was ultrasensitive about his looks—particularly his baldness. Whitson finally decided to shell out some serious bucks for a toupee, and I must admit, he acquired a rather handsome weave.

The funny thing was that after going to all the trouble to get a rug, Whitson continued to wear a ball cap on his head eighty percent of the time. Noting this oddity, I asked him one day: "Eddie Lee, why didn't you just buy a few strands of hair and Velcro them to the bill of your cap?"

"Screw you, Goose," he said.

I thought at the time it was a fair question. Still do.

In March 1987 the Padres made their annual pilgrimage to Phoenix, which, as I mentioned, combined some Cactus League games with the annual St. Patty's Day Fun Run. One day, new manager Larry Bowa took most of the squad down to Tucson for a game with the Cleveland Indians.

Guys who weren't scheduled to play that day—mostly pitchers and reserves—stayed back in Phoenix, lounging around the swimming pool at the hotel. We ordered a few beers. And a few more. Between the beers and the Arizona sun, we started to get fried. Around four-thirty P.M. we decided to start making dinner plans.

Eddie Lee was standing right by the pool, as close to the water's edge as Joan Kroc had been that night I pulled her in. Bochy, still in his swimsuit and feeling no pain, spied Whitson. I could see what was coming.

Bochy, his legs flying outward as usual, made a run at Whitson, wrapped Eddie Lee in a big bear hug and ran him halfway across the pool. He airmailed him.

They were underwater for several seconds. When they came to the surface they were probably ten feet apart. Bochy immediately started pointing and laughing. Whitson's expensive new toupee had slid back on his head and the front of it stuck up like a pompadour.

"Hey, Eddie Lee," Bochy shouted, "you didn't tell us you bought the flip-top model."

Whitson reached up and felt his scalp. From where I stood, it looked like a drowned rat had crawled on top of his head.

I knew Bochy had gone too far. One look at Eddie Lee told me he was ready to start swinging. Just as they climbed out of the pool, though, here came Trader Jack McKeon, Larry Bowa, and the rest of our teammates.

The arrival of the team bus from Tucson averted a major commotion. I spent that entire evening calming down Whitson and commiserating with him about his toupee.

———

The previous year during spring training, I got into a different kind of scrap. After practice one day several Bingers retired to Johnny's Bar and discovered—much to our delight—that it was Mud Wrestling Night.

Johnny's Bar had imported a carload of beautiful girls from San Diego. They were decked out in skimpy bikinis and were gorgeous. Tens. After a few seconds in the pit, though, some of their loveliness was hidden behind a thick layer of mud.

The emcee came out and announced that for the evening's big finale some lucky soul in the audience of five or six hundred would get to wrestle one of these babes (at least that's what I thought he said). That lucky individual would be highest bidder in an auction about to commence.

I slipped $150 to Bochy and told him that we were going to win the auction and designate Tim Stoddard to wrestle for us. Stoddard was as big as a ponderosa pine, six-foot-seven and maybe 270 pounds. I figured he would make a fine specimen in the mud pit.

What I didn't know was that Stoddard had decided to enter the bidding war himself, with the intention of designating me as the wrestler. And a bunch of Marines were pooling their resources to send in one of the platoon leaders.

The bidding quickly got to $100. Then it reached $150, and Bochy, being the cheap bastard he is in situations involving money, dropped out. He wouldn't put up any of his own cash.

The Marines were left to bid against Stoddard, but in the end it came down to the difference in pay scales between enlisted men and baseball players.

I was all over Bochy. "You idiot!" I screamed. "Why the hell did you drop out?"

Just then the emcee pointed at Stoddard and shouted, "Sold! To this gentleman!" Tim looked over at me and started laughing. I thought, Oh no, he's not going to get me in that damn pit.

While Stoddard went to settle up, I got on my hands and knees and started crawling out of Johnny's Bar. I nearly made it. I'd almost reached the front door, but people shouted, "Here he is, here is," and I was scooped up and strong-armed to the mud pit.

First I had to go back to a little dressing area and put on a pair of boxing trunks that were two sizes too small. I looked like ten pounds of manure in a five-pound bag.

Then came worse news: Instead of wrestling one of the lovelies from San Diego, they wanted me to tangle with Mother Earth.

My opponent was huge. The only woman I've ever seen as large was the center for China's Olympic basketball team, who shakes the floor every time she moves.

This beast came out from behind a curtain wearing platform heels that made her about six-foot-six. I bet she hadn't seen 200 pounds since puberty. She looked like a cross between Stoddard and Bochy, only uglier.

She was clumsy too. Prancing around the pit, inciting the crowd, she managed to catch one of the platform heels and twist her ankle. Now, in addition to being ugly, she was pissed.

The emcee brought us to the center of the pit and in a stage whisper told us to just play around a little and not to get too rough. He stepped back and signaled for us to start wrestling. The crowd started going crazy.

So much for instructions. Mother Earth became rougher

than a corncob pipe. She picked me up and slammed me straight down into the pit. Then she stomped on my stomach.

As I lay there sucking for air, she picked me up by the hair and buried my face in her cleavage. Her breasts, like the rest of her, were enormous. As she was rubbing my head back and forth, playing to the crowd, a piece of mud caked to her chest scratched my eye.

Now I got pissed. I wrapped my arms around her huge frame, lifted her up and brought her down with a full body slam. It was like leveling a giant redwood. When she hit the pit, mud went flying.

She couldn't get up, and after writhing around for several minutes finally had to be carried out. I thought it would take a forklift to move her. Meanwhile, I rubbed my aching eye, which would need several days to stop watering.

I was the talk of the town in Yuma for the rest of spring training. Wherever I went, people would say "Hey, Goose, I saw you the other night at Johnny's. You were awesome, brother."

Maybe so, but I should have known I was in for another long year when the most memorable part of spring training was my wrestling, not my pitching.

Toward the end of my tenure with the Padres, I returned to the Grand Hyatt Hotel in New York one night, after a game with the Mets, and suddenly realized upon entering the lobby that a Manhattan bartender had poured me one too many.

I had urgent need of a men's room, but there was none in sight. What's worse, I couldn't make a dash to my room because the hotel elevators weren't working.

So, as discreetly as possible, I sauntered over next to a large potted plant and relieved myself.

House security must have caught my act on a video camera, and apparently didn't think much of my idea of discretion. No sooner had I zipped my fly than a bulky security guard, who resembled Chicago Bears star William "Refrigerator" Perry, shouted, "Hey, Goose, you gotta come with me." I'd been busted.

The guard had instructions to escort me to my room. He led me to a stairwell on the far side of the lobby.

"Are you sure you have to do this?" I asked. "I'm on the twenty-third floor." I knew he'd have trouble climbing that many steps.

He had his orders, though, so we started up. By the fifteenth floor he was huffing and puffing. By the twentieth he was gassed. I thought I'd have to carry him up the last couple of flights. Now that would have been something to see on video.

When we got to my room, my security pal was drenched with sweat. I invited him to sit down and brought him a towel and a glass of water. "Looks like you've had enough for one night," I told him. He didn't disagree.

The most unforgettable incident during the San Diego years, though, concerned the team's ban on beer in the clubhouse during the summer of 1986, which ultimately earned me a suspension and $25,000 fine. It became a real brew-haha.

One day I walked into the clubhouse and discovered a memo on my chair that read, in part, "As of this day, no alcoholic beverages will be available in the clubhouse."

The Birchers had one-upped the Bingers. Taking beer

away from a ballplayer would be like taking cigarettes away from a manager. An important part of baseball is talking about the game, over a couple of beers, as soon as it's over. Players have to wind down and get things out of their system. Clean the slate for tomorrow.

"What kind of bullshit is this?" I roared. "Somebody tell Ballard Smith to get his ass down here. Now!"

I started putting on my uniform. Then I heard a mousy voice ask, "Did I hear that you wanted to see me?"

It was Ballard, the Padres president by virtue of his being Joan Kroc's son-in-law. He certainly had no other qualifications for the job. He'd never played the game and wouldn't have known which end of the bat to hold.

"Take it easy, Goose," he said. "Let's go into Steve's [Boros's] office and talk."

Once inside, I demanded to know whose idea it had been to ban beer from the clubhouse. Ballard said the team's lawyers had insisted on it for liability reasons. They were concerned the Padres would be at risk if a player were involved in an alcohol-related traffic accident.

We went back and forth for several minutes. I didn't buy Ballard's liability bit; I think he thought up the beer ban just to bust our chops. Maybe the front office wanted to punish the players for our poor performance on the field that year.

As the conversation was winding down Ballard leaned toward me and said, "Goose, if having a beer's so important to you, just sneak it into the clubhouse."

I couldn't believe my ears. "You want me, a grown man, to sneak beer into the clubhouse?" I exclaimed. "What about the new team policy you've just been talking about? Liability, remember? Now you're telling me to sneak beer in? This is ridiculous."

I stormed out.

It didn't take long for the Padres beat writers to get wind of the beer ban and the fact that I'd confronted Ballard. After the game that night they came swarming around my locker like locusts in a wheat field.

Always glad to oblige, I filled their notebooks with wild rantings, including these memorable words: "She [Joan Kroc] is poisoning the world with her hamburgers, and we can't even get a lousy beer."

It had to have been my greatest quote. As I recall, Graig Nettles helped me polish it.

Later that summer I got fed up with the Padres lack of competitiveness and its goody-two-shoes image. I gave an interview to a reporter, who had the national baseball beat for one of the New York dailies, in which I complained, in an oblique reference to the Bircher/Binger feud, that the Padres were only interested in signing "choirboys."

"I never sang in choir," I said. "I didn't know you had to go to church before you could play baseball. George [Steinbrenner] could wear you down. Things could get old [in New York], but this is ridiculous."

I also took several shots at Ballard Smith, who earlier had announced that the Padres would sign only one-year contracts until a new drug agreement had been reached with the Players Association.

"If we don't sign some free agents, we're going to be worse next year than we are now. And who's going to sign here for a one-year contract?" I said.

I added a few uncomplimentary observations about the

state of the San Diego franchise and scoffed at the management's supposed open-checkbook policy, which never attracted any new talent.

When that interview hit the newsstands—and the San Diego paper picked up on the story—the shit hit the fan.

The Padres had flown back East to begin a road trip in Montreal. The next morning, at our hotel, I received a call from Steve Boros, who asked if he could come to my room. Sure, I said, come on up.

Boros brought with him an envelope. I opened it and read that, effective immediately, the San Diego Padres had suspended me without pay for the rest of the 1986 season.

I was livid. "Suspended?" I shouted at Boros. "For what?"

"Calm down, Goose, it's not my decision," Steve said. "It's because of the comments you made in today's papers in San Diego."

I called my agent, Jerry Kapstein, who told me to sit tight and await further instructions. He was going to try to set up a meeting with Ballard and Joan to get me reinstated.

My Padres teammates, including some of the Birchers, rallied around me. Bircher Dave Dravecky, the player rep, issued a statement on their behalf:

"The organization suspended Rich because he said what he believes. Some of us might not agree with what Rich said. Some of us may agree with this, but not the way he said it. But all of us agree he has the right to say what he believes. We call upon the organization to reinstate Rich Gossage immediately."

Steve Garvey, neither a Bircher or Binger, chimed in: "Obviously, the biggest concern is the abuse of the First Amendment right of speech. Our concern is with freedom of speech. This could be a precedent-setting situation. His rights have been taken away."

While my teammates finished the series with Montreal and went on to Philadelphia, I flew back to San Diego to face the brass. Kapstein met me at the airport and we, along with my attorney, Bob Teaff, drove directly to Ballard Smith's home. Joan, Ballard, and Jack McKeon were joined by Beth Benes, an attorney for the Kroc family.

The tone was civil and cordial, at least for a while. Then feelings began to escalate.

I felt like getting a few things off my chest, so I went over a list of management's blunders, beginning with the firing of Dick Williams, the inability to attract free agents like Rick Sutcliffe and Tim Raines—both of whom had indicated an interest in joining the Padres—and the lack of leadership at the top of the organization.

"You people don't care about winning," I said. "We had a chance to dominate this division and now look at us. We can't beat anybody. We're a joke."

Joan Kroc interrupted me and changed the focus of the meeting to my situation, not the team's. She informed me that McDonald's Corp. executives were furious about my "poisoning the world with hamburgers" crack and were demanding a public apology.

Tough, I said. I had no intention of apologizing to anyone.

"You embarrassed McDonald's, not to mention me, my family, and this team," Joan said.

"You're a hypocrite," I countered. "You have a big Budweiser sign in the stadium that brings you, what, $1 million a year in revenue? Beer commercials run on every single TV or radio broadcast of a Padres game. You're making a freaking fortune from beer, and yet the players can't have a beer in the clubhouse?"

The meeting quickly degenerated into Joan and me calling each other uncomplimentary names. I suppose we could have continued exchanging pleasantries indefinitely, but someone was smart enough to break off the meeting.

I drove home to await my fate. The only statement I gave the media was: "My goal is to play again this year."

That didn't happen for three weeks. I had to sit out twenty-one days, missing series with the Expos, Phillies, Mets, Giants, and Astros. Good thing the Padres weren't in a pennant chase.

In the meantime we had another meeting or two with Padres management. On September 5, I emerged from one of the discussions and said, "Meetings with Ballard and Joan . . . have been very productive in establishing a much better understanding among all of us. I know we are focusing on the future in a positive manner. I am looking forward to returning to playing as soon as possible, and I am optimistic about the prospects."

But the Padres refused to lift the suspension, so the Players Association filed a grievance against the club. It looked like the case was headed for arbitration, mediation, or some other polysyllabic word that ends in *tion*.

Then Jerry Kapstein stepped in.

From the beginning of this episode Jerry was in my corner, saying my free speech had been abridged. One day in mid-September, though, Kapstein did a 180-degree turn. He advised me to play ball with Joan and Ballard. He told me McDonald's would come after me with its big legal guns and blow me away.

They won't sue me, I insisted. They won't want the negative publicity associated with a trial.

"They might, Goose," Kapstein said. "And if they do, they'll wipe you out. Everything you worked so hard to get, they'll take away. You'll be broke. Is that really what you want for Corna and the boys?"

At Kapstein's urging, I caved in. We set up another meeting with Joan and Ballard, at which I agreed to make an apology to them and McDonald's Corp. I agreed to make a public statement saying that McDonald's was a swell place and my kids, wife, and I ate there all the time. Joan Kroc made me write a personal check for $25,000, payable to the Ronald McDonald House.

The Padres reinstated me. Joan gave me a hug and said there were no hard feelings. Right.

As for Jerry Kapstein, he later resigned as my agent (he also handled Carlton Fisk, Fred Lynn, and several other All-Stars) to handle the sale of the Padres for Joan Kroc. And he married Joan's daughter, Linda.

After the beer ban took effect in the clubhouse, several of us Bingers began tailgating after games in the Jack Murphy Stadium parking lot. We rotated responsibility for bringing a cooler of beer. We'd sit in lawn chairs, and as the parking lot traffic thinned out, we'd kick back with a couple brewskis and unwind. Or we'd talk to fans who wanted to hang around and visit. Just as Bill Veeck would have done.

Once or twice we smuggled some beer into the clubhouse and hid it in the ice dispenser. But none of the Bingers ever got drunk or abused alcohol in the clubhouse. None of us was involved in a traffic accident driving home either. The Padres attorneys could sleep well at night.

On August 17, 1986, Pete Rose played his last game with the Cincinnati Reds. Father Time had finally caught up with the speed of his bat. Sooner or later it catches up with everyone.

Rose, perhaps more than any major league player in the postwar era, personified a hard-nosed competitor. He played like someone from the old school.

When he came up in the early 1960s, Rose attracted attention by sprinting to first base on walks. He never stopped running. His nickname—Charlie Hustle—suggests the boyish enthusiasm with which he played.

When Pete stepped into the box for the final time, he owned the major league record for at-bats (14,053) and hits (4,256). He was hitting .217. Batting left-handed, he struck out on three pitches. The last was a nasty backdoor slider. A bastard pitch.

Here's a trivia question for the ages: What San Diego Padre relief pitcher punched out the great Pete Rose in his final at-bat?

CHAPTER 9

1988–89

FREEZE-OUT

San Diego's sad-sack season in 1987 left a bitter taste. As nin-compoopish and half-baked as the Padres could be at times, nobody connected with the organization wanted to endure another agonizing and embarrassing summer like that one.

I spent that fall and winter working out as hard as I had in many years, under the enthusiastic supervision of Padres trainer Dick Dent, one of the best trainers in baseball. I ran, stretched, and spent extra sessions on a stationary bicycle. I wanted to make amends for my performance: 5 wins, 11 saves, a 3.12 ERA.

Thirty-six years old, missing a foot off my old fastball, I figured I had one last shot to be a top gun out of the bullpen. I felt like a gunslinger in the Old West facing the challenge from itchy-fingered, trigger-happy kids looking to make a name for themselves.

I assumed my last stand would take place at Jack Murphy Stadium with the Padres. I assumed wrong.

On December 8, 1987, wheels were set in motion that would take our family back to Chicago, where my career had begun sixteen seasons earlier. Corna and I didn't know it, as we huddled around the tree that Christmas morning, watching Jeff, Keith, and Todd unwrap their presents, but we were headed back to the future. Instead of Comiskey Park on the South Side, however, we were bound for the brick-and-ivy walls on the North Side. Wrigley Field.

The Cubs started this chain of events by shipping Lee Smith, their veteran closer, to the Boston Red Sox, in exchange for starters Calvin Schiraldi and Al Nipper. Chicago's pitching rotation heading into 1988 featured an ace in Rick Sutcliffe and a terrific prospect in young Greg Maddux but little else. After that one-two punch came slim pickings— and I don't mean the actor.

Swapping one reliever for two starters seemed sound enough strategy, even if it meant the Cubs had to surrender Smith, who led the National League in saves in 1983 and finished among the top five in that category virtually every year.

Smith, a six-foot-five right-hander from Louisiana, possessed a 95 mph fastball and excellent control. He kept the bill of his cap pulled low on his forehead and, except for when he decided to blow someone away with high heat, kept his pitches down in the zone. Smith would later star for St. Louis, leading the National League in saves in both 1991 and 1992. At the close of the 1990s, he remained baseball's career leader in saves with nearly 500.

Smith's departure left the Cubs with a significant void in short relief. Of Chicago's 48 saves in 1987, Lee had accounted for 36, exactly three-fourths. The remainder of the Cubs staff offered little hope for filling Smith's large shoes; although Frank DiPino had been effective as a closer with the Houston Astros in the early 1980s, he was better suited as a setup man.

With the new tandem of manager Don Zimmer and director of baseball operations Jim Frey making decisions, the

Cubs began looking for a closer. Not surprisingly, my name made a blip on their radar screen.

Zimmer had been the Boston skipper for the A.L. East playoff game in 1978 and probably had Yastrzemski's pop-up as committed to memory as I. He had also been a Yankee coach during my tenure in New York.

Frey had been the Royals manager during the heyday of the rivalry between Kansas City and New York. "There's only one thing that keeps us from beating the Yankees," Frey once said. "That's Goose." (Of course, Frey made that particular remark before George Brett's massive home run in 1980.)

Both Zimmer and Frey remembered my dominating prime. They began to wonder if I had any of that ability left.

San Diego, meanwhile, had reached the conclusion that for the right price, I was expendable. The Padres had been grooming a hard-throwing right-hander named Lance McCullers—dubbed "Little Goose" by some—to replace me as the team's main closer. McCullers had, in fact, led the 1987 Padres with 16 saves.

The Padres also were bringing along a left-hander named Mark Davis, who showed both promise and plenty of guts. Within two years Davis would lead the league in saves and be named the N.L. Cy Young winner.

With McCullers and Davis both needing the ball, I became the odd man out in San Diego's bullpen plans. On February 12, 1988, shortly before the start of spring training, the Cubs and Padres engineered a trade that sent pitcher Ray Hayward and me to Chicago for infielders Keith Moreland and Mike Brumley.

The key man in the deal for San Diego was Moreland,

who had hit 27 homers, with 88 RBIs, in 1987. The Padres immediately inserted Moreland into their everyday lineup as part of a first base/outfield rotation with John Kruk.

Moreland, in 511 plate appearances, managed only 5 home runs and 64 RBIs in 1988, meaning San Diego could not have been pleased with the fruits from the trade. Neither, as I'm about to explain, were the Cubs.

I had a decent spring training with Chicago in Mesa, Arizona. My specific memories are dim, other than being frightened half to death by a Doberman pinscher while walking to breakfast one morning.

I was headed from the team's hotel over to a Denny's to chow down on some eggs and pancakes. As I walked through the parking lot, the Doberman, standing in the bed of a pickup truck, began snarling at me and baring his long, sharp teeth. He must have believed his space had been invaded.

The Doberman tugged on his chain like he wanted to come after me. Apparently, he had breakfast plans of his own: Goose pâté.

I moved past the truck briskly, avoiding any further eye contact with the Doberman and trying my best not to think about what would happen if he broke free.

Just then I heard a growl and felt something sharp digging into my hamstring. I nearly wet my shorts.

What I didn't know was that Cubs pitcher Mike Bielecki had seen the Doberman barking at me and decided to play a little joke. He raced up behind me and dug his fingernails into my leg.

When we got to Denny's, I made sure Bielecki paid for breakfast. "I'll get you back," I promised, though I never did.

The Cubs opened the 1988 season on the road in Atlanta. One of the Chicago beat writers noted: "The Goose has had a good spring. The scowl is in mid-season nastiness." Another writer suggested that the keys to any success Chicago might enjoy would hinge on starting pitching and if "Rich Gossage does the job in the bullpen."

As it turned out, what kept the Cubs over .500 in the early part of the 1988 season were the pitching of Greg Maddux, the defense of shortstop Shawon Dunston, timely hitting from third baseman Vance Law, and the all-around excellence, despite ailing wheels, of outfielder Andre Dawson.

Maddux was nothing short of sensational. He opened the season pitching back-to-back complete games, becoming the first Cubs pitcher to do so since Milt Pappas in 1971. Dunston, while not as agile or rangy as Garry Templeton, nevertheless showed that season he could play a top-drawer brand of shortstop. Often overshadowed by Ryne Sandberg, Shawon earned my vote for the team's MVP. Dawson and Law drew on their experience and savvy to make major contributions, finishing one-two in RBIs.

The Cubs also received a boost from the arrival of Mark Grace, a sweet-swinging, left-handed first baseman. Grace, who can hit .300 as easily as blowing his nose, replaced Leon Durham in the lineup and made a strong bid to best Cincinnati's Chris Sabo as N.L. Rookie of the Year.

All their fine efforts went to waste, however, because of subpar pitching. Calvin Schiraldi struggled with injuries and never hit his stride. He won nine games. Al Nipper had arm problems and won only two games.

Even so, I may have been the biggest disappointment of the trio of new hurlers the Cubs had acquired via trade. The guy asked to replace Lee Smith instead pitched like a cross between Lee Meriwether and Jaclyn Smith.

By the end of training camp, Don Zimmer started confiding to reporters that I no longer threw like my old self. Not exactly a news flash, but a strange remark for a manager to make nonetheless. By the second week of the regular season, Zimmer announced, out of the blue, "Les Lancaster may work late relief in tandem with Goose Gossage."

Remember what I said earlier about a team having more than one closer? How it doesn't have any? Those comments by Zimmer weren't words a guy struggling with his confidence needed to hear.

The first in a series of setbacks occurred on the opening road trip. Rick Sutcliffe, without his best stuff, gutted us into the ninth inning with a 7-4 lead at Montreal. He got the first two outs, then surrendered a single to Herm Winningham.

Sutcliffe's next pitch was a ball to Tim Raines. Zimmer, deciding the fuel indicator on Rick's dashboard had finally reached E, made the call to the bullpen. Here I came.

I missed on the first pitch, taking the count to 2-0, and then grooved a fastball over the middle of the plate that Raines rammed into the cheap seats.

Relax, I told myself. Get it together. We're still ahead 7-6.

Not for long we weren't. I walked the next batter, Wallace Johnson, and promptly balked him to second base. Umpires that season were cracking down on enforcing the rule that pitchers had to make a complete pause at the set position. I had a bad habit of bringing my arms down and then going directly into my windup without a pause. Granted, it was pure carelessness on my part; but as I mentioned, I got so locked-in on the batter, I paid no mind to base runners. Those swine.

Hubie Brooks lined the next pitch to the outfield, plating Johnson and tying the score. The Cubs pushed across three runs in the tenth inning to win, 10-7, but I took no consolation from getting the W that day.

"There's nothing I hate more than coming in after a guy pitches his heart out for eight innings and screwing it up," I told reporters, my dejection as obvious as the Fu Manchu.

When the team came back to Chicago in mid-April for the first home stand, I began hearing it from the Wrigley Field faithful. The chilly reception couldn't compare with my brutal introduction at Yankee Stadium in 1978, but intermingled with a few "GOOOOSE" cries were unmistakable boos. Schiraldi and Nipper got an earful too. The Lee Smith chorus had shown up in fine voice.

Catcher Jody Davis tried to inject some confidence in my fragile psyche. "It's important to any team that's going to contend to have somebody who can come in and shut the door," Davis told one of the writers. "I think Goose can still do that."

God knows, I wanted to. But I couldn't get batters out with merely good intentions. I had to make good pitches.

That became more difficult to do after I developed a persistent pain in my neck. I can't recall a specific event that either caused the injury or kept reaggravating it. One day I had full range of motion, the next day I didn't.

It's difficult to pitch comfortably, or find a decent rhythm, when there's a burning sensation shooting from the upper part of the shoulders into the neck and head. I wouldn't wish that on anyone—not even Don Zimmer.

(Speaking of burning, I was lounging around in the clubhouse one day when nature called. I grabbed a copy of *The Sporting News* and sauntered into the can. As I went about my business, I flipped through the pages of the so-called baseball bible. Suddenly, *TSN* erupted in flames. I had heard of hot copy, but this was ridiculous. I jumped up off the pot and dropped the crispy pages on the floor. Ryne Sandberg had crawled under the stall door and set the paper on fire. I don't know how Sandberg got a match—or lighter—going without me hearing it, but he did. That happened to be one of Ryno's favorite pranks. I wasn't the only Cub he torched in the john that summer.)

The Cubs medical staff ran all the standard tests on my neck. The Cubs trainers put me through the usual rehab exercises. The precise cause of the problem couldn't be pinpointed and—what's worse—the pain wouldn't abate.

I might be driving to the ballpark, hit a little bump in the road, and immediately feel a stabbing sensation that wouldn't go away for hours. I could be sitting on a team charter, and if we hit a patch of bumpy air, the slight jarring would be enough to make me see my own inflight movie.

To combat the constant discomfort, I ate aspirin by the handful and drank beer by the fistful. That didn't help.

By the middle of summer, my season had become a mess. I had an ERA over 4.00 and a save total stuck in single digits. My manager and coaches had no more confidence in my pitching than Cubs fans, who were still clamoring in vain for the return of Lee Smith.

Meanwhile, Greg Maddux continued to be a marvel.

Even at the tender age of twenty-two, he showed the command and composure that would subsequently earn him four consecutive Cy Young awards (1992-95) and stamp him as baseball's best pitcher in the 1990s.

Maddux had good movement on his pitches and excellent control. It seemed like he always worked from ahead in the count, which is one of the keys to success. Plus, Maddux could paint the outside corners of the plate like Andy Warhol painted soup cans.

Maddux, a fine all-around athlete, fielded his position as well as anyone this side of Jim Kaat, another perennial Gold Glove winner. Those two may be the best fielding pitchers I've ever seen.

Over the course of a season, Maddux probably saves himself a quarter point in ERA just with his glove. His quick reflexes enable him to stab wicked shots through the box, pounce on sacrifice bunt attempts, climb the ladder to take away big choppers—you name it.

(I, on the other, never fielded worth spit. With my wild-ass windup and big fall toward the first-base line, I'd be off balance for a split-second after release. By then, hopefully, the ball was past the batter and in the catcher's mitt.)

Greg Maddux is not a big man. He's probably six feet tall and maybe 175 pounds. He brings to mind mild-mannered reporter Clark Kent; put Kent in a telephone booth and he turns into Superman. Put Maddux on the pitcher's mound and he does the same.

How does Maddux perform at such a high level year after year? With competitiveness and craftiness. I used to refer to him as the Tasmanian Devil, because Greg's as ferocious a competitor as any I ever played with. By craftiness, I mean he mixes pitches and changes speeds so well that hitters wonder what's coming next.

Basically, there are only two ways to pitch—at any level. Either a pitcher overwhelms batters with raw power or keeps them off-stride with finesse. That's it in a nutshell.

In the power category are pitchers like Bob Gibson, Tom Seaver, Steve Carlton, Nolan Ryan, Randy Johnson, Roger Clemens, Ron Guidry, and the young Doc Gooden. In the finesse category you find pitchers like Juan Marichal, Whitey Ford, Luis Tiant, David Cone, and Tommy John.

Relievers, too, tend to be either power pitchers (Lee Smith, Jeff Reardon, Dennis Eckersley, Tom Henke, Rod Beck, Trevor Hoffman, John Wetteland) or finesse pitchers (Bruce Sutter, Dan Quisenberry, Gene Garber, Kent Tekulve, John Franco).

What all successful pitchers, power and finesse, share is an ability to throw strikes. Few pitchers hang around in the majors if they can't find home plate. Ask poor Steve Blass, who after winning nineteen games for the Pirates in 1972 was out of baseball by 1974. Ask Mark Wohlers, the Atlanta Braves reliever who struggled so mightily in 1998 that he went back to the minor leagues. Those guys suddenly and mysteriously lost the knack for throwing strikes.

Compounding my difficulties in 1988 was that, in addition to lacking the overpowering fastball of a true power pitcher, my control with my slurve—the combination slider/curve I used as an off-speed pitch—was pretty spotty. Nor did I improve matters much by failing to throw enough change-ups.

Those factors allowed batters to sit on my fastball. And if major league hitters only have one pitch to worry about, they can catch up with anyone's fastball, even Nolan Ryan's.

That August would produce some of the highlights—and lowlights—of my entire career.

On August 8, 1988, the Cubs hosted the Philadelphia Phillies for a historic occasion at Wrigley Field. So historic that bunting, usually reserved for World Series games, adorned the stadium walls. (As former NFL coach and current pro football analyst John Madden likes to point out, when a spectator sees bunting ringing a ballpark or arena, he knows the game is a big deal.)

What had drawn Commissioner Peter Ueberroth, National League President Bart Giammati, a host of major league dignitaries, city officials, and more than five hundred journalists to the venerable ballpark at Clark and Addison that day was night baseball.

The Chicago Cubs had been playing afternoon games at home for seventy-two years, ever since the team moved from the West Side Grounds to Weeghman Park (later renamed Wrigley Field, in honor of chewing gum magnate William Wrigley Jr.) in 1916.

Ernie Banks had never hit a homer after sundown in Chicago. Fergie Jenkins had never pitched a complete game there under the lights. Harry Caray had never had the opportunity to rise for the seventh-inning stretch and warble "Take Me Out to the Ball Game" by moonlight.

All that was about to change. Back in February, Chicago's City Council had repealed antinoise laws that for decades had kept Wrigley Field the only ballpark in the major leagues without lights. The Cubs were scheduled to play eight night games in 1988 and expand the schedule to eighteen games a year through 2002; this would be the first.

———

A sellout crowd of more than 40,000 watched Harry Gross-man, a ninety-one-year-old Cubs fan, throw a switch and il-luminate the field, after which Cubs legends Ernie Banks and Billy Williams threw out the ceremonial first ball.

Many Chicagoans believed that day baseball at Wrigley Field was a tradition worth perserving. Devout Cubs fans considered night games at Wrigley Field unnatural. What would come next, dogs and cats sleeping together?

Others in the city, however, maintained that a steady menu of day games during hot, humid Chicago summers took the starch out of Cub teams—perhaps never more obvi-ous than in 1969, when the Cubbies led the N.L. pennant chase until fading in September and being passed by the Amazin' New York Mets. These people argued that giving Cubs players a chance to perform occasionally in the cool, cool, cool of the evening might help with their stamina.

Ryne Sandberg hit the first night homer at Wrigley Field in the first inning. When Sandberg came up again, Morganna, the notorious Kissing Bandit, shimmied out of her seat down the right-field line and made a beeline for the batter's box. Before she reached the infield, two stadium guards inter-cepted her and—as the crowd hooted—escorted her off the field.

I have a few questions about Morganna: Why were the objects of her affection always hunks like Ryne Sandberg, Steve Garvey, and George Brett? Why didn't she go after relief pitchers? Did she have a bias against moustaches? Morganna had a penchant for picking on clean-cut, all-American types—which ruled out most relievers.

Shortly after Morganna's ouster, a cloudburst dampened

the grand occasion. Play was halted, tarps were rolled out on the field, and everyone waited around to see if the game would resume.

Well, not exactly everyone. Four of my teammates got into the spirit of the occasion and raced on the field, launching themselves in headfirst dives on the slippery infield tarpaulin. They hydroplaned into second base, third base, and home plate, reenacting a scene in the popular baseball movie *Bull Durham*. The soggy crowd roared in appreciation and delight.

The rain never did let up, though, and the game had to be cancelled. Cubs fans and players alike went home unfulfilled. A few residents in the neighborhood around Wrigley Field complained about the noise of night baseball, but their protest was mild.

On August 9 we tried again to get the first official night game at Wrigley Field into the record books. This time we succeeded.

A smaller (36,000), more subdued crowd watched Chicago beat New York, 6-4. The Mets took a quick lead off Mike Bielecki on a two-run homer by Lenny Dykstra. The Cubs rallied in the middle innings for five runs off Sid Fernandez and reliever Roger McDowell, stringing together singles by Rafael Palmeiro, Shawon Dunston, Ryne Sandberg, and Mark Grace with a two-run double by Jody Davis.

In the ninth inning Zimmer brought me in to protect a 6-3 lead. I gave up a double to Gary Carter and RBI single to Dave Magadan but got my 301st save! Three nights earlier against the Phillies I had registered my 300th career save. That made me only the second relief pitcher to attain that particular milestone. Rollie Fingers, pitching for the Milwaukee Brewers in 1982, had been first.

It gave me great pleasure to be in such select company.

Any hope that those saves would propel the rest of my 1988 season was short-lived. I immediately crashed and burned.

On August 11, with the Mets still in town, the Cubs carried a 6-4 lead into the ninth inning. New York ignited a rally with consecutive hits off Frank DiPino, whom Zimmer replaced with Pat Perry. Perry surrendered an RBI single to Len Dykstra before getting Tim Teufel to pop up.

Perry, a left-hander, proceeded to walk Keith Hernandez, loading the bases. He got Darryl Strawberry for the second out, but Zimmer, rather than let Perry pitch to right-handed Kevin McReynolds, put in another call to the bullpen. My turn.

I went to a 1-1 count on McReynolds, then the human couch potato planted my next pitch straightaway in the center-field bleachers more than 400 feet away. Kevin's grand slam, which accounted for the final score of 9-6, had barely cleared the wall when boos showered down on me from all corners of the stadium.

The headline across the front of the Chicago Tribune sports section the next morning read METS COOK THE CUBS' GOOSE. (I have to hand it to newspaper headline writers, they always had a field day whenever I fouled up. "Goose Is a Turkey" was another one of their favorites.)

Postgame reactions varied.

McReynolds: "He's one of the great relievers of all time. But everyone in the league knows he's fastball/slider."

Zimmer: "I said this spring he doesn't throw the ball like he did six years ago. Who does? Ain't nobody trying harder in the world to do something right."

Me: "I get paid to get McReynolds out and that's the bottom line. I didn't get him out. I can't second-guess myself on the pitch [a fastball] or anything. He just hit it out."

In the meantime, Jim Frey had handed out fines for the four players—Greg Maddux, Al Nipper, Les Lancaster, and Jody Davis—who had been splish-splashing on the soaked tarpaulin during the rained-out game with Philly.

Frey said that in addition to possibly injuring themselves, the four naughty boys had risked inciting fans to join in the lark. As a matter of fact, several Chicago fans were detained for running on the field that first night; but they had been collared before the rain delay, not after.

Frey, in my opinion, should have let the incident, well, slide. But he and Zimmer lacked a sense of humor. They were so serious and determined to cut into our fun that they tried to impose a ban on pranks—hotfoots and Ryne Sandberg's torchings, for example—that season. That's right, a ban.

Two baseball veterans like Frey and Zimmer should have known better. Expecting ballplayers not to pull pranks would be like expecting fifth graders not to act up the moment the teacher steps out of the room. Who were they trying to kid? Boys must be boys.

One of the biggest pranksters on the Cubs was pitcher Al Nipper. Maybe his being left-handed had something to do with his nuttiness.

Nipper was always up to something. He liked to glue coins—quarters, dimes, nickles—to the clubhouse floor. Cubs players or staff would see a coin lying there and bend over to pick it up. The coin, thanks to Al and his handy bottle of super glue, wouldn't budge.

Nipper also liked to amuse himself in airports by leaving five or ten dollar bills on the floor. Airline passengers walking through the terminal would reach out to grab the bill only to have Nipper, sitting maybe twenty or thirty feet away and hiding behind a newspaper, pull it away. (He used a thin piece of fishing line, reminding me of the gag Dave Parker pulled with his bat.)

The passenger would look around sheepishly, wondering what the heck was happening. We used to roar, watching Nipper make people look like such fools.

My lowlight that year came on August 30 in Houston. The Cubs were locked in a tight game with the Astros, trailing 4-3 in the seventh inning, when Zimmer brought me in.

I didn't have good stuff that evening—or even average stuff. I walked Billy Hatcher on four straight pitches and then hit the next batter, Glenn Davis. After Buddy Bell hit into a force play, Kevin Bass sent a rocket down the right-field line into the corner. Bass wound up with a triple, clearing the bases and extending the Astros lead to 6-3.

Before Ryne Sandberg's relay throw had made it to Vance Law at third base, I saw the squatty Zimmer, with a look of disgust on his face, shuffling out of the dugout to give me the quick hook.

That really pissed me off.

If he's going to show me up, I thought, two can play the same game. I took the ball from Law and, before Zimmer even got to the mound, I flipped the ball about thirty feet straight up in the air.

That was, of course, a major breach of baseball etiquette. Emily Post and Miss Manners insist that a pitcher not surrender the ball until his manager or pitching coach arrives at the mound. Some managers prefer that the pitcher hand them the ball; others insist that the departing pitcher hand the ball to the relief pitcher.

Whatever, a pitcher isn't supposed to flip the ball to the skipper—or pitching coach—and skulk off the mound.

Zimmer followed me back into the dugout and got in my face. "Don't you dare ever show me up like that again!" he shouted.

"Me?" I roared back. "You're the one who showed me up! I'm tired of you letting me get into a jam and not have the chance to get out of it."

Just as I said that, I noticed the red light shining on the TV camera in our dugout. That meant our rapidly escalating exchange was being broadcast over WGN, the Cubs superstation.

Baseball fans all across the country had a good look at the fireworks, and that wouldn't do. "Let's take this underneath and finish it," I told Zimmer.

Hearing that, several Cub players and coaches quickly moved in and tried to break things up. They mistakenly thought I wanted to take Zimmer into the tunnel and punch his lights out. That's absolutely the last thing I intended. I just wanted to get our argument out of range of the TV cameras.

I never punched anyone in baseball—not even Billy Martin, who gave me plenty of reason to. No way was I going to deck an old-timer like Don.

After the game, Zimmer was livid. He called a team meeting and dressed me down. He humiliated me in front of my teammates like no manager before or after.

"What you saw out on the field today was a total disgrace," Zimmer told the Cubs. "Your teammate here has had a Hall of Fame career, but now he's nothing more than an old drunk. A fucking alcoholic."

I took it quietly, like a man. There was no use making another scene.

When reporters came into the clubhouse, the team meeting was mentioned and I was asked about the confrontation the TV camera had so vividly captured. "I'm here to pitch and get people out, and the bottom line is I haven't been doing the job," I said. Addressing the exchange with Zimmer, I added, "It's unfortunate. I'm frustrated and it's an emotional game. I'm a very emotional player and have been all my life. I had to vent some frustration."

The upshot of the incident was that Zimmer hit me with a $250 fine for flipping the ball. And Jim Frey called me in to his office for a powwow about my future with the team.

"We had a positive meeting," I told the press afterward. "[Frey] wants me to get to thinking how I can help the team next year. We both have some ideas."

Zimmer didn't hold a grudge. He brought me into nine games in September, and I picked up a couple more saves. After the Astrodome incident, however, fans at Wrigley Field rode me like a flea rides a dog. And a Chicago sportswriter, listing fifty reasons to feel good about the Chicago Bears chances in the 1988 NFL season, smugly wrote: "Because Goose Gossage is not in the bullpen."

Whatever plans Frey and Zimmer had for me in 1989, they quickly went by the board. In December the Cubs engineered a deal with Texas, sending Rafael Palmeiro, Jamie

Moyer, and Drew Hall to the Rangers in exchange for six players, including closer Mitch "Wild Thing" Williams.

Williams threw hard (mid-nineties) and, like me, had an awkward delivery that created a bit of panic on the part of hitters. The downside to Mitch was that he had a nodding acquaintance with the strike zone, which caused pitching coaches to turn prematurely gray.

Williams's arrival set the stage for my release. I returned to spring training with Chicago in 1989, but as we were preparing to break camp, Zimmer called me in and said the Cubs were going to cut me loose.

I could accept being rejected by Chicago, because I knew I hadn't pitched well. What really steamed me, though, were reports that filtered back that Frey and Zimmer had been on the banquet circuit that winter blaming me for Chicago's 77-85 record in 1988.

"We'll be contenders in 1989," they assured ever-hopeful Cubs fans in the Midwest, "because we're bringing in Mitch Williams to replace the Goose."

That really fried my bacon.

The funny thing was, the Cubs did indeed have a banner season in 1989, winning 93 games under Zimmer. Maddux, Sutcliffe, and Bielecki all had outstanding years. Mitch Williams came through with 36 saves, second most in the league behind Mark Davis of the Padres.

The Cubs got drilled in the NLCS, however, by San Francisco, which in turn got swept by Oakland in the 1989 World Series. That was the Series when a devastating earthquake, which registered 6.9 on the Richter scale, hit the Bay Area only a half hour before game three was scheduled to start. The Series didn't resume for ten days.

———

By the time the earthquake struck, I had been on a wild ride to San Francisco and New York. My coast-to-coast journey began when the Giants picked me up shortly after the Cubs let me go.

I was glad to be reunited in San Francisco with Giants GM Al Rosen, who had been with the Yankees front office back in the late 1970s and early 1980s. Rosen thought I could add depth to the Giants bullpen, which featured lefty Craig Lefferts, my ex-Padre teammate, as the closer.

Manager Roger Craig, though, had little use for my services. Craig never made me feel wanted. He was a pal of Don Zimmer's, which probably explained the cool attitude he exhibited toward me.

Although I picked up a couple wins and a couple saves for San Francisco, for the majority of the time I wore a Giants uniform I did almost as much sitting as the Supreme Court.

San Francisco enjoyed a splendid 92 win season in 1989, keyed by outfielder Kevin Mitchell, the National League's MVP. Mitchell led the league with 47 homers and 125 RBIs. Brett Butler was a terrific lead-off hitter, rising young star Matt Williams had 18 homers, and Will Clark hit .333 with 111 RBIs. Veteran Rick Reuschel, who turned forty that season, led the staff with 17 wins, and Scott Garrelts chipped in with 14.

The Giants were a great bunch of guys. They won that year not because of Roger Craig but in spite of him. His idea of leadership was to call clubhouse meetings to remind everybody what a gutsy guy he was by rehashing stories of how he pitched with blisters on his fingers. His primary claim to fame had been to teach the split-finger pitch to Mike Scott and Jack Morris, among others. Roger sang that tune as often as Tony Bennett sings "I Left My Heart in San Francisco."

Will Clark provided me with my most vivid memory of that summer. Corna, the boys, and I had gone to dinner one evening at the Hard Rock Cafe in San Francisco. We were standing in a big crowd, waiting for a table, when someone grabbed me, spun me around and planted a big, wet, juicy kiss full on my lips.

It was Will the Thrill, just being his normal, nutty self. "Goose, how you doing? I love you, man," Clark gushed. He gestured at the people standing around us, "Hey, everybody, it's the Goose."

Everyone laughed except for me. "Don't you ever do that again," I glowered, wiping off my lips. "Or I'll kill you."

The Hard Rock patrons suddenly got real quiet. They must have thought we were going to have a fight. Then Will and I burst out laughing and slapped each other on the back.

By August, Roger Craig had decided the Giants wouldn't need me for the stretch drive. He called me into his office one day and told me I was being released. I can't say I was heartbroken at parting company with Roger, but I still wanted to find a job in baseball.

That's when Yankee boss George Steinbrenner intervened. George told GM Syd Thrift to pick me up off the waiver wire as a free agent on August 11, which gave me the chance to return to New York for a last hurrah.

I arrived just in time to read in one of the New York papers this quote from Yankee manager Dallas Green: "The Giants are in the middle of a pennant race and don't want Gossage. What are we going to do with him? My gut feeling is he won't be able to contribute."

Thanks, Dallas. Good to see you too.

Within a week, though, Dallas Green was the guy out on the streets looking for work. Steinbrenner axed Green and most of his coaching staff and chose Bucky Dent to be the Yankee skipper.

I can't tell you how weird I felt playing for one of my oldest friends in baseball. Bucky and I had both signed with Chicago in 1970—he out of junior college, me out of high school.

We had been roommates together with Terry Forster in Appleton. Teammates with the White Sox. Teammates with the Yankees. Both of us had played key roles in the 1978 playoff game with Boston, Bucky the biggest of all.

Now there he was, my manager. My boss. It was another unmistakable sign that I was getting old.

By 1989 the Yankee franchise had fallen on hard times. The crosstown New York Mets were a hotter ticket. The once-potent Yankee attack had been reduced to Don Mattingly and little else.

Camaraderie among Yankee players—an often overlooked ingredient in the team's success in the late 1970s—was missing too. Players went their own way and did their own thing. Cohesion in the clubhouse was virtually nonexistent.

Corna, the boys, and I spent the last six weeks of the 1989 season living with our friend Debbie Perry and Debbie's three children in Franklin Lakes, New Jersey. It was quiet, peaceful, and mellow—totally unlike my earlier tenure in New York. I got a win in my only decision with the Yankees and picked up a save or two.

At the end of that season, Bucky Dent let me know that I wouldn't be part of the Yankees plans for 1990. I'd have to look elsewhere for work.

If I hadn't quite reached the end of the road, it seemed to be coming up fast on the horizon.

CHAPTER 10

1990

PASS THE SUSHI

George Steinbrenner had brought me back to the Yankees in 1989 for what he believed would be my swan song in the major leagues. He once made the remark that his two biggest mistakes during the 1980s were not re-signing Reggie Jackson after 1981 and letting me get away to San Diego after 1983.

What George perhaps failed to realize was that wild horses couldn't have kept me in New York after my original six-year contract with the Yankees expired. There wasn't enough gold in Fort Knox to change my mind.

While I appreciated George's gesture and generosity in putting me back in Yankee pinstripes for an encore performance at the end of the 1989 season, I promptly deviated from the script. I didn't retire from baseball, after all.

I kept looking for work. After Bucky Dent told me I didn't fit into New York's plans for 1990, I started making inquiries to other clubs. I wasn't ready to give up the game I loved dearly. Aches and all, I felt I still had something to contribute.

That belief, I quickly discovered, was shared by a majority of one. Teams treated me like a pariah. Apparently, word on the street ever since the run-in with Don Zimmer at the Astrodome had me pegged as troublesome, quarrelsome, nettlesome, and a negative influence in the clubhouse. I begged to differ—but no one would hear me out.

Adding to the uncertainty about my employment prospects in early 1990 was another work stoppage. Owners locked out players from spring training camps in mid-February because terms of a new collective bargaining agreement couldn't be reached. (Camps would ultimately open six weeks late, pushing the start of the season back one week in April.)

As spring blossomed I waited for a call from some player personnel director with an opening in the bullpen. The phone never rang. To keep busy—and to keep from pulling out my thinning hair—I coached the youth baseball team of my sons Jeff and Keith.

I was pitching batting practice to Keith one day and he kept stepping into the bucket—a baseball term that refers to pulling away from the pitch—time after time.

I stopped throwing and walked in to the batter's box. I picked up a bat and demonstrated to Keith what he was doing wrong, which was bailing out with his left (front) foot. I showed him how to stay locked-in at the plate by not opening up with the left shoulder or left leg.

Then I went back to the mound and resumed throwing. Keith kept swinging—and stepping into the bucket. He made no adjustment to his swing and no contact with the ball. This startling development upset me greatly; I expected my boys to be able to pick up the finer points of the game. After watching Keith make six or seven more futile swings, I'd seen enough.

I got mad at his indifference and decided to hum one down the middle of the plate. Give him a wake-up call, if you will.

I put on my game face and went into the mode I reserved

for big-league hitters. I rared back and fired the kind of fast-ball I would have thrown to Kirk Gibson or George Brett. Unfortunately, the pitch got away from me a teeny bit, and I watched as the ball tattooed the left thigh of my eleven-year-old son.

When Keith went down writhing in pain, I suddenly felt about one inch tall. I wormed my way in to home plate to check on him. All Keith's teammates, including Jeff, were gathered around him, watching him bawling and blubbering.

Keith finally regained his composure and, through all his tears, said, "Dad, you're an asshole."

I couldn't disagree with that assessment. I certainly felt like one. What kind of father drills his own son?

After we drove home, Keith immediately ran into the house and informed Corna about what had happened.

"Dad drilled me!" he shouted.

"He what?"

"He hit me with a pitch. Right here." Keith unbuckled his pants and showed Corna the ugly purplish bruise form-ing on his upper thigh.

Corna shook her head. "You hit your own kid? Not on purpose, I hope?"

I shrugged my shoulders. I didn't think it had hap-pened on purpose—but then again, I couldn't say for sure. I'd been hot.

"You know something, Rick," she said disgustedly. "You're sick. Really sick."

Corna covered Keith up with kisses and gave me the cold shoulder for several days. Who could blame her?

———

That same spring, my adviser, Bob Teaff, and I had a brainstorm: We would contact baseball people in Japan and inquire about openings in the Japanese League. I still owned that large ranch near Canon City—the scene of Eddie Lee Whitson's misadventure and the prank on Big Buck Bochy—and the cattle industry in Japan, like the rest of the economy, was booming.

Teaff and I figured that while playing baseball in Japan I could make contacts with that country's large meat manufacturers—the equivalent of an Armour or Swift—about setting up a cattle-breeding program. Baseball and beef sounded like a good twofer to pursue.

The Japanese baseball season stretches from April through September and encompasses roughly 130 games. The rainy season in Japan in late summer generally creates a large number of postponements, games that are made up in early October. After which follows the Japanese World Series, which pits the winners of the Pacific League and Central League.

Americans had been playing baseball in Japan for decades. Larry Doby and Don Newcombe were two of the first American stars to go over in the early 1960s. Through the years, such well-known American players as Frank Howard, Dick Stuart, Clete Boyer, Willie Davis, Jim LeFebvre, Reggie Smith, Roy White, Don Money, and Bob Horner, to name a few, have played for yen.

Rules permitted each Japanese team to carry two foreign players—*gaijin*—on their roster. Bob Teaff and I flew over to Japan in March, and I worked out at four or five training camps.

The Daiei Hawks, a Pacific League team based in

Fukuoka, a coastal city on the northwest side of the island of Kyushu, showed the most interest. But Daiei, like all the other Japanese teams, didn't have any roster openings. All the spots for *gaijin* had been filled. Nevertheless, Hawks officials said they would keep in touch.

A couple months later, during which time some Japanese meat executives came to Colorado to inspect our ranch and feedlot, Daiei contacted me again. The Hawks had decided to release *gaijin* Willie Upshaw, a veteran first baseman from Texas who had played most of his major league career with the Toronto Blue Jays.

Was I still interested in playing in Japan? You bet.

By the time the details of a contract could be worked out, it was early June. I immediately discovered how seriously Japanese fans take their baseball. A welcoming committee hailed my arrival to Fukuoka like I was Marco Polo on his first visit to the Orient. City fathers rolled out the red carpet at the airport. TV crews were on hand to cover my arrival, as if a foreign dignitary had dropped in. The club had assigned me an interpreter, Mr. Ojimi (whom we called Jimmy), and through him I told everyone how thrilled and delighted I was to be playing baseball in Fukuoka. It's doubtful whether U.S. President George Bush would have received a bigger welcome.

I stood out like Gulliver among the Lilliputians, towering over the Japanese people like an NBA center. With my size and flowing moustache, to them I must have seemed like a character who'd stepped out of the pages of a comic book.

Shortly thereafter, Corna and the boys flew over and we began a great summer adventure. Jeff and Keith hung out with me at the ballpark every day and traveled with the team on road trips, while Todd, our youngest, roamed all over the city and countryside with Corna. They became experts at riding subways and bullet trains.

Our family's new home was a three-bedroom apartment in a high-rise building. The apartment, about 1,500 square feet or so, would have been commonplace back in the States, but it was spacious and prohibitively expensive for most residents of Fukuoka. Our fellow tenants were doctors, executives, and other professional people. When several members of the Hawks clubhouse staff came to visit us one day, they oohed and aahed at our luxurious accommodations. We had sliding doors and tile floors covered with tatami mats. The apartment overlooked a park and the manicured grounds, on which Corna liked to jog, of an abandoned castle.

Corna was jogging one day when she happened upon a group of elementary school students out on a field trip. As she approached them she saw several children pointing toward her as they called out to their teacher, *"Gaijin! Gaijin!"* As Corna ran by, the teacher orchestrated a formal greeting, having the children stand up and in say, in unison, "Hello!"

Our building stood less than a mile from the Hawks stadium. When I'd walk to work each day, residents of Fukuoka would stare and gawk. Some parts of Japan— Tokyo, for instance—are fairly cross-culturalized; you can find a McDonald's, Burger King, or Hard Rock Cafe at every turn, and enough Americans are there on business, or as tourists, to spark conversation with familiar faces in a native tongue.

Not so in Fukuoka. We were pretty much strangers in a strange land. About the only English-speaking people we encountered on a regular basis were Tony Bernazard, the other *gaijin* on the Daiei Hawks team, Tony's interpreter,

Cota, and Cota's girlfriend, Susan. Bernazard, who played for several clubs in the majors, including the Expos, White Sox, and Indians, hails from Puerto Rico.

Later we discovered the International Bar in Fukuoka, at which karaoke was the main attraction, and befriended its owner, Mary. Both Mary and her boyfriend spoke English.

When the boys, all towheads at the time, arrived in Japan that summer, residents of Fukuoka would come up to them and study their features. Many of the townsfolk were intrigued because they had never seen people with blond hair or fair skin. They would politely ask Corna or me if it was okay to touch the boys' hair—a phenomenon that was quite endearing but took a bit of getting used to.

When I started pitching for the Hawks, who used me as a closer—the Japanese, being keen students of the game, had adopted major league relief patterns—I found I didn't have to make many adjustments. The dimensions of the pitcher's mound and home plate were no different. The umpires called pretty much the same strike zone, and like their counterparts stateside, missed a call here or there.

The biggest difference was that the comparatively small stature of Japanese players made the strike zone look about the size of a peanut hull. Tony Bernazard, at five-foot-nine and 150 pounds, would be considered a smallish guy in the major leagues; in Japan he was about average size. (Keep in mind that one of Japan's leading sports figures, golfer Masashi Ozaki, is called "Jumbo" by his countrymen. Jumbo stands six-foot-two and goes 200 pounds.)

My Hawk teammates, because of their low-fat diets and

feverish conditioning programs, sported lean bodies. So did the majority of players in the Japanese League. All these whippets racing around the bases makes for an exciting game. True, there have been some sluggers in Japan—the great Sadaharu Oh, for one—but the emphasis there has always been more on speed than power.

Japanese play what amounts to small ball. Prevailing strategy is built on moving runners along from station to station, often by bunting. If the home run is the main symbol of American baseball, the bunt holds the same distinction in Japan.

Bunting boils down to an act of sacrifice (hence the term *sacrifice bunt*), which is central to the Japanese way of life. A Japanese player feels honored to have the opportunity to give himself up for the good of the team. Conversely, I've see American players get pissed off when a bunt sign is flashed at them.

In Japan the entire culture is based on selflessness, not selfishness. People make their contribution not by standing apart from the crowd but by blending in. The Japanese are born to conform: That philosophy drives the economy, corporations, and baseball teams. A Japanese player's attitude never concerns *I* or *me*, it's always focused on *we* or *us*.

Even with having to endure nagging pain in my neck and shoulders, I still threw heat in the low nineties, which made me one of the fastest pitchers in the Japanese League. The majority of the starting pitchers I saw in Japan threw fastballs in the high eighties; only a handful topped 90 mph.

Japanese pitching, like hitting, was more finesse-oriented than power-oriented. The most successful pitchers in Japan were Tommy John and Greg Maddux types, guys who changed speeds well and varied the location of their pitches. Almost all the pitchers had good control. Working with such a small strike zone, they had to.

The first major hurdle to clear in Japanese baseball was getting over the communication barrier. The manager of the Daiei Hawks, Mr. Tabuchi, didn't speak any English, and I didn't speak any Japanese. To facilitate dialogue between us is where Mr. Ojimi came in.

In theory, at least. I had some reservations about Jimmy's effectiveness as a translator. He was ready and willing, if not able. I have a hunch that more than a few conversations I attempted to have with Tabuchi during a game went something like this:

Me: Jimmy, ask Tabuchi if he wants me to work these guys inside or outside.

Tabuchi (not in English): What did he say?

Jimmy: Goose-san wonders if he should hire a housekeeper or a gardener.

Tabuchi: How should I know?

Me: What did he say?

Jimmy: He doesn't know.

Me: What do you mean he doesn't know? He's a manager. He should know them like the back of his hand.

Tabuchi: What did he say?

Jimmy: Goose-san said he has something wrong with the back of his hand.

Tabuchi: His hand! Is he okay? Can he still pitch? Let's warm him up and see if he's all right.

Me: What did he say?

Jimmy: He wants you to warm up. He thinks you may be getting cold. Here, put on this jacket.

Goose: And then pitch the batters inside or outside?
Jimmy: He didn't say.
Tabuchi: What did he say?

Speaking of warming up, during my first appearance with the Hawks, I learned one of the differences between baseball in Japan and baseball back home. I went out to the mound to start an inning, and as soon as I threw my first warm-up pitch, the catcher held on to the ball and the umpire came running out from behind home plate waving his arms and shouting, "No! No! No!"

I didn't have a clue what was happening. Jimmy had to come out and explain that warm-up pitches weren't allowed. Each inning begins the moment the lead-off batter steps in. No pitches may be thrown until then. If a pitcher wants to warm up, he has to throw in front of the dugout while his own team is still batting. Oh.

Another difference between our game and theirs is that Japanese teams delight in running up the score. Here in the States, when a team gets way ahead, it generally calls off the dogs. Managers make substitutions, starters lose some of their edge, and the final few innings usually are played without a lot of intensity. Not so in Japan.

In one of my first outings I found out about the Japanese way of doing things. The Hawks were trailing something like 9-1 late in a game when Tabuchi sent me in for a little bit of work. The other team immediately proceeded to start bunting.

With my big windup and delivery, I wasn't exactly a model of nimbleness and grace coming off the mound, which the opponents quickly grasped. Time after time a batter would push the ball down the third-base line and beat my throw to the bag.

I got pissed. The madder I became, the more the other team bunted. And, as runner after runner crossed home plate, the opposing players sat in their dugout roaring with laughter. They were having a ball at my expense.

When I finally got the third out of the inning—after giving up a total of six or seven runs—I came down into the Hawks dugout, slammed down my glove, and headed for the tunnel below the grandstand that connected the two dugouts. I was ready to kick ass.

Tabuchi: Where's he going?

Jimmy: Where you going?

Me: I'm going to kill their manager.

As soon as Jimmy relayed that message, Tabuchi and several Hawks coaches came running up and restrained me before I could do anyone harm. They settled me down and explained they had no problem with the other team's tactics.

In America, the other team would have been guilty of showing me up. There it was standard procedure.

One of the first things *gaijin* notice when they start playing baseball in Japan is the outrageous difference in their training regimens. It represents a gulf as wide as the Sea of Japan.

Japanese players train every bit as hard as the athletes who qualify for the Ironman Triathlon in Hawaii. They make American baseball players, even those most dedicated to year-round conditioning, look like loafers by comparison.

The Japanese method of training is hard to imagine until you've seen it with your own eyes. Players take the field two or three hours before game time and undergo rigorous workouts. They complete fielding drills, batting practice, bunting practice, then they work on their baserunning and sliding.

Next, they run wind sprints in the outfield and go through a strenuous series of calisthenics. Then—believe it or not—they repeat the entire cycle.

The way Japanese players prepare for a game, every game, would be the equivalent of the NFL's Denver Broncos going through an eighty-play intrasquad scrimmage just a couple hours before kicking off against the Kansas City Chiefs.

Robert Whiting's insightful book on the culture of Japanese baseball, *You Gotta Have Wa*, quotes Warren Cromartie, the former Montreal star who later became a MVP-type player in Japan, saying the conditioning programs in Japanese baseball "made military camp seem like a church social."

He wasn't kidding.

Such fanaticism about conditioning could have its downside, however, especially when it came to the welfare of Japanese pitchers. One of the key ingredients to successful pitching, as I mentioned earlier, is recognizing what your body is telling you and giving your arm proper rest.

Shortly after I joined the Daiei Hawks, Mr. Tabuchi— through Jimmy, of course—asked me to work with one of the team's young starters. This kid threw in the low nineties and had good stuff, but for some inexplicable reason he could never get beyond the second or third inning.

I worked with the kid in the bullpen one afternoon for

about forty-five minutes. He had a good, live arm and plenty of movement on his pitches. There was nothing glaringly wrong with his mechanics either. With the arsenal at his command, this kid should have been able to set the world on fire. He had overpowering stuff.

Before Daiei's outing the next evening, I looked out in the Hawks bullpen and noticed the same kid warming up.

"What's he doing throwing?" I asked Jimmy.

"He's our starting pitcher tonight," came the reply.

The mystery had been solved. The kid was overworked. Gassed, plain and simple.

"No wonder he can't get past the second or third inning," I told Tabuchi through Jimmy. "He's been throwing on the side too much. You've got to give him some rest. He's worn-out."

Tabuchi, upon hearing my report, shook his head. Rest, apparently, is not a word contained in the vocabulary of a Japanese manager. (The answer to any problem in Japan, I learned, is to work harder.)

After that day, Tabuchi never again asked me to help work with a Daiei pitcher. Nor did he solicit any of my advice on pitching. The kid, by the way, got shelled in the second inning that night.

Looking back, I'd have to say the most memorable part of my introduction to baseball in Japan came from the fans. They were exuberant and incredible.

Daiei Hawks fans—not just some of them, practically all of them—dressed in team colors. They brought flags and banners to the stadium and waved them with pride. The fans sang, chanted, and engaged in rhythmic clapping throughout the entire game.

The fans kept one eye on the field and one on the team's cheerleaders, adult males who wore white gloves and used whistles to organize and coordinate the cheering. Japanese fans, ever eager to go with the flow, followed the cheerleaders' prompts and gestures to the letter. Rarely, if ever, did a fan let out a spontaneous cry.

The Daiei fans didn't hand out any Bronx cheers either, no matter how sloppily we performed. Fans in Japan didn't boo the home team or cuss at the players (a welcome change, I might add).

In keeping with Japanese custom, the worse the Daiei Hawks played during a game, or the further we fell behind on the scoreboard, the harder our fans cheered. They acted like they felt a responsibility to overcome our misfortunes with positive reinforcement and good vibes. In America, by contrast, the worse a team plays, the harder its fans jeer. Or the sooner they leave for the parking lot.

In Japan, fans stayed to the end (bitter or otherwise) of every game. They typically were cheering as loud, or louder, on the final pitch as they did on the first pitch.

During that summer, Corna and I went out one evening with Mr. Tabuchi and his wife. Ojimi and his girlfriend, Marnie, came along to interpret. We had a pleasant time seeing some of the city's sights, hitting golf balls at a driving range, and eating a tasty meal that consisted of several courses.

After dinner Tabuchi insisted that we stop at another restaurant for dessert. Corna tried to beg off, saying she was too stuffed to eat another bite, but Jimmy explained to us that Japanese custom dictates that if a host wants dessert, everyone in his party must have some too. Protocol demands as much.

At the end of the evening, Corna told Mrs. Tabuchi, through Jimmy, how much she'd enjoyed meeting her and that she would look forward to seeing her again at a Hawks game.

Mrs. Tabuchi looked aghast. Jimmy had to explain to Corna that wives of Japanese players, managers, and team officials never go near the stadium. The Japanese have strict codes of behavior that discourage mixing family and business. Mrs. Tabuchi and the other baseball wives were considered persona non grata at Daiei games.

Corna, on the other hand, went to every Hawks home game and most of our road games. She even entered the Hawks clubhouse (becoming perhaps the first female, *gaijin* or otherwise, to do so) to receive acupuncture treatment for a separated shoulder.

Corna was sitting in the stands one night when a woman seated next to her volunteered, "In the United States, you people like to shoot each other. Bang. Bang." She made a gesture with her thumb and forefinger to suggest a pistol firing.

Corna tried to explain to the woman that America, unlike Japan and its homogenous culture, is a melting pot. American society, with so many people of such varying backgrounds and ethnicities, is going to have serious differences, Corna explained, and violence is often a product of those differences. The woman shook her head like she didn't understand. Corna dropped the subject.

People in Japan were extremely proud of the relative lack of crime. And, I must say, we did discover that we could walk anywhere, at any time of day, without fearing for our safety.

Everyone was mortified, therefore, when Corna lost her camera on a road trip to Kawasaki. We were already back at the team hotel after the game before she realized she had left it at the ballpark.

Don't worry, Jimmy assured Corna, your camera will still be there tomorrow. No one would think of stealing it. But the next day the camera remained missing, and people at the stadium were stunned. Everyone apologized profusely.

Despite feeling safe and secure in Japan, Corna and I still needed to arrange for baby-sitters for the boys when we went out. One member of the Hawks clubhouse staff, Sakata, frequently volunteered to look after them.

Jeff and Keith were terribly impressed that no matter where the Daiei Hawks traveled on the road, Sakata seemed to have a girlfriend in each city. Jeff took an immediate liking to one of Sakata's friends, primarily because the woman spoke English fluently. Jeff told Sakata he thought he was a lucky man, indeed.

"But Jeffrey," Sakata said, shaking his head. "Small breasts. No sanks."

During the All-Star break that summer, we flew to Korea and went to an amusement park in Seoul that must have been the Korean equivalent of Disneyland. During our stay in Japan we also had a moving experience visiting the Peace Park and Museum in Nagasaki.

The solemness of our visit was interrupted by Todd, who kept asking excitedly in a loud voice, "Mom, when we dropped the bomb on Japan—"

Ssssh, we'd quickly interrupt. Not here, Toddie. We'll tell you later.

One problem I didn't experience in Japan was keeping up my weight, even though the climate in Fukuoka was humid and steamy and conducive to shedding pounds.

I developed a taste for the local cuisine, like udon, a soup with chewy noodles in broth. I munched on fish flakes with my beer, ate raw eggs, and even learned to like goldfish cocktails, where you swallow live goldfish. (Cleans the system, I was told.) I also tried octopus balls, which are pretty tasty and not to be confused with Rocky Mountain oysters.

Steak, which was served in small cubes, was something of a rarity. Most restaurants in Fukuoka specialized instead in fish—steamed, raw, broiled, baked, fried—you name it. We ate so much fish that summer, it's a wonder we didn't grow gills. The worst part for Corna was watching live shrimp being thrown on a grill, crying out in agony in their last moments alive.

One morning on the road, Corna came to the table complaining she'd had too many fish flakes with her beer the previous night. When my breakfast order of a raw sea urchin topped with a raw quail egg arrived, she took one look and made a dash for the ladies' room.

Overall, we led an idyllic lifestyle on a beautiful island in the summer of 1990. Corna, with her innate sense of adventure, mastered the art of transportation. Once she discovered she could make sense out of train schedules and subway signs, she and Todd were free to go where they pleased.

They would take off in the morning on their bicycles and come home in the evenings with stories of great adventure. Once, they traveled to a beach on Noko Island, taking a train, subway, and ferry to reach their destination.

The beach on Noko Island was gorgeous. A man with a camera took several pictures of Todd playing in the sand with Japanese kids—all of whom like to flash the peace sign—and then asked Corna to write down our address in Colorado. Several months later we received a batch of photographs from their memorable day at the beach.

Wherever we went in Japan, people were polite and courteous. They treated us all royally. After Corna took the boys home and reenrolled them in school in Colorado Springs, she came back to Japan in September with Debbie Perry, our friend from New Jersey, and my sister Paula.

The three of them went on an extended tour of Japan. They rode the *shinkazen* (bullet train) to most of the major cities and had a great time exploring and sightseeing. More than once, Japanese approached them in the street and, because they were fascinated with fair skin, gave them gifts—fans, bells, and little trinkets.

One day, Corna, Paula, and Debbie rode the *shinkazen* into the mountains and went hiking. On the return trip they encountered a group of giggly schoolgirls. As the train approached a large open field, the schoolgirls started shouting, "Oooh-foe. Oooh-foe."

Corna figured out the Japanese girls were saying "UFO." And, sure enough, a large circle had been burned into the middle of the field. The next day, Corna saw a photograph in a local newspaper reporting a possible UFO landing.

About the only downside to our summer in Japan was that the meat manufacturing business Bob Teaff and I had envisioned failed to materialize. Even though I conducted several meetings in Tokyo, we were unable to get anything going.

That didn't diminish the total experience, though. Each of us brought back memories that we'll cherish forever. It's like I tell Corna: We'll always have Fukuoka.

CHAPTER 11

1991–94

THIS GUN'S FOR HIRE

The 1990 season in Japan proved to be a pleasant diversion and provided our family with a summer of adventure and cultural enlightenment. It also gave my confidence and self-esteem a much needed boost.

Japanese fans offered a hero's welcome and treated me with appreciation and respect. Their responsiveness represented a nice change of pace from the abuse I had endured in 1988 and 1989, when I'd been derided and dissed for no longer being the mighty stopper of old.

I had a good season in Daiei, ranking near the top of the Japanese League in saves. My fastball, if not overpowering, still had plenty of pop. I returned from my season abroad determined to find another job in the majors. I didn't harbor any grand illusions about becoming some team's go-to guy either. I just wanted to try to help out as a setup man.

Relief pitching during the 1980s had undergone further refinement. Remember how, at the beginning of the 1970s, teams had begun to develop closers? Guys like Terry Forster and me were asked to take over for a tiring starter and work two or more innings to ensure a victory.

That had changed. By the beginning of the 1990s, most closers came in to pitch only the ninth inning—if the score was tied or their team was ahead. A closer, unless he needed some extra work after several days off, usually sat out on nights his team got hammered.

Starters, meanwhile, increasingly were treated with kid gloves. Most of them were asked to throw six or seven innings, tops. With the rapid escalation in players' salaries that occurred during the 1980s, teams typically had millions invested in starting pitching. No one wished to overwork the poor darlings, lest their investment go down the crapper. Consequently, complete games joined the snail darter and spotted owl on the list of endangered species.

Funny thing, management never worried much about the workload when starting pitchers made $20,000 or $30,000 a year. Give a starter a seven-figure salary, though, and the bosses start treating him like Bonnie Prince Charlie.

Needing to bridge the gap between starter and closer, both of whom enjoyed shorter workdays, teams developed a new type of relief specialist: the setup man.

The setup man's task is to keep his team afloat until the call goes out to the closer. The setup man is as anonymous as the guy who runs the third leg on a sprint relay—the only time you pay attention to either one is when he blows a lead.

A few setup men are actually closers-in-waiting. One of the reasons the New York Yankees won the world championship in 1996 was the spectacular work of setup man Mariano Rivera, who pitched mostly in the seventh and eighth innings. Rivera became a black hole, a fastballer who took the Yankees to the ninth inning and then turned things over to closer John Wetteland. When Wetteland signed as a free agent with Texas before the 1997 season, Rivera became the Yankees closer. He remains one of the best in baseball, as he demonstrated during New York's world championship season in 1998 and 1999.

Some of the best setup men are left-handers—guys like Paul Assenmacher, Rick Honeycutt, Mike Stanton, and Dennis Cook come immediately to mind—whom managers like to bring in to face a series of tough left-handed hitters.

A few setup men are tweeners. Their stuff is not quite good enough for starting pitching, and they lack a big enough out-pitch for closing. They have just enough stuff to contribute.

That's how I envisioned myself as the calendar turned to 1991: a contributor, a role player, a setup man.

I hooked up with Tony Attanasio, an agent based in San Diego, who represented my pal Bruce Bochy. Tony had a friendship with Texas Rangers manager Bobby Valentine, and that relationship landed me a tryout in early 1991 at Arlington Stadium, in which I threw in front of Valentine and pitching coach Tom House.

My performance earned me an invitation to the Rangers spring training camp in Port Charlotte, Florida. Over the next five weeks, I kept my focus on winning a roster spot and apparently impressed enough people. I signed a one-year contract with Texas worth around $200,000.

Who was I to quibble about money? I just wanted to work.

Bobby Valentine had been named the Texas skipper in 1985, shortly before his thirty-fifth birthday. He had swarthy good looks, which connected with TV viewers and made him a heartthrob to all the teenyboppers who frequented major league parks.

Valentine had come up through the Los Angeles Dodgers organization, where he'd been a favorite pet of Tommy Lasorda. (Small forests have been depleted to make all the newsprint devoted to speculation that Lasorda will one day arrange for Valentine to take over as Dodgers manager.)

Valentine played for Los Angeles in 1971 and 1972, then was one of several players, including Frank Robinson and Bill Singer, traded to the California Angels for Andy Messersmith. Bobby got off to a great start in 1973, but broke his leg crashing into an outfield wall. His caliber of play never reached the same level after the injury. He had a ten-year career in the bigs.

Valentine amounted to a walking contradiction. Behind all his polish and bravado, Bobby was insecure and paranoid. He was famous for walking through the Rangers clubhouse and interrupting a conversation between players by saying, "Are you guys talking about me again?"

Valentine's exact words of welcome to the team at spring training that year were: "I forgot more baseball than you guys will ever know." I recoiled at such smugness and arrogance. I was tempted to tell my new teammates, "Better buckle up the seat belts, boys, we're in for a bumpy ride."

For once, though, I kept my mouth shut.

Valentine that season proved to be the absolute worst handler of a pitching staff I'd ever been around. He ran everyone into the ground. For example, Valentine would have two right-handers, or two left-handers, warming up at the same time. What was he planning to do, bring them both in the game? That was totally unnecessary. Over the course of the season, all those dry humps wore out the bullpen.

Bobby would get Ranger relievers busy at the first hint of trouble. Sometimes, before the first hint, as if he expected bad things to occur. I would have hated to be a starting pitcher for Valentine, because it would have been difficult to concentrate on business while watching all the guys warming up in the bullpen. Talk about a total lack of confidence.

Bobby Valentine should have been the lookout on the *Titanic*. He always spotted trouble up ahead.

There were numerous occasions when Tom House wanted to work with the Rangers pitchers on our mechanics. But it was impossible to put in a fifteen- or twenty-minute throwing session with House before a game and then have to endure all the dry humps you'd get with Valentine during the game.

The other thing I disliked about Valentine was that he had one set of rules for Nolan Ryan—who had been Bobby's teammate with California in the early 1970s and who, by 1991, had taken on a semi-mythical status in the major leagues—and another set for the rest of the team. It's no secret that Valentine had his head so far up Ryan's ass that he could see through Nolan's eyeholes.

I never got real close to Nolan, but I had a great deal of respect for his ability and accomplishments. Who wouldn't? His truly was a one-of-a-kind talent. His election to the Hall of Fame in 1999 was a foregone conclusion; the only surprise to me was that it wasn't unanimous.

Valentine let Ryan keep his own schedule and pretty much do his own thing, which I felt was detrimental to team unity. Nolan traveled with us on the road part-time, but he sometimes stayed at home. And he never spent as much time on the bench, pulling for his teammates, as he should have. Ryan always seemed to be back up in the clubhouse, working out or doing whatever he did.

Nolan could have provided more leadership for the Rangers, but he wasn't a consummate team player. He focused on himself more than the club. He kept a separate agenda.

One day before a game, Nolan confronted me about the grumbling I'd been doing about his not going on the road with the team.

"I heard you have a problem with me," he said, in that trademark Texas drawl, as I was in the training room getting treatment.

"My problem's not with you," I answered. "It's with the double standard around here. You get to go on the road when you want to. And you get to use your own set of signs. I don't think that's right."

Ryan shrugged. He turned around and walked away without saying one word. Then again, Nolan never was much of a conversationalist. I tried several times to get him to talk about the art of pitching, but he never had much to say.

(Ryan may not have been a talker but, lord, could that man grunt. When he let go of his fastball, he sounded like a woman giving birth. Or a beast in the jungle.)

Valentine's signs were another pet peeve of mine. You needed a course in hieroglyphics to decipher them. Bobby was so paranoid that opponents might be picking up our signs that he had the Ranger catchers, Geno Petralli and Mike Stanley, go through a series of slaps and taps with their mitt before giving the actual hand signal for each pitch.

That drove me nuts. I didn't want to wait around for a series of signs, I wanted to get the ball and go. With all the phony signs Ranger catchers flashed before the real sign, in the back of my mind I sometimes wondered if I'd read the signs correctly. It's hard to be committed to throwing a pitch if you're not a hundred percent certain it's the right one.

I finally went to Valentine and asked if he'd let me have my own signs. He had a one word answer: no.

"Nolan has his own set of signs, why can't I?"

"Yeah, well, he's got three hundred wins," Valentine smirked.

"I think I can come up with three hundred of something," I replied, referring to my save total.

Valentine didn't budge. I had to keep going through the same drawn-out process as the other pitchers.

Nolan Ryan performed another one of his miracles early in the 1991 season. On May 1, at Arlington Stadium, he pitched the *seventh* no-hitter of his illustrious career, a 3-0 whitewashing of the Toronto Blue Jays. Ryan struck out 14 batters, including Roberto Alomar for the final out.

His timing couldn't have been better. It was Arlington Appreciation Night, which meant the stadium was completely sold out. Ranger fans were on their feet, roaring with every pitch, from the seventh inning on. When he got Alomar with a fastball, Ryan broke into a wide grin and was immediately mobbed by his teammates. I joined the happy throng.

Seven no-hitters is an astounding feat. It might be one of the most remarkable records in baseball. Keep in mind that only one other pitcher, Sandy Koufax, has had more than three no-hitters. Ryan nearly doubled Koufax's total of four.

The arcs of Ryan's career and mine would intersect, albeit briefly, later in the 1991 season. We hosted Boston for a night game on July 23, and with Nolan on the mound, more than

40,000 turned out. Valentine told me beforehand to be ready to step in as closer, because Jeff Russell, who had pitched in three of the previous four games, was getting a much needed rest.

Ryan fell behind the Red Sox 3-0 after two innings but then found his rhythm. He started mowing Boston down like crabgrass. Texas rallied with four runs in the fifth inning, keyed by a two-run double by Ruben Sierra.

Mike Jeffcoat relieved Ryan in the seventh inning, and then I took over from Mike with two outs in the bottom of the eighth. I gave up one hit in the one and a third innings, preserving a 5-4 Rangers win. "This is what a team is all about," I told reporters afterward. "You have to pick each other up."

What I didn't know, until informed by John Blake, the Rangers' crack publicist, was that Nolan and I had each picked up something special that evening. He had his 308th career victory; I had my 308th career save.

We had photographs taken to celebrate the numerical co-incidence, each of us holding a baseball inscribed 308. It's a popular item on the collectible circuit. I have one of the cards in my personal collection.

Four days earlier, Nolan had signed a ten-year personal services contract with Texas, which specified he would pitch for the Rangers in 1992 and 1993 (at least) and then become a goodwill ambassador for the team through 2001.

The deal with Ryan was announced by Rangers managing general partner George W. Bush, whose father occupied the Oval Office at that time and who himself would later become governor of Texas. He's now the front-runner for the Republican party's nomination for president.

Ryan had another ten years to spend with the club; I had another ten weeks. My dissatisfaction with Bobby Valentine's paranoia, which included his frequent sitting in a chair next to the clubhouse so he could watch players interact—bringing to mind a study hall monitor in junior high—came to a head late in the season.

We were on a road trip in Oakland. One evening at a bar (naturally), I ran into Valentine and got in his face. Granted, I may have been overserved by the time I saw him. I gave him both barrels of my frustration.

I told Bobby, in front of several Texas teammates, "Your shit is so tired, man. The way you treat people is fucking ridiculous. You expect players to respect you, but you don't give them any respect in return. And the way you spy on us, how ridiculous is that? I'm sick of this bullshit, Bobby. And it's all your fault."

Valentine didn't say a single word. He finished his drink—he'd been snooping on us again—and left the bar.

To the surprise of no one, especially me, the Rangers decided not to renew my contract after 1991. They let me go at the end of the season with little fanfare. I'd burned another bridge.

In the spring of 1992, I arranged for a tryout with the Oakland A's, who trained in Phoenix. It boiled down to another do-or-die situation, like the one with Texas a year before.

Chuck Tanner remembers an exhibition game the A's played during that camp against Milwaukee, where Tanner had signed on as bench coach under Brewers rookie manager Phil Garner. The game was on the line in the final inning when I got the call from manager Tony La Russa. It was a chance to show him, and Oakland pitching coach Dave Duncan, that I still had the goods.

My old boss Tanner, surveying the scene unfolding on the field, turned to Garner and whispered under his breath, "If you don't mind me saying so, I hope he gets us out."

"You know what? I hope he does to," replied Garner, my ex-Pirate teammate.

I did get the save that day for Oakland and ultimately got two years of employment from La Russa. I settled comfortably into the role of setup man for the A's in 1992–93. My personal highlights were few, but I played on a great Oakland team that won 96 games and the A.L. West in 1992, then lost to Toronto in six games in the ALCS.

Dennis Eckersley excelled as the A's closer that season, posting 51 saves, a 7-1 record, and a glittering 1.91 ERA. Eck so dominated hitters that year—his eighteenth in the majors—that he became the first reliever since Detroit's Willie Hernandez in 1984 to win both the Cy Young and Most Valuable Player awards.

Eck combined a sinking fastball and sharp slider with pinpoint control. He could shave the corners like a Remington or Norelco. In addition, he possessed the supreme confidence that a closer needs to do his job. He feared no one.

Plus, Eck never got gay. He kept everything on an even keel, neither celebrating his victories nor dwelling on his defeats. While he might occasionally get touched for a big hit, he never let that faze him. The pitch Kirk Gibson planted off Dennis in the 1988 World Series might have undone another closer; not Eck.

The Oakland A's teams of the late 1980s and early 1990s featured the Bash Brothers, Mark McGwire and Jose Canseco. Still in their twenties, they had already made their marks on the history of the game. McGwire hit 49 home runs in 1987, setting a record for rookies still on the books. Canseco in 1988 became the first 40-40 man in history, hitting 42 homers and stealing 40 bases. Together the two strongmen helped carry Oakland to three consecutive A.L. pennants (1988–90) and a world championship in 1989.

While McGwire worked constantly to improve all aspects of his game, Canseco mailed in his effort. Jose came from the Kevin McReynolds school of rigorous exercise; he relied on his natural ability (which was extensive, no doubt about it) to take him as far as it would.

Canseco represented the breed of selfish superstar that emerged in baseball during the 1990s. He had little respect for the game or its history. He treated veteran players like fossils or museum pieces. He paid the manager and coaches little, if any, mind. Canseco was as self-centered as a rock star—something he must have learned from hanging out with Madonna—and expected to be treated like one.

La Russa finally had his fill of Jose's selfishness and shipped him to Texas during the middle of the 1992 season. Jose would have some misadventures with the Rangers, blowing out his arm while pitching an inning against Boston, and having a ball bounce off his head and over the fence for a home run against Cleveland.

In exchange for Canseco, the A's acquired another noted slacker, Ruben Sierra. Sierra ranks as the worst defensive outfielder I ever saw. (Jorge Orta was a misplaced infielder, so we'll give my ex–White Sox teammate the benefit of the doubt.)

When Sierra stood out in the outfield—the operative word being "stood"—his mind must have focused on making up tunes for the Latino albums he recorded during the off-season. He obviously paid little attention to batters or game situations. He spent more time out of position than a contortionist.

Canseco and Sierra were prime examples of the kind of ballplayers who have emerged now that defensive ability no longer enters into the payroll equation. They knew that to make big money, all they had to do was put up big numbers. They didn't have to be complete players, so they just went through the motions on defense.

The cast of characters in Oakland also included the King of I: Rickey Henderson. One of the most productive lead-off hitters in history, and baseball's all-time base stealer, Henderson set a new standard for selfishness. He made Jose Canseco look like a social worker by comparison.

Henderson liked to test Tony La Russa's patience by skipping workouts and showing up late for games. He would further test Tony by taking himself out of the lineup at the slightest ache or twinge. Henderson could be obstinate and surly on his good days. Just a joy to be around.

I remember the day I asked Rickey to autograph a baseball for a friend. "Would you sign it on the sweet spot?" I asked, a reference to the narrowest spot between the seams. Henderson chose to sign his name elsewhere on the ball, which he handed back to me without a word. His body language, however, fairly shouted, "Don't you ever ask me for an autograph again!" I didn't.

With all the prima donnas in our dugout and selfish attitudes loose in our clubhouse, Oakland unraveled in 1993. The A's won a measly 68 games, putting them on my personal putridometer next to such squads as the 1976 White Sox and 1986 Padres.

La Russa and Duncan came up short in starting pitching in 1993. Two of the rotation's mainstays of 1992—Mike Moore and Dave Stewart—signed free-agent contracts after the season. Moore went to Detroit and Stewart to Toronto.

That left Oakland with more retreads than a Goodyear factory. Bobby Witt, the erstwhile ace of the staff, was the only A's starter with a winning record (14-13) and an ERA under 5.00. The A's managed to compile both the league's lowest team batting average (.254) and the league's highest team ERA (4.90). Among recipes for disaster, that combination ranks with the tastiest.

With the pitching cupboard bare, his star slugger Mark McGwire on the shelf with injuries, and the team going nowhere, La Russa relieved one of his headaches in midseason by sending Henderson to Toronto for two minor leaguers. We missed Rickey and his moods like an outbreak of shingles.

A funny thing had happened during the winter of 1992 that affected my performance throughout the 1993 season and beyond: I got healthy.

Through a referral from Robert Howsam of the Colorado Springs Sky Sox, whose dad, Bob, was a former GM of the Cincinnati Reds, I was introduced to a kinesiologist named Dr. Mike Vidmark.

Mike has his practice in Longmont, a city of about 50,000 located roughly forty-five minutes north of Denver. He began working with me to correct pain I'd been experiencing in my right bicep and right shoulder—which he later discovered stemmed from a reduced blood flow—as well as pinched nerves in my neck.

I went back and forth to Longmont for several weeks, spending two or three days at a time living at Mike's house. I would work out in his home gym in the early morning hours and then go to Mike's office in the late afternoon for treatment.

When we went to dinner, Mike would talk about research he was doing on how consumption habits—what athletes eat and drink—affect their overall health and performance. I'd have a couple of beers and mull over what he was saying. I'd never given the topic much thought.

One morning as he was leaving for work, Mike said he had some information to share with me and asked that I stop by his office later that day. I showed up around noon.

"I've got good news and bad news, Goose," Mike said. "Which do you want to hear first?"

"Gimme me the bad news, Doc."

"Okay. You've got to quit drinking beer."

I burst out laughing. Me? Without beer? That would be comparable to a Florida summer without sunshine or a Colorado winter without snow.

"I can't quit drinking beer," I said. "That would kill me!"

"If you want your arm to feel better, cutting out beer will help you tremendously," he insisted.

"C'mon, Mike. I've been drinking it all my adult life."

Then Mike dropped the real bombshell—I have an allergy to barley and hops. Somehow, he had figured that out from the resistance-training work we'd been doing. He said that because of my allergy, beer robbed my muscles of their natural strength.

I sat back in the chair, dumbfounded. Me? Allergic to beer? That's like Robin Williams being allergic to ad-libs or Willie Nelson allergic to guitars. Beer was an essential part of my being. Or so I believed.

"You may have had this allergy for years and not known it," Mike explained. "It's just that you're getting older and your body can no longer compensate for the harm beer has been doing."

Jesus, Mary, and Joseph. No more beer?

As you may have surmised, the list of things in life I love more than beer is short. One of the few items on it, however, is baseball. If my being physically able to pitch hinged on giving up beer, so be it. That's what I'd have to do.

The good news? Dr. Vidmar didn't think I would have to undergo surgery. Good thing, because at my age I didn't have a year to spend in rehab.

I went cold turkey in early 1993. I popped the top off of one last Coors Light, took a cold taste of the Rockies, let out a loud, satisfying belch and said, "See ya." I tossed the can in the garbage and sent brewskis into oblivion.

Not surprisingly, in the next couple of weeks I dropped a few pounds and lost an inch off my waistline. By the time I reported to spring training in February, I had a new lease on life. I felt great—like I'd made a deal with the devil to remove ten years of wear and tear.

There was absolutely no comparison between the Goose who had finished the 1992 season and the gosling who showed up for 1993.

Dave Duncan, after watching me go through running and fielding drills one day, pulled me aside and said, "What's up, Goose? You look like a young kid out there."

I felt energized all year and remained free of injury or pain. By the time the 1993 season ended, my fitness and health were at such a high level, I didn't blink about staying off the sauce. It's been seven years since my last beer (or alcohol of any kind).

Too bad I didn't meet Mike Vidmar ten years earlier. I might still be pitching in the big leagues today. Believe me, I feel good enough to give it a try.

I went back to spring training with Oakland in 1994, but after a few days in Phoenix, Tony La Russa and Dave Duncan let me know that the A's were planning to undergo a youth movement with their staff. They promised, however, to use me in some game situations where other teams could get a look at my stuff. That was a nice gesture on their part.

I caught on with the Seattle Mariners, managed by Lou Piniella, my pal from our days with the Yankees. Sweet Lou, who had saved the 1978 playoff win over Boston with his remarkable defensive play, had piloted the Cincinnati Reds to a world championship in 1990 before getting his fill of owner Marge Schott.

Piniella signed with Seattle at the beginning of 1993 and immediately turned the Mariners around after their atrocious 64-win season in 1992. It didn't hurt Lou's rebuilding program one bit to have Ken Griffey Jr. in center field. Or, for that matter, to have Ken Griffey Sr. in uniform as a base coach. The Mariners weren't idiots; if seeing his pops on the premises made Junior happy, they knew enough to keep Senior around.

Ken Griffey Sr. and I had been teammates with the Yankees in 1982 and 1983. Junior, then entering his teens, hung around Yankee Stadium every day. He once told his dad, "That Goose guy, he scares me." (Corna would remind me frequently during the 1994 season, "You know you're getting old when you're playing with your ex-teammates' kids.")

Junior is one of the two best athletes I've ever seen in a baseball uniform. Bo Jackson, before he got injured playing football and had to have a hip replacement, is the other.

I consider Junior, without a doubt, the best ballplayer of the current generation. He does everything that needs to be done offensively, hitting for power, average, and in the clutch, plus he plays the best defensive outfield since Willie Mays or Paul Blair.

In my one season in Seattle, I saw Junior catch balls in the gaps that no other player could have reached. I saw him go over the wall and take away home runs. I swear I saw him sprout wings and fly.

The people connected with the Hall of Fame in Cooperstown might as well start planning for the Ken Griffey Jr. exhibit. He's going to require a lot of extra space. Maybe his own wing.

One of the best and most personally rewarding things that happened in 1994 took place just before opening day.

The Mariners were in Vancouver, playing a two-game

exhibition series with the Colorado Rockies, who were beginning their second season as a National League expansion team.

I was just taking the field for warm-ups when I heard someone shout, "Hey, Goose." I looked around and stared straight into the rosy, puffy cheeks of Rockies coach Don Zimmer.

Zim! I hadn't seen or talked to him since he practically ran me out of Chicago at the end of 1988. I'd made a silent promise never to speak to him again.

"Goose," he said, extending his right hand. "I want to bury the hatchet. I'm sorry about everything that happened between us in Chicago. Forgive me."

You might be surprised by what took place next. I know I was.

I saw a hand that looked a lot like mine reach out and shake Zimmer's. I heard a voice that sounded like mine say, "I'm sorry too, Zim. I deeply regret that things didn't work out. I thought I would have been able to help the Cubs more than I did. I let you guys down."

The vintage Goose Gossage would either have snarled and snapped at Zimmer—or ignored him. The new (beer-free) me accepted Zimmer's apology and offered one of his own. Could it really be possible? Had the Goose mellowed?

I thought I detected tears welling up in Don Zimmer's eyes, but he turned away and went back toward the Rockies dugout. I decided it must have been the late afternoon light playing tricks. As for the dampness I momentarily felt on my cheek? Must have been sea mist blowing in off the Strait of Georgia.

The downside to the 1994 season for me was having to play indoors at the Kingdome. I loathe indoor baseball. Baseball is a game that should be played in fresh, open air, on green grass, in the natural elements—rain, fog, or shine. All this climate-controlled, artificial surface stuff is a load of manure. It's not real baseball.

I'm not picking on the Kingdome either. I hate all indoor stadiums. The Astrodome in Houston—dreary. The Skydome in Toronto—plastic. The Metrodome in Minneapolis—ridiculous. All of them ought to be imploded.

The Metrodome may be the worst. Take me down to a hardware store and give me a few minutes and I could build a better stadium. When that place opened, the carpet on the outfield had a trampoline effect. Routine singles would bounce over fielders' heads for doubles and triples. Shots to the gap would bounce over the fence for ground-rule doubles. When we played the All-Star Game there in 1985, the field was still the topic of running jokes among players. Jim Kaat, my old White Sox teammate, probably said it best: "Playing baseball in the Metrodome was like playing marbles in a bathtub."

The dark cloud hovering over the 1994 season was the prospect of another labor dispute—which would ultimately result in the eighth work stoppage and fifth general strike since 1972. The ongoing war between the Players Association and major league owners had been escalating to a point of no return. Big issues on the table were salary caps for teams (which the owners wanted and the players opposed) and changes to arbitration and free agency requirements (vice versa).

On the field the biggest news was the realignment of each league into three divisions: East, Central, and West. That and the pace at which Matt Williams of the San Francisco Giants and Ken Griffey Jr. hit home runs. By midsummer each looked capable of taking a serious run at Roger Maris's record of 61. So many balls were leaving the yard that season people were convinced the ball had been "juiced." (My own take is that with all the advances in technology through the years, balls are being wound tighter. By 1994, you could bounce a ball off a hard surface, like concrete, and see a noticeable difference.)

Meanwhile, no progress had been made toward a new collective bargaining agreement. In fact, things started falling apart.

We were hosting the Baltimore Orioles on July 19 when four large acoustic panels fell out of the Kingdome roof, forcing the first cancellation in Kingdome history. I was out on the field, doing stretching exercises with fellow reliever Bobby Ayala, when I saw something flash out of the corner of my eye and then heard a resounding crash.

Fortunately, the accident happened about four o'clock, a couple hours before the stadium would normally begin filling up.

The structural damage forced Seattle to rearrange its schedule while the situation was assessed and repairs got under way. We flopped around a couple series with other clubs and went on the road for an extended three-week stay. In a sense, we never got back home.

On July 28 the Players Association executive board set an August 12 deadline for reaching a new agreement with owners. Donald Fehr, executive director, termed the looming strike a "last resort" and insisted the players wanted to play ball. It was those darn owners messing things up, Fehr insisted.

The owners countered with statistics showing that average salaries had risen to $1.188 million and that players were a bunch of greedy bastards. In the battle for public opinion, the owners seemed to hold the upper hand. Most baseball fans, though, didn't care which side won or lost the battle. They just wanted to see a product on the field. They wanted to see management and labor quit their bitching and play ball.

Our extended road trip while the Kingdome roof was being repaired took us to Texas in early August. On Monday, August 8, at the Rangers shimmering new stadium—called The Ballpark in Arlington—we hammered our hosts, 14-4. The bats were smoking, as Junior Griffey, Jay Buhner, Luis Sojo, and Tino Martinez all left the yard. Martinez's massive three-run shot in the fifth inning turned the game into a laugher.

I earned my 310th career save that day. I came in after Jeff Nelson, Bob Wells (who got the win), and John Dettmer. I pitched three hitless innings and earned a save, at the official scorer's discretion, for effectiveness. My line read:

	IP	H	R	ER	BB	K	NP
GOSSAGE	3	0	0	0	0	1	36

The save, my first since April 27, 1993, with the A's, would be the final one of my career. The game would also be my last.

As the strike deadline neared, we left Arlington and traveled to Oakland for a three-game series. I never got out of the bullpen. On Thursday, August 11, the Mariners beat the A's 8-1, with Randy Johnson pitching a complete game.

Johnson, the Big Unit, has to be the most intimidating pitcher in the game today. He's an imposing six-foot-ten left-hander, and he throws a fastball in the high nineties. Plus, when he pitches, he has a mean streak the size of the Suez Canal. Facing Johnson must be similar to what it was like facing me in the late 1970s and early 1980s. A batter better have his jockstrap on tight.

My locker in the Mariners clubhouse was right next to Randy's. The day he made his first start of the season, he came walking in and I cheerfully said, "Hey, Randy, how you doing, buddy?" He gave me a withering stare that could have cut glass. Okay, I thought, nice talking to you, bud.

I never again uttered a single word to him on days he pitched. I gave him a wide berth to put on his game face.

Our game in Oakland ended after midnight Eastern Time on August 12. We were the last people in the majors playing ball before the strike began. Then we put away all the balls and bats and waited for a resolution to the dispute. And waited. And waited.

I went home to Colorado Springs to wait with Corna and the boys. We were still waiting in October, when the World Series should have been played. Baseball had managed to stage World Series games during World War I, the Great Depression, World War II, the cold war, the Vietnam War, the Watergate scandal, and the Middle East hostage crisis— every single year since 1904—but there was no World Series in 1994.

Things remained in a state of flux all winter. Owners kept taking steps to try and break the players' union solidarity, like lining up replacement players, to be paid something like $600 a game, for the 1995 season. To his everlasting credit, Detroit manager Sparky Anderson said he wouldn't work with replacement players; the Tigers put Sparky on an involuntary leave of absence. The Baltimore Orioles, too, refused to carry on the charade with replacement players and cancelled their exhibition schedule. Bravo for the Birds.

In late March, with scabs in training camps and owners insisting they were going ahead with the 1995 season, the National Labor Relations Board filed for an injunction to restore the previous collective bargaining agreement. The Players Association immediately voted to return to work—if a federal judge supported the NLRB stance.

That ruling, by U.S. District Judge Sonia Sotomayor, came on March 31. While owners appealed her decision, they agreed on April 2 to let players go back to work. The abbreviated 1995 season got started on April 24.

The strike, which lasted 234 days, was the longest and most expensive in professional sports history (at least until the next one comes along). Owners lost an estimated $800 million in revenue. Players lost roughly $350 million in salary. As for baseball fans, many of them lost, in addition to a World Series that year, some of their passion for the game.

I wanted to get back to baseball, but I discovered that baseball no longer had a place for me. After the strike began on August 12, 1994, I never put on another major league uniform.

My goose was cooked.

CHAPTER 12

1995–Present

DON'T CRY FOR ME, COLORADO

Among Yogi Berra's many memorable quotes is the oft-repeated "It ain't over till it's over."

For me it was over on April 18, 1995. Two weeks elapsed after the strike finally ended and spring training camps belatedly opened, yet I found myself without work. Seattle, which had assured me over the winter that I figured in its poststrike plans, decided not to invite me to camp.

I suddenly and unexpectedly felt like I was stuck in the refrain of a Meat Loaf song: "All revved up with no place to go."

My agent, Tony Attanasio, spent several days calling various teams, including the expansion Colorado Rockies, but he found no takers for his well-traveled forty-three-year-old client. Unable to catch on as a setup man, I retired after twenty-two years and 1,002 games. I was the only player whose career spanned all eight major league work stoppages between 1972 and 1994; the last one, however, had tripped me up.

"I'm not voluntarily retiring," I told several reporters in Colorado Springs. "I'm just retired. It's a bittersweet feeling, but I'm not disappointed. I loved every minute of this game. But if there's no job out there for me, I can't play. Everybody in baseball faces it sooner or later. Here I am."

(Had any team contacted me that day or the next, I would have hopped a jet plane and been on my way to training camp faster than you could say Jackie Robinson.)

I did feel a keen disappointment that the expansion Colorado franchise wouldn't give me a tryout. I wanted a chance to earn a spot on the Rockies roster based on merit. Ending my career playing at Coors Field in Denver would have meant a great deal to this native Coloradoan. But I guess my disappointment at being rejected by the Rockies falls under the heading of "things never meant to be."

Several reporters asked me that day if I had any regrets about my career. No, I said, not a single one. I wouldn't have changed a blessed thing. As I told them, playing in the major leagues was like getting aboard the best ride at Disney World and not getting off for twenty-two years.

I sincerely wish that every true fan of baseball had the opportunity, if only for one day, to put on a big-league uniform and walk between the white lines. There's no greater feeling on earth.

Some people questioned why I remained in the majors for so long, especially since my last dominating season had been back in in the mid-1980s with the San Diego Padres. Did I feel that I took up a roster space at the end?

Hell, no. While I hadn't been overwhelming in the last few years, I wasn't chopped liver either. I had done some pretty decent work, right up through the 1994 season with Seattle. I made a contribution to each team—if not with wins and saves, then by sharing experiences about how to play winning baseball with my teammates, some of whom were young enough to be my sons.

My attitude about longevity went back to something I had heard Chuck Tanner say during my first spring training

camp with the Chicago White Sox: "You guys don't appreciate how fortunate you are to get to play this game for a living. You have the best job in the world. Don't ever give up
that uniform you wear voluntarily. Make somebody tear it
off your back, because nothing you do in your life will be as
good as this. Nothing will ever take the place of baseball."

I took Tanner's advice to heart. I pitched until every one
of the twenty-eight teams in the major leagues said I couldn't
pitch anymore. Then I took my ball and glove and went
home. Thanks for the memories, guys.

My retirement received extensive coverage in sports pages
across the country. The *New York Times*, *Wall Street Journal*, and *USA Today* wrote stories recapping my career. So
did the *Denver Post*, *Rocky Mountain News*, and *Colorado
Springs Gazette*.

The nicest and most flattering parts of the coverage were
tributes from ex-teammates, managers, and coaches. Don
Baylor, my teammate in New York who had since become
the first manager of the Rockies, described me as "at the top
of the list" of intimidating pitchers. "He was one of the best
teammates I ever had," Baylor said. "He cared more about
the team than he did about stats. If you beat him, you knew
you would have to come right back the next day and beat
him again. He wasn't going to back down. Guys like that,
you wish could go on forever."

"He was a leader," said Dave Duncan, the Oakland A's
pitching coach. "In a very special way, he has taught a lot of
younger pitchers what the game of baseball and the game of
pitching are all about. They probably didn't even know they

were learning it from him. What he said meant so much because of his stature. It came from the heart."

Tony La Russa, the Oakland manager, praised me as an ultimate warrior: "When he went to the mound, he was out there like a warrior, scrapping and competing and doing it for the love of the contest."

La Russa also included me in some select company: "He helped revolutionize the closer role. You think of closer, you think of [Bruce] Sutter, [Rollie] Fingers, and Gossage. And if the trend had been different, you're talking about four hundred saves at least. That needs to be brought up more."

Graig Nettles chipped in with: "[Goose] was always a no-nonsense kind of guy. What I thought was particularly good was that he didn't make excuses. There were times when he got hit hard, like everybody did, and he never made an excuse for it. He just said, 'Hey, I didn't do the job today.' "

Willie Randolph, who's now a coach for the Yankees, recalled: "So many times, Goose would come on in the bottom of the ninth and blow everybody away. He never deviated from his style. Everybody in the ballpark knew he was coming at you, with that fastball and hard slider, all arms and elbows. He was one of those who could say, 'Here's my best pitch. See if you can hit it.' "

Don Mattingly, who joined the Yankees in 1983, my final year in pinstripes, touched on a more personal side. "Goose pretty much took me under his wing, as far as making sure I felt comfortable," Mattingly told the *Denver Post*. "His wife did the same thing for my wife. They took care of us."

I would like to have heard how Billy Martin remembered my contributions, but Billy had perished in a automobile accident in upstate New York on Christmas Day, 1989. But

Yankee boss George Steinbrenner told the *Wall Street Journal*: "Reggie Jackson was the best at his trade, Thurman Munson was the leader, but no player was any greater than Goose Goosage in his role." Reading those words from George meant a great deal to me.

My career had ended—not my life. I didn't need anyone's sympathy. I had too many irons in the fire to feel sorry for myself. Besides, all good things must come to an end, right?

On July 8, 1995, three months after my retirement and three days after my forty-fourth birthday, Colorado Springs honored me and my family with the dedication of the city's Richard M. Gossage Youth Sports Complex.

It was a grand occasion. An army band from nearby Fort Carson played the national anthem, and bunting covered the screen behind home plate. Bunting, as you know, signifies big deal.

Corna and the boys were there for the public unveiling of the twenty-four-acre site which includes five baseball diamonds and nine soccer fields. So was Sue Gossage—whom my teammates lovingly referred to as "Mother Goose"—my sisters Paula and Lavonne, and my brother Jack, who had nurtured my pitching talent all those many years earlier.

Don Baylor came down from Denver and took part in the dedication. Mayor Robert Issac, another product of Colorado Springs youth ball, read a proclamation and then said, "We couldn't have picked a better person to name this complex for. We're proud of you, we think the world of you, and we're glad you're back here to work with our youth, because we need you."

I can't think of a nicer tribute than to be recognized by

your own hometown. The only thing that would have made that day better was if my dad had been around to see it.

It would have touched him as deeply as it did me.

Aftershocks of the 1994 strike were felt for the three years following my retirement. The breach between baseball and many of its former fans remained wide.

Fortunately, however, baseball enjoyed a renaissance during the 1998 season. The best two things that could possibly have happened to the game came along that summer: Mark McGwire and Sammy Sosa. Or, take your pick, Sammy Sosa and Mark McGwire.

Not only did they push Roger Maris and Babe Ruth two rungs down the ladder of single-season home runs, but McGwire and Sosa made history in such a manner as to rekindle passion for America's pastime. Their feats leaped from sport sections in metro dailies around the country and landed on the front page, not an easy maneuver when you consider they competed for space with independent counsel Kenneth Starr's report to Congress on Bill Clinton.

What McGwire and Sosa did equally as well as crunch baseballs into the next zip code was communicate the awesome joy they each experienced during their quest for the home run record. Both did a masterful job sharing their feelings and emotions with fans.

By empowering fans—connecting with them as few players in memory have been able to do—the duo became the best goodwill ambassadors baseball has seen in decades.

Their home run race filled stadiums around the country. McGwire and Sosa brought baseball lovers to a fever pitch and aroused even the casual sports fan. Finally—and this was no small feat—they brought back to baseball legions of former fans who had been embittered by the 1994 strike.

I'm sorry, but if you didn't get a lump in your throat seeing McGwire blast his 61st home on the same day his father, John, celebrated his 61st birthday, check your pulse. If you didn't get teary-eyed watching McGwire embrace the children of the late Roger Maris after hitting number 62, call for an ambulance.

If you didn't get the shivers when fans at Wrigley Field kept bringing back Sammy Sosa for more curtain calls after he launched his 62nd out on Waveland Avenue, prepare to receive last rites.

McGwire finished with 70 home runs; Sosa hit 66. Amazing.

Major league baseball, thanks to Sosa and McGwire, is riding the crest of a big wave. Regardless of whether I get back into the game as a coach or in a front-office capacity, I hope that resurgence continues well into the next century.

People frequently ask me if I'd like to put on a uniform again, perhaps as either a pitching coach, bullpen coach, or roving minor league instructor. To be honest, I have mixed feelings on the subject. I suppose I'm still sitting on the fence (although to date I have turned down a couple of job offers).

If I became a pitching coach, I might have trouble keeping a pitching staff intact. My guys would either be suspended all the time or broke from paying too many fines.

I'm overstating the case to make a point, but I believe it's imperative that pitchers learn how to throw effectively inside. Many of them don't know how to come in with their pitches.

In today's game, hitters have the upper hand so much that they feel free to dive out over the plate without fear of reprisal. It's not unusual anymore to see batters duck out of the way on pitches called strikes. That's how much they crowd the plate.

A few pitchers, like Roger Clemens, work the inside of the plate, but most have either never learned or have forgotten how. I would take it upon myself to reintroduce that aspect of pitching to the game.

I also know that if I became a pitching coach, I'd probably develop ulcers, or some kind of gastrointestinal disorder, watching major league umpires call balls and strikes. When a belt-high pitch right over the middle of the plate is no longer a strike, it's time to reset the clocks. Because something's cuckoo.

The lords of baseball, in their desire for high-scoring games, have gone overboard on behalf of offense. Not only are virtually all new stadiums—like Jacobs Field, Camden Yards, and Coors Field—batter-friendly, but the strike zone has been shrunk several sizes.

We're not talking about a little nip and tuck either. We're talking about a reduction as startling as the one to Tommy Lasorda's midsection after he went on that Slim-Fast diet several years ago. The strike zone's nearly vanished. It's on the endangered species list.

A small strike zone and bandbox ballparks lead to more home runs. Those two factors—more than tightly wound balls or corked bats or anything else you read about—are responsible for turning ordinary hitters into sluggers.

Don't misunderstand me—Mark McGwire and Sammy Sosa would get their home runs regardless. Those guys have more bat speed than Bruce Wayne. So, for that matter, does Junior Griffey.

But if the strike zone were larger and fences farther back, you wouldn't see so many six, seven, and eight hitters in the lineup swinging from their heels. And, I guarantee, there wouldn't be so many balls leaving the yard.

The only solutions I see are getting hitters out of their rocking chairs by pitching inside and returning to the spirit of the rule book by calling the strike zone as it's written. That's with the top of the zone at the letters—or armpits—not south of the equator.

On the other hand, one motivation for becoming a coach is that I really do enjoy working with young talent. One of the greatest satisfactions in my career came after the 1994 strike. Several young pitchers on the Seattle roster—guys like Bobby Ayala, Jim Converse, and Bill Risley—contacted me that fall and expressed their gratitude for the help I'd volunteered.

I appreciated hearing from them, but I didn't deserve any special commendation. I simply tried to carry on a time-honored tradition—passing along knowledge gained through experience. Twenty years earlier, when I had been in their shoes, veteran White Sox pitchers like Wilbur Wood, Jim Kaat, and Stan Bahnsen showed me the ropes in Chicago.

Baseball fans might not remember the name Ray Berres, who had an eleven-year career as a catcher in the 1930s and 1940s, but he probably helped me as much early in my career as Johnny Sain and Larry Sherry did later on.

Ray Berres was the pitching coach in Sarasota, my first

stop in professional ball. I showed up for the Rookie League in 1970 as raw and unrefined as crude oil.

Berres came from the old school. He kicked ass and took names. Within a few days' time Ray had me feeling like I'd never picked up a baseball. "Stay back," he shouted whenever I threw on the sidelines or in a game. "You got that, kid? Stay back!"

I didn't know what he meant.

"I'm staying back, coach," I protested.

"Like hell you are," he'd snarl. Then Berres would patiently demonstrate how, by allowing my body to get too far forward, my arm dragged behind. My pitches, consequently, lost some zip.

When I finally learned the feel of what Berres had been trying to teach—when I stayed back—I was headed on the road to success. Which didn't happen overnight, of course. I got sent to Appleton later that same summer, and my new manager, Ira Hutchinson, was so impressed with my work (an ERA over 6.00) that at the end of the 1970 season he recommended my release. Hutch thought my future would be as a stock clerk in a supermarket.

You couldn't necessarily blame him for his viewpoint. Making my first appearance at Appleton, I threw a curveball that missed home plate so badly it went into the dugout down the third-base line. Seriously.

The opposing team's manager, who was coaching third base, called time-out. He went down into the dugout, and when he reemerged, he'd put on a batting helmet. The crowd roared with laughter, but Ira Hutchinson nearly had a stroke.

Ray Berres was one of several members in the White Sox organization, along with Joe Jones and Sam Hairston, who stood up for me. "Don't let this kid go," they argued. "He's going to be a big-time pitcher some day." Ira Hutchinson got overruled.

Sure enough, the next year I impressed Chuck Tanner at spring training, went 18-2 at Appleton and won the league's Player of the Year honors, didn't kill Ernie Banks that day at Wrigley Field, started dating Corna in the fall, and the rest, as they say, is history.

Based on how much people like Ray Berres, Larry Sherry, and Johnny Sain meant to me and my career, I'd be proud to serve as a pitching coach. I have wisdom acquired over two decades to share. So it's conceivable that some major league team could make an irresistible offer. For the time being, though, I'm content to stay on the sidelines and confine my teaching to my son Todd's teams in youth baseball.

Anyway, my plate these days is pretty full. Between autograph sessions, memorabilia shows, speaking engagements, and charity fund-raisers, I stay busy enough.

One of my pet projects is helping raise money for a new youth sports complex in Colorado Springs. We've earmarked a fifty-four-acre site on which we plan to build soccer fields and baseball diamonds. In the November 1998 general election a referendum passed that will generate additional revenue for the site.

It's no secret that many children in our society feel lonely and neglected. Colorado Springs is not alone in having scores and scores of disaffected kids, teenage and younger.

Youth sports programs are a mechanism through which kids feel better about themselves. The self-esteem, self-confidence, and discipline kids acquire through athletics serves them well in every endeavor in life. Studies also show that kids involved in organized sports are less likely than their peers to develop drug dependency, join gangs, or commit crimes.

Sports, in other words, helps build character and values. If we build fields and organize leagues, children in our cities will have a head start in life.

One of the many activities created to raise funds for the youth sports complex is the annual Goose Gossage Celebrity Pro-Am. It's a two-day golf tournament played at the Broadmoor, the famous resort located in Colorado Springs. I'm grateful to all the former major league players, including Hall of Famers like Bob Gibson and Phil Niekro, and former NFL stars, like Ted Hendricks and John David Crow, who play in the tournament. We had to miss 1999 because of scheduling conflicts, but we'll tee it up again this year and for as long as we can help raise money for kids.

Another activity to which I devote as much time as possible is speaking to youth baseball leagues. I'm happy to hop on a plane and talk to kids about my experiences and the lessons I've learned. When I was seventeen years old, I heard Warren Spahn speak at a baseball banquet at the Air Force Academy. His remarks that night inspired me and helped fuel my ambition.

I try to give something back to the game that's been so good to me and my family. If I'm able to motivate young ballplayers to push themselves and strive for excellence, I'll feel I've made a small contribution.

What do I say to eager, fresh-faced audiences? Plenty.

I talk about the mental toughness and concentration required to play the game properly. I tell kids that while it's fine and dandy to be saints—or Boy Scouts—off the field, when they step across the white line they need to adopt a different attitude and mental makeup. To be successful, they'll need a desire to bury their opponents.

I remind kids that success doesn't just happen. A large amount of hard work and dedication is involved. You can't just step out on a field and expect to be successful. If you put little effort into baseball, you'll get little in return.

I talk about how to develop self-confidence and believe in your ability. I tell kids how to silence the little gremlins of self-doubt and focus on the immediate task.

"Challenge yourself!" I'll demand, my voice rising. "See how really good you can become. You don't want to have to look back later in your life and say, 'Well, if I would have worked harder, I might have made it.'

"Would have, should have, could have, might have— those are some of the saddest words in the entire English language," I'll say.

I tell kids how to deal with the fear of failure. Fear is, of course, a powerful motivator. All of us are afraid of failing in front of our peers. It's really no different for a twelve-year-old in Little League ball than a thirty-year-old playing in the World Series.

I know what I'm talking about because I've been there. I've looked fear in the eye and stared it down. I've stood alone on the mound in front of 50,000 people in a hostile environment, with millions more watching worldwide, and won the war of wills with fear.

I also tell kids about the feeling when so much adrenaline races through your body that you actually become frightened. And how to take adrenaline and corral it, harness it and ultimately channel it so it works as your ally.

Adrenaline, which manifests itself in the form of controlled aggression, is what enables athletes to throw harder, run faster, jump farther, or hit a baseball out of sight.

I try to explain to young ballplayers that nervousness comes with the territory. If a ballplayer doesn't have butterflies before a game, he's in the wrong line of work. Butterflies are as much a part of baseball as squeeze plays and stolen bases.

"Say you come up in the bottom of the last inning, with two outs and the winning runs on base," I'll say. "You can either be the hero or the goat. Take a deep breath. Stay within yourself. See the ball and hit the ball hard. Don't let doubt or fear of failure creep in, because they'll try. Don't be saying to yourself, 'Gee, what if I make the last out?' Keep your thoughts positive and stay focused on the task."

I like to share with kids a mental technique I used early in my major league career. When negative thoughts tried to elbow their way in, I would step off the pitching rubber and say to myself, "No, I don't have time for you right now. I'm going to put all you negatives in a little black bag, zip it up, and set it aside."

That kind of self-dialogue helped me a great deal early in my career. Later, after I'd hit my stride as a closer, my self-talk sounded much different. I would silently mouth to each batter, "Okay, buddy, I'm going to bury you." Negative personal thoughts never entered the picture.

I stress that a major component of being mentally tough is remaining focused on the task and expecting good results. Once you start thinking about how things can go wrong, they will. Why? Because you've lost your focus by allowing negative thoughts to creep in.

I guess word has gotten around that I bring a great

amount of energy—as well as credibility—to my baseball talks, because the phone keeps ringing. That's flattering. And I'm always happy to go, especially if I can help inspire just one kid to follow his dream.

As a former New York Yankee player, the highlight of each season is being invited back to Yankee Stadium for Old-Timers Day in July. I'm approaching the half-century mark, but when I get around all those Yankee greats in the clubhouse, I tingle with excitement like a teenager on a first date. The fan in me comes out.

During New York's 1996 championship season I was able to visit at length on Old-Timers Day with closer John Wetteland. I admired Wetteland's approach to the game, his composure and competitiveness, even before I got to know him.

He had my old locker in the Yankee clubhouse. As soon as he saw me come in, Wetteland jumped up and said, "Goose, this is still your locker. It belongs to you, man."

After the Yankee old-timers were introduced on the field and the exhibition game began, John and I went back into the clubhouse and talked about pitching. We discussed the burdens a closer has to shoulder and how doing the job successfully is such an exercise in positive thinking. We were still talking when the real Yankees game began.

It was obvious that Wetteland respects baseball, and that's why I respect him. My main beef with some of today's players is the lack of respect they have for the game.

I recall being in spring training in Phoenix in 1992 and meeting up with Tony Attanasio and several of his clients, young pitchers with bright futures. One of them said that he wanted to play in the majors just long enough to amass enough money to start his own business.

I nearly came unglued. "Don't ever play this game from here," I shouted, slapping my wallet. "You have to play it from here," I said, tapping on my heart.

My other beef with ballplayers is directed at those who either ignore fans or treat them like dirt. Fans are the lifeblood of this game, baseball's heart and soul. The great managers I played for—like Chuck Tanner, Dick Williams, and Tony La Russa—were always quick to remind their players about the importance of interacting with fans and involving them in the process.

There's not a service business I know that will ever reach its potential without having good customer relations. Baseball is no different. Players—and owners—have to grasp that fact.

Besides the great home run chase, baseball's other headline story in 1998 was the sparkling performance of the New York Yankees. By winning an American League record 114 games during the regular season and waltzing through the playoffs, the 1998 Yankees took their rightful place among the handful of best teams in baseball history.

Now Yankee fans can spend the next few decades arguing which New York team was better—the 1927 club with Babe Ruth and Lou Gehrig, the 1939 team with Bill Dickey and Joe DiMaggio, the 1961 squad with Mickey Mantle and Roger Maris, or the 1998 Yankees with Derek Jeter, Bernie Williams, Paul O'Neill, and the rest.

Me? I'm still partial to the 1978 team.

In the 1998 World Series the Yankees ripped through San Diego like a tornado. I would have preferred to see a closer and more competitive Series, one in which the Padres won a couple games at home, in front of their own fans. Bruce Bochy, the Padres manager, remains one of my closest friends, and he and Tony Gwynn were teammates of mine when San Diego made its only other appearance in the World Series in 1984.

But even with a soft spot in my heart for San Diego, my feelings weren't mixed and my loyalties weren't divided. I definitely wanted the Yankees to win another world championship. I've been a Yankee fan ever since those Saturday afternoons in the late 1950s and early 1960s when I'd watch their games on TV with my parents. That allegiance will never change.

Watching the Series, I felt particularly gratified for Yankee owner George Steinbrenner. With George, you always know he's going to do anything in his power to win. I don't think a player can ask any more of an owner than to put the best possible team on the field. I commend him for that.

I'm also glad that George shows such respect for the calm and steady leadership manager Joe Torre provides. I've seen the job of Yankee manager turn some guys inside out, but Torre somehow manages to take everything in stride and keep the team focused on its primary job. I think George realizes what an asset he has in Joe.

When Corna, Todd, and I traveled back to the Big Apple for Old-Timers' Day in August 1999, we encountered a more subdued atmosphere in and around Yankee Stadium than on previous such occasions. The absence of Joe DiMaggio, who died on March 8 after a lingering illness, left a void impossible to fill.

I never saw DiMaggio play, of course—his last season with the Yankees in 1951 was the same year I was born—but I grew up listening to my dad talk about the gracefulness of Joltin' Joe.

A dark cloud seemed to hover over the Yankee family. Not that anyone needed a reminder, but 1999 was the twentieth anniversary of Thurman Munson's death. A few days before the Old-Timers game, Whitey Ford's son, Tommy, died suddenly. Catfish Hunter, already suffering the debilitating effects of Lou Gehrig's disease, had fallen at his home in North Carolina and suffered acute cranial damage. (Catfish was in the intensive care unit, fighting to hold on. He would pass away, at age fifty-three, a month later. I'll always be indebted to him for pulling me out of that deep funk in Toronto.)

One development that lifted our spirits was that Yogi Berra returned for the annual Old-Timers celebration after a long boycott, and George Steinbrenner welcomed Berra back like the prodigal son. With Joe D. gone, there's no doubt about who inherits the tag as greatest living New York Yankee. And no, it's not Reggie Jackson or Don Mattingly. Not yet, anyway.

The 1999 postseason served as a showcase for the Yankees and demonstrated that the team's true strength can be found in its absence of weakness. New York had the whole package—offense, defense, pitching (starters and relievers), a deep bench, cool, capable management on the field, and leadership from Joe Torre, who set the tone for their success. By steamrolling Texas in three games and Boston in five, then sweeping the Atlanta Braves in the World Series, the Team of the Century sewed up Team of the Decade honors for the 1990s as well. New York extended its World Series winning streak to 12 games, tying a major league record, and joined the 1927–28 and 1938–39 Yankees as the only teams to register back-to-back sweeps.

Underscoring once again the importance of relief pitching, closer Mariano Rivera was selected Series MVP. Virtually untouched in the past two postseasons, Rivera has become a black hole for batters. Moreover, when Atlanta jumped out to a 5-1 lead in game three, threatening to make the Series competitive, Yankee relievers Jason Grimsley and Jeff Nelson silenced the Braves while Yankee bats started massaging Tom Glavine's pitches. When Chuck Knoblauch's two-run shot in the bottom of the eighth tied the score, everyone in Yankee Stadium could sense another Yankee win, which came two innings later on Chad Curtis's game-winning blast.

The names and faces in baseball's big show slowly change with each passing year, and I've had my time at the top. Now, with contemporaries such as George Brett, Nolan Ryan, and Robin Yount being inducted into Cooperstown, people are asking about my Hall of Fame chances.

If it happens, fine. If not, that's okay, too. I have many fond memories from my long years of service in the major leagues, and not a single regret. If the future is filled with frequent Yankee appearances in the World Series, that's good enough for me.

INDEX

McBride, Bake, 104
McCullers, Lance, 245
McDaniel, Lindy, 88
McDowell, Roger, 255
McEnaney, Will, 140
McGraw, Tug, 131, 158
McGwire, John, 314
McGwire, Mark, 29, 130,
    222, 295, 297,
    313–14, 316
McKeon, Jack, 214, 219,
    221, 222, 231, 239
McLain, Denny, 48, 49
McMahon, Don, 88
McPhail, Lee, 173–74
McRae, Hal, 130, 176
McReynolds, Kevin, 197,
    208, 216, 256, 257,
    295
McSherry, John, 201, 202
Melton, Bill, 13, 15, 16, 22,
    27, 67
Messersmith, Andy, 288
Michael, Gene "Stick,"
    159–60, 162, 163,
    167, 189
Millan, Felix, 98–99
Miller, Galen, 4
Miller, Marvin, 5
Milwaukee Braves, 52
Milwaukee Brewers, 70,
    164, 165, 255

Minnesota Twins, 28, 32,
    36, 77, 82
Minoso, Orestes "Minnie,"
    83–84
Mitchell, Kevin, 262
Molitor, Paul, 164
Monchak, Al, 103–4
Money, Don, 114, 269
Monge, Sid, 84
Moore, Mike, 297
Moreland, Keith, 203,
    245–46
Morgan, Mike, 186
Morganna, 254
Morris, Jack, 207, 263
Moyer, Jamie, 260–61
Munson, Diane, 145, 147
Munson, Thurman, 83, 114,
    117, 118, 120, 126,
    128, 129, 144–50,
    163–64, 171–72, 188,
    312, 325
Murcer, Bobby, 184
Murray, Eddie, 203
Murtaugh, Danny, 86

Namath, Joe, 40
Narron, Jerry, 146
Nelson, Connie, 183
Nelson, Jeff, 305, 326
Nelson, Roger, 61
Nelson, Willie, 3, 183–85